TUTANKHAMEN

TUTANKHAMEN

THE SEARCH FOR AN EGYPTIAN KING

JOYCE TYLDESLEY

BASIC BOOKS

A Member of the Perseus Books Group
New York

Published in 2012 by Basic Books
A Member of the Perseus Books Group
387 Park Avenue South
New York, NY 10016

Published in 2012 in Great Britain by Profile Books Ltd

Hardcover ISBN: 978-0-465-02020-1

Book Club Edition

To the memory of Robert 'Bob' Partridge
(1951–2011)

*'May your spirit live, may you spend millions of years,
you who love Thebes, sitting with your face to the north wind,
your eyes beholding happiness.'*

CONTENTS

ACKNOWLEDGEMENTS

Many people have contributed to the development of this book. I would like to acknowledge the particular help of Paul Bahn, Dylan Bickerstaffe, Victor Blunden, Audrey Carter, Robert Connolly, Steve Cross, Rosalie David, J. Fox-Davies, Robert Loynes, Jaromir Malek and the Griffith Institute, the late Bob Partridge, Bryan Sitch, Steven Snape and Angela Thomas. I would also like to express my thanks to the on-line Egyptology students of Manchester University, for their animated and always thought-provoking discussions.

At Profile Books I would like to thank my editor, the ever-patient Peter Carson, Penny Daniel and Annie Lee.

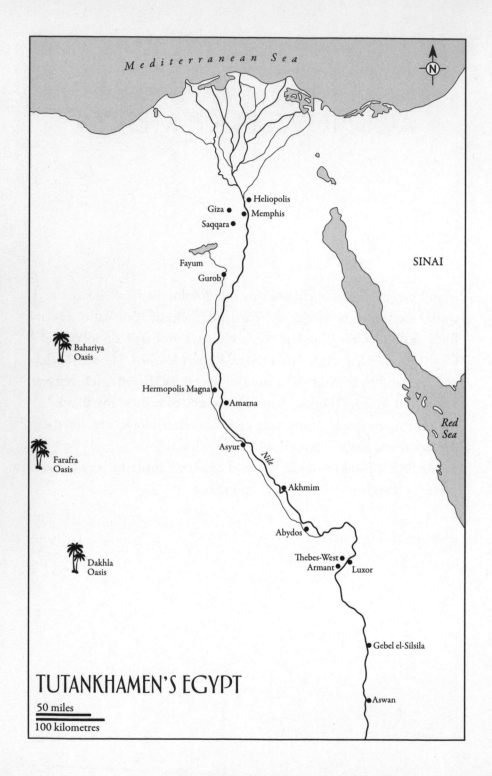

Mediterranean Sea

N

SINAI

Heliopolis
Giza •
• Memphis
Saqqara •

Fayum
Gurob •

Bahariya
Oasis

Hermopolis Magna •
• Amarna

Red
Sea

Farafra
Oasis

Asyut •
Nile

Akhmim •

Abydos •

Dakhla
Oasis

Thebes-West •
Armant • • Luxor

• Gebel el-Silsila

TUTANKHAMEN'S EGYPT

50 miles

100 kilometres

• Aswan

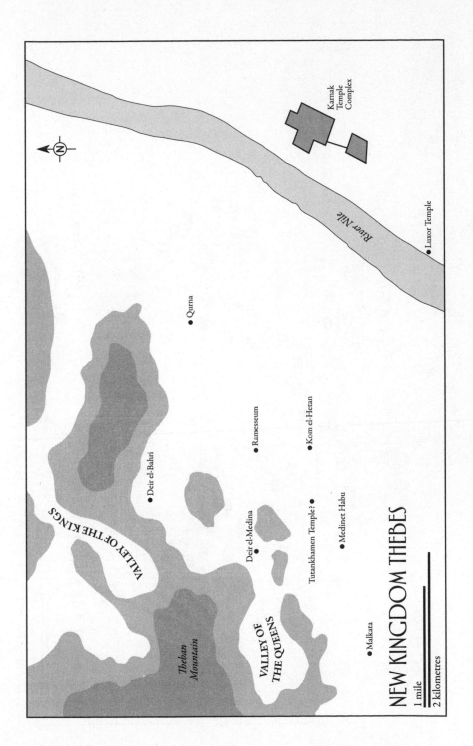

NEW KINGDOM THEBES

1 mile

2 kilometres

Theban Mountain

VALLEY OF THE KINGS

VALLEY OF THE QUEENS

Deir el-Bahri

Deir el-Medina

Ramesseum

Qurna

Kom el-Hetan

Tutankhamen Temple?

Medinet Habu

Malkata

River Nile

Karnak Temple Complex

Luxor Temple

N

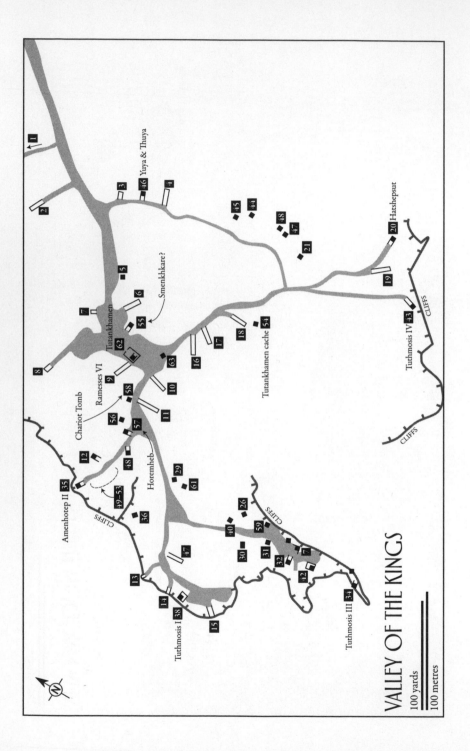

VALLEY OF THE KINGS

A NOTE ON NAMES

The Egyptians omitted vowels from their hieroglyphic texts: like modern emailers and texters (txtrs), they saw no need to waste time, energy and space writing sounds – and sometimes even words – that would have been obvious to everyone. Lol.

Unfortunately, ancient Egyptian is now a long-dead language, and the missing sounds are far from obvious to modern readers. Egyptologists therefore have to guess which vowel goes where. Generally, we insert 'e' as the vowel of choice, but this may not be the vowel that the Egyptians used, and we might not insert it in the correct place. As a result, all but the shortest Egyptian words have several variant English spellings, all equally acceptable. Throughout this book I use the spelling Tutankhamen, and I refer to Tutankhamen's god as Amen. In so doing, I follow the precedent set by Howard Carter. I have taken the liberty of extending this preferred spelling to all quotes within the text. Others prefer the spelling Tutankhamun (and Amun) or Tutankhamon (Amon); more exotic variants – Touatânkhamanou, Tut.ankh.Amen, Tutenchamun, etc. – will be found in the older literature. All refer to the same man.

The king that we know as Tutankhamen (living image of [the god] Amen) was born Tutankhaten (living image of [the god] Aten) but changed his name during the first few years of his reign. His consort,

Ankhesenpaaten, became Ankhesenamen at the same time. Others had already changed their names. The king that we today know as Akhenaten was originally Amenhotep IV; Akhenaten's consort, Nefertiti at the time of her marriage, expanded her name early in her husband's reign to become Neferneferuaten Nefertiti. To avoid unnecessary complications I will refer to these individuals as Tutankhamen, Akhenaten, Nefertiti and Ankhesenamen throughout the text, unless it is inappropriate so do.

At his coronation Tutankhamen assumed a series of five names that served as a formal statement of intent or propaganda for his reign. His last two names, known today as the prenomen and the nomen, are the names that are given in cartouches (distinctive oval loops) on his monuments and inscriptions. His prenomen (Nebkheperure) is the name by which his people knew him:

Horus Name: Image of births
Two Ladies Name: Beautiful of laws who quells the Two Lands/
    who makes content all the gods
Golden Horus Name: Elevated of appearances for the god/his
    father Re
Prenomen: Nebkheperure: Lord of manifestations of [the god]
    Re
Nomen: Tutankhamen: Living image of [the god] Amen

A NOTE ON DATES

Egypt's dynastic age started with the unification of the country by the southern warrior Narmer in approximately 3100 BC, and ended just over 3,000 years later with the suicide of Cleopatra VII in 30 BC. Following the scheme devised by the Ptolemaic historian Manetho, Egyptologists divide this dynastic age into 'dynasties': lines of kings who are in some way linked together. They may be, but are not always, blood relations. It is important to remember that these dynasties are artificial, modern divisions; the ancients did not divide up their history in this way.

The dynasties are grouped into times of strong, centralised rule (the Old, Middle and New Kingdoms and the Late Period) separated by periods of decentralised or foreign control (the First, Second and Third Intermediate Periods). Tutankhamen ruled during the late 18th Dynasty, the first dynasty of the New Kingdom (Dynasties 18–20, *c.* 1550–1069 BC).

The Egyptians dated events by reference to the current king's reign: Year 1, Year 2, Year 3, etc. When the old king died and a new king took his place, the dating system began again with a new Year 1. Although this is by no means a perfect system, it is the most accurate means that we have of dating Egypt's past, and it is the system that will be used throughout this book.

It is notoriously difficult to tie the Egyptian regnal dates into our modern calendar. As there is no universally accepted chronology the following, based on the dates suggested by Ian Shaw in the *Oxford History of Ancient Egypt* (2000: 481), is used:

Kings of the 18th Dynasty (*c.* 1550–1295 BC)
Ahmose *c.*1550–1525 BC
Amenhotep I *c.*1525–1504 BC
Tuthmosis I *c.*1504–1492 BC
Tuthmosis II *c.*1492–1479 BC
Tuthmosis III *c.*1479–1425 BC
Hatshepsut *c.*1473–1458 BC
Amenhotep II *c.*1427–1400 BC
Tuthmosis IV *c.*1400–1390 BC
Amenhotep III *c.*1390–1352 BC
Amenhotep IV/Akhenaten *c.*1352–1336 BC
Smenkhkare *c.*1338–1336 BC
Tutankhamen *c.*1336–1327 BC
Ay *c.*1327–1323 BC
Horemheb *c.*1323–1295 BC

A NOTE ON TOMBS AND
TOMB NUMBERS

The Theban west bank is honeycombed with tombs of all ages, some royal and some private. Starting in the 18th Dynasty, the New Kingdom pharaohs chose to be buried alongside some of their more important courtiers in rock-cut tombs cut into the remote Valley of the Kings. During the 19th Dynasty the nearby Valley of the Queens was developed as a cemetery for some of the more important royal wives and their children.

In AD 1827 John Gardner Wilkinson surveyed the twenty-one known tombs in the Valley of the Kings. Each tomb was given a number, allocated as he came to it. Today it is possible, by following his number sequence, to see that he walked first from the Valley entrance southwards, then turned towards the east. His system has continued into modern times, with the tombs now being numbered in the chronological order of their discovery, so that in 1922 Tutankhamen's tomb was designated KV (or King's Valley) 62. When, in 2005/6, the next 'tomb' was discovered by a team led by Dr Otto Schaden, it became KV 63. KV 64 is a suspected tomb, discovered by radar, while KV 65 is a suspected tomb entrance. The next tomb to be discovered will become KV 66, and so on. Just twenty-five of the KV tombs are royal tombs. The others were built for

Egypt's non-royal elite; KV 46, for example, is the tomb of Yuya and Thuya, parents of the formidable Queen Tiy and, perhaps, great-grand-parents of Tutankhamen. Some are not even tombs; KV 54 is a simple, stone-lined pit, while KV 63 appears to be a storage chamber.

The tombs in the Western Valley, an offshoot of the main or Eastern Valley, are given interchangeable WV or KV numbers, so that the tomb of Amenhotep III can be either KV 22 or WV 22, the tomb of Ay either KV 23 or WV 23. Tombs in the Valley of the Queens are given QV numbers, tombs in the Deir el-Bahri bay are given DB numbers and other Theban tombs have TT numbers.

A NOTE ON THE NUMBERING OF TUTANKHAMEN'S GRAVE GOODS

Tutankhamen's tomb yielded 5,398 separate finds. Howard Carter assigned every object, or group of objects, a number from 1 to 620, with letters used for subdivisions (atypically, Find 620 was given numbered subdivisions). The finds were numbered as they were recorded, as follows:

Find 1–3: Outside the tomb and staircase

Find 4: First doorway

Find 5–12: Passageway

Find 13: Second doorway

Find 14–170: Antechamber (28 being the blocked doorway to the Burial Chamber)

Find 171: Annexe blocking

Find 172–260: Burial Chamber (256 being Tutankhamen's mummy)

Find 261–336: Treasury

Find 337–620: Annexe

Subsequently, as they were received by Cairo Museum, each object was given a '*journal d'entrée*' museum number. For example, the first object to be officially removed from the tomb, a beautifully painted chest filled with children's garments, was Carter's number 21, and this became JE61467.

The vast majority of Tutankhamen's grave goods are currently displayed in Cairo Museum. There is a subsidiary exhibition in Luxor Museum, and the botanical material is in the Cairo Agricultural Museum. Some of the larger shrines are in storage in Luxor. Tutankhamen himself still rests in his tomb in the Valley of the Kings.

Even today, the tomb and its contents remain substantially unpublished, although there are occasional volumes written by experts and dedicated to individual and somewhat diverse components of the grave goods such as footwear, chariots and gaming boxes. The Griffith Institute at Oxford University, repository of Carter's papers, has done a great deal to remedy this deficiency by making Carter's diaries and his meticulous records and drawings, plus the diaries of Arthur Mace, notes taken by Alfred Lucas and the numerous photographs taken by Harry Burton, available online in *Tutankhamun: Anatomy of an Excavation:* www.griffith.ox.ac.uk/gri/4tut.html. Meanwhile Nicholas Reeves's comprehensive *Complete Tutankhamen* (1990) provides a scholarly yet accessible introduction to the tomb and a detailed analysis of its contents for non-specialist readers. There are many other Tutankhamen-themed works aimed at different audiences, some good, some less so, others decidedly bad. The difficulty, for the non-expert, is to sort the wheat from the chaff. As a general rule of thumb, any book that refers to the king as 'Tut', and his wife as 'Ankhy' or 'Patty', and any book that includes the word 'truth' on its cover, is best avoided.

INTRODUCTION: TUTANKHAMEN'S MANY CURSES

It was a thrilling moment for an excavator. Alone, save for my native workmen, I found myself, after years of comparatively unproductive labour, on the threshold of what might prove to be a magnificent discovery. Anything, literally anything, might lie beyond that passage, and it needed all my self-control to keep from breaking down the doorway and investigating then and there.

Howard Carter[1]

On 4 November 1922 labourers employed by Lord Carnarvon and his archaeological partner Howard Carter discovered a flight of steps leading down to the lost tomb of the 18th Dynasty Egyptian king Tutankhamen. The tomb was virtually intact and Tutankhamen's mummified body still lay within, protected by a nest of golden coffins and surrounded by a vast array of slightly dusty but still glittering grave goods. This discovery – Egypt's first near-complete royal burial – provoked unprecedented media interest. Reporters flocked to Egypt, where they perched on the stone wall surrounding the tomb and irritated the naturally taciturn Carter almost to breaking point. Pushed by their editors to write about the most exciting discovery ever made, yet denied access to the tomb and its contents, the journalists published a highly entertaining mixture of fact and fiction spiced with a dash of vitriol aimed at the archaeologists.

Tutankhamen's was by no means the first mummy to be discovered, nor the most important, yet he quickly became a celebrity and, like all celebrities, was featured relentlessly in newspapers and journals. As 'Tut-mania' gripped the West, Egyptology, no longer the dull refuge of earnest scholars and library-bound academics, acquired a popular appeal that was reflected in fashion, architecture and fiction. Meanwhile in Egypt, an increasingly independent country struggling to enter the modern world, the discovery raised uncomfortable questions about colonialism, the ownership of Egypt's past, and the right of the archaeologist to mine a foreign land for knowledge, profit or personal glory. Things would never be quite the same again.

For me, like many of my generation, Tutankhamen provided an introduction to the hot and glamorous world of the pharaohs. I was born and raised in Bolton, Lancashire, some 2,600 geographical miles from the Valley of the Kings, and far, far away in terms of heat and glamour. Damp, prosaic Bolton – an ex-mill town – is, however, a remarkably good place for an aspiring Egyptologist to live. The nineteenth-century entrepreneurs who made their fortunes from the cotton trade developed a strong interest in ancient Egypt and its possible links to the Bible. Driven by a need to amass not just knowledge but actual artefacts, they sailed along the Nile collecting souvenirs ranging from the smallest of beads to full-sized coffined mummies. Back home they expanded their collections by buying from antiquities dealers, and they financed archaeological digs that entitled them to a share of the excavated finds. Their private acquisitions eventually made their way into local museums, so that Bolton, Burnley,

Blackburn, Liverpool, Macclesfield and Manchester (to name just a few) are today blessed with extraordinarily rich Egyptology collections. As a child, of course, all this passed me by. It seemed perfectly natural that Lancashire's museums should be packed with exotic Egyptian treasures. If I thought about it at all, I assumed that all museums were similarly well endowed.

In 1972 the 'Treasures of Tutankhamen' exhibition arrived at the British Museum, bringing with it an assortment of artefacts including the king's iconic funerary mask. Almost overnight, a new wave of Tutmania swept over Britain. Colour television, still something of a novelty, showed the grave goods in all their golden glory and, as Tutankhamen invaded the nation's living rooms, viewers were introduced to a past very different to the classical history learned in school. Well over a million visitors were inspired to make their way to the British Museum to see for themselves. So infectious was the atmosphere that the brave (some might say foolish) decision was made to take my entire school to London. A train was chartered, and by the time it was realised that we could not travel on the day that schools had priority access to the Museum, it hardly seemed to matter. Off we went, hundreds of girls armed with packed lunches and waterproof coats. The day itself could not be counted as an unqualified success: having first visited the Science Museum and the Tower of London we ran out of time and, after queuing for an hour or so in the grounds of the British Museum we left, clutching posters and postcards but without having actually seen the king himself. It would be another ten years before I gazed at Tutankhamen's golden face in an almost empty Cairo Museum. Nevertheless, my latent interest in Egyptology had been kindled, and there was no going back. This Tutankhamen-inspired fixation with ancient Egypt may well be my own, personal version of Tutankhamen's curse.

I am able to make the suggestion that I have been cursed by Tutankhamen quite lightly, because I don't believe that ancient curses

– either real or imagined – can have any effect on the modern world unless we allow them to. In fact, I have to come clean and admit that I don't believe in curses at all. However, there are many who do indeed believe, and who see Tutankhamen's curse as a very serious matter: a deadly protection derived from an archaic, esoteric knowledge, used by the necropolis priests to guard the dead king and his tomb. This protection can take many forms, ranging from the magical and unverifiable (deadly spells and elemental spirits) to the more scientific and physical (hidden 'biosecurity' measures, pathogens and poisons). Believers – and a quick trawl of the internet confirms that there are many, each armed with a slightly different version of 'the truth' – accept that this curse somehow killed Lord Carnarvon within five months of the opening of the tomb, simply because he financed the archaeological mission that desecrated the burial. The curse then went on to kill others linked either directly or indirectly with Tutankhamen, using a variety of ingenious and, to the sceptic, needlessly perverse means.

Carnarvon's sudden death thrust his archaeological partner into an unwelcome limelight, so that today we remember Carter as the driving force behind the Tutankhamen mission while Carnarvon is relegated to the role of genial and generous backer with a passing infatuation for ancient Egypt.[2] Their contemporaries, however, understood that the tomb belonged fairly and squarely to Carnarvon. The initial report of the discovery, published in *The Times* on 30 November 1922, makes this very clear. Headlined 'Great find at Thebes. Lord Carnarvon's long quest', it tells how 'for nearly sixteen years Lord Carnarvon, with the assistance of Mr Howard Carter, has been carrying out excavations on the west bank of the Nile at Luxor'. The next day's *Times* carried a 'tribute to Lord Carnarvon', written by Sir E. A. Wallis Budge, Keeper of Egyptian Antiquities at the British Museum, which started 'The news of the very important Egyptian discovery which has been made by Lord Carnarvon and his trusty helper, Mr

Howard Carter, is one which will send a thrill of pleasure throughout the whole of the archaeological world.' This is Tutankhamen's story, and not Carter's. Yet Carter's personality and behaviour so influence our understanding of the discovery and emptying of the tomb that it is impossible to consider one without the other. Anyone interested in reading more about Carter's life should start with James's thought-provoking biography *Howard Carter: The Path to Tutankhamen* (1992). Unfortunately, there is no equivalent biography of Lord Carnarvon and, as much of the family archive was destroyed during the Second World War, there may never be one.

For Carter, the discovery of a warehouse-like set of chambers crammed with fragile artefacts proved both a blessing and a curse, as it forced him to assume a diplomatic role for which he was supremely ill-suited. Tutankhamen brought Carter a great deal of fame and some fortune, but little of the academic recognition that he might reasonably have expected. Effectively, his great find brought his career as an excavator to an end. He was to devote the rest of his life to Tutankhamen's grave goods, dying before the academic publication of his work was anywhere near complete. This means that much of our information about the excavation of the tomb comes from popular sources: private writings, Carter's own books, and contemporary newspapers, *The Times* in particular, which carried regular reports of events in the Valley. I have used these writings to convey a flavour of the wonder and excitement with which the excavators, and the general public, welcomed Tutankhamen to the modern world.

Many Egyptologists would argue that the true curse of Tutankhamen is the fixation that the general public, thoroughly egged on by the media, has developed with the king at the expense of the rest of Egypt's long history. Our overwhelming interest in Tutankhamen has effectively distorted our perception of the past so that, almost a century after his rediscovery, and more than 3,000 years after his death, 'Tut' – we are so familiar with him that we even accord him a friendly nickname – remains the ultimate ancient-world celebrity. Only Nefertiti and Cleopatra VII can approach his superstar status. Ramesses II 'The Great' lags some way behind, while Senwosret III and Pseusennes II and many others – magnificent, heroic god-kings once widely celebrated for their mighty deeds – are remembered only by those who have made a special study of Egyptian history. As the newly revealed Tutankhamen surfed the zeitgeist, two spectacular, near-contemporary discoveries, Leonard Woolley's 1920s excavation of the royal death pits in the Mesopotamian city of Ur, and Pierre Montet's 1939 excavation of the near-intact Third Intermediate Period royal tombs at the Egyptian city of Tanis, failed to capture the public imagination.

While it is understandable that in 1939 the eyes of the world were not focused on ancient Egypt, the lack of interest in Woolley's work is at first sight baffling, given its obvious connection to Biblical archaeology. However, three important differences distinguished the two excavations. First, unlike the anonymous servants buried in the grim death pits, Tutankhamen was a named individual: an ancient yet curiously modern young man, revealed to the Western world at a time when the West had lost so many of its own young men. The art and fashions of his age – the Late Amarna Period – fitted neatly with the art and fashions of post-war Europe, allowing him to appear both glamorously remote and reassuringly familiar. Second, while Tutankhamen was by no means the first pharaoh to be discovered – Cairo Museum already had an entire gallery full of kings – he was the first to be discovered with a vast amount of gold. Treasure, and treasure-hunting, has a universal, timeless appeal that cuts across boundaries of age, race and gender, and it seems that it was Tutankhamen's gold death mask, rather than his actual face, which so captured the public imagination. Finally, Carter's excavation was conducted under an intense media scrutiny, which ensured that, even if they wished to, the public could not forget about ongoing events in the Valley of the Kings.

In many ways this fame has been a good thing. Tutankhamen, and the study of his life and times, have brought a great deal of pleasure to many, me included. His instantly recognisable brand has proved particularly valuable to the Egyptian economy. In January 2011 tourism accounted for 11 per cent of the Egyptian national income, with visits to the Cairo Museum (home of Tutankhamen's grave goods) and the Valley of the Kings (modern Luxor: home of Tutankhamen's tomb) an important part of all itineraries.[3] It is therefore an unfortunate paradox that Tutankhamen's very popularity threatens to destroy his legacy. The tourists who make their way to the Valley of the Kings disembark from vibrating, polluting coaches to breathe and perspire in his cramped tomb, causing incalculable damage to the fragile decorated walls. The negative effects of tourism – the Valley's own curse of Tutankhamen – are an ongoing and very serious problem for the Egyptian Antiquities Service (EAS), the government agency with responsibility for the care and protection of Egypt's ancient monuments.[4] In response, and as a way of balancing the needs of the visitors with the needs of the conservators, the EAS has recently announced ambitious plans to build a full-sized replica of Tutankhamen's tomb in a nearby valley. This false tomb will allow visitors an 'authentic' experience while preserving the genuine tomb.

It is sad, but perhaps predictable, that his celebrity status has resulted in some Egyptologists drawing away from Tutankhamen lest they be perceived as pandering to, exploiting or even (perish the thought) enjoying popular taste. Confessing an interest in Tutankhamen is, for a few, the equivalent to confessing a preference for television soaps over Shakespeare or musical theatre over opera, while writing about Tutankhamen may be interpreted as a venal attempt to make money, which, in the world of academia, has not always been seen as a good thing. This elitism is, however, rare. Many others have simply dismissed Tutankhamen as insignificant: a short-lived boy, weak, manipulated and unworthy of any detailed study.

He is a 'sensitive youth, a Hamlet totally unequal to the crushing responsibilities he was called upon to bear'; a 'youthful nonentity'; a king who simply does not deserve to serve as the representative of the Dynastic Age.[5] This criticism is in part true. His was a short reign that started at a young age; much of what he accomplished must have been done under the guidance of others. However, while Tutankhamen's decade is brief when compared with the thirty-eight-year (prosperous but, perhaps, slightly dull) reign of Amenhotep III, it compares favourably with the seventeen-year (far from dull) reign of Akhenaten and the four (presumably dull: we know little about them) years of his successor Ay. Ten years, in a land where elite males had a life expectancy of approximately forty years, was a long time. While it would be going too far to regard the twenty-year-old Tutankhamen as middle-aged, he outlived many of his contemporaries, and he died a man, not a boy.

Tutankhamen's decade was far from dull. It was the turning point between the unique religious certainties of the Amarna Age and the traditional polytheism of later reigns.[6] It included a change of capital city and a return to traditional royal propaganda that was reflected in the development of official art and writings. Tutankhamen's own curse is surely the early death that stopped him achieving his destiny. Had he lived for twenty more years there is a fair chance that he would have succeeded in restoring his country to its former prosperity. He may even have been hailed as the first king of the 19th Dynasty. Instead, his brief reign did not allow him sufficient time to distance himself from the 'heresies' of his predecessors Akhenaten and Smenkhkare. Forever linked to them and their unorthodox ideas, he was deliberately excluded from the 19th Dynasty King Lists – the official record of Egypt's rulers – and effectively became a non-person. This, to a king who believed that he needed to be remembered if he was to have any hope of living beyond death, was a serious matter indeed.

Although the evidence is complex, and there are gaps in our

knowledge, there is enough archaeological and textual evidence to allow us to reconstruct Tutankhamen's reign with a fair degree of accuracy. There are many areas of scholarly disagreement – Tutankhamen's parentage being a subject of continuing, vigorous discussion even after the recent publication of DNA tests, for example – but on the whole, the bare bones of his story are agreed and we know much about his life and times. Yet alongside this orthodox and entirely satisfactory history Tutankhamen has developed a second, very different 'history'; an intuitive, post-discovery cultural construct that makes him the subject of a whole spectrum of interpretations including murder plots, archaeological conspiracies and the occult. Modern technologies – the internet in particular – have helped these constructs to spread so that, in just ninety years, Tutankhamen has advanced from long-dead, barely remembered king to cultural phenomenon.[7] This is an important contemporary, and still evolving, aspect of Tutankhamen's legacy, but conspiracies and curses sit uneasily alongside biomedical Egyptology and the forensic examination of ancient texts. I have therefore divided this book into two complementary but entirely separate sections. The first deals with the evidence for Tutankhamen's life and death. The second considers the development of the post-discovery Tutankhamen. Together they tell one complete tale.

The king of Egypt (or pharaoh: the two words are interchangeable) had many duties. As the earthly representative of the gods he was the head of the army and the civil service, and the chief priest of every state cult. But his principle, overriding duty, the duty that linked all other duties and justified his existence, was the maintenance of *maat.* The constant conflict between *maat,* the correct order of being, and its opposite *isfet,* or chaos, was fundamental to Egyptian thought.

Chaos is easy for us to understand: in ancient Egypt this concept encompassed all uncontrolled behaviour, including illness, crime and the strangeness of foreigners. *Maat* is more difficult; with no equivalent English word it is best defined as a powerful combination of truth, rightness, status quo, control and justice.

The Theban god Amen, 'The Hidden One', smiled on the 18th Dynasty kings, allowing a series of mighty warriors (Ahmose, Tuthmosis I, Tuthmosis III) to be interspersed by monumental builders and astute diplomats (Hatshepsut, Tuthmosis IV, Amenhotep III). With an empire stretching from Nubia in the south to Syria in the north, 18th Dynasty Egypt was to all intents and purposes invincible and her kings were wealthy as Egypt's kings had never been before. The treasury was filled with gold, the granaries were overflowing and the people were peaceful and content in a land whose ancient mud-brick towns and cities were now dominated by imposing stone temples built to house the cult statues of the many gods.

Amenhotep III succeeded to the throne as the richest and most powerful person in the eastern Mediterranean world. He ruled Egypt for thirty-eight peaceful and extremely prosperous years, his reign characterised by diplomacy and great building works. A series of impressive stone temples and sumptuous mud-brick palaces made it obvious to all that Amenhotep was truly blessed by the gods. While remaining loyal to, and investing in, the traditional state deities, Amenhotep showed a growing devotion to the solar cults. At the same time, he developed an unprecedented interest in his own divinity.

Amenhotep III was succeeded by his son, Amenhotep IV. The new reign started conventionally enough, but within five years Amenhotep had made radical changes to state theology. There was now to be one main god; a faceless solar disc known as the Aten. Amenhotep changed his name to Akhenaten and retreated with his consort, Nefertiti, to worship the Aten in the purpose-built Middle Egyptian city of Amarna. It is highly likely that this is where Tutankhamen was born.

Akhenaten and Nefertiti are such strong characters, and there is so much that one can write about their deeds, beliefs and even appearance, that they threaten to overwhelm any biography of Tutankhamen.

Akhenaten ruled Egypt for seventeen years: years which are extremely ill-documented outside the claustrophobic Amarna court. The end of his reign is something of a mystery, but there is good archaeological and textual evidence to suggest that he was associated with a co-regent named Smenkhkare. It is not, however, clear who Smenkhkare was, and we do not know if he – or even she – lived long enough to enjoy an independent reign. Smenkhkare's death goes unmentioned and, after a brief period of confusion, the next historical certainty comes when, in approximately 1336 BC, the young Tutankhamen inherits the throne as the sole surviving male member of the nuclear royal family. His ten-year reign will be dedicated to erasing all obvious memory of Akhenaten's unfortunate religious experiment. His untimely death will plunge his country into a succession crisis which will cause the 18th Dynasty to fall.

PART I

TUTANKHAMEN:
LIFE AND DEATH

What matters it to any save Egyptologists and archaeologists that LORD CARNARVON and MR HOWARD CARTER should have discovered in Egypt the tomb of KING TUT-ANKHAMEN, who reigned and died more than thirteen centuries before our era? What avails this new proof that, in days so distant, the silver cord was loosed, the golden bowl broken, or the pitcher shattered at the fountain? Vanity of vanities, all is vanity, and there is no new thing under the sun. These ancient kings and their peoples, with their strivings, ambitions, and conquests, their heresies and their orthodoxies, their jewels and their State couches, have they not all passed away, leaving only the fragments found by seekers among their tombs? They and their civilizations are gone, like other civilizations that followed them, as our civilization, too, may go, deep-founded though it seemed to be a decade since. Why, if naught endures, if there be no pledge of permanence in thought or deed, if our little systems have their day and cease to be, should men delve into bygone ages, seeing that, with all their probings, they may bring to light nothing which can serve as a guide to the future, and establish no principle save that of the ceaselessness of change. To questionings such as these there is no answer in logic that is not, in its way, a paraphrase of the counsel to eat, drink and be merry in our several ways. Therefore if the archaeologist's or the Egyptologist's form of mirth is to dig among tombs and painfully to collate and compare their findings, let no man grudge them their sad pastime, but rather ride his own hobby as best he may.

— The Times, 1 December 1922

The worthy conclusion is that there is indeed a purpose to all human activity, no matter how pointless it may initially seem, as:

Dead kings in their tombs, past civilizations and their records, however much they may enlighten us upon the history of mankind, are in themselves of less import than the activity that leads to their discovery.

LOSS

Clearly enough we saw that very heavy work lay before us, and that many thousands of tons of surface debris would have to be removed before we could hope to find anything; but there was always the chance that a tomb might reward us in the end, and, even if there was nothing else to go upon, it was a chance we were quite willing to take. As a matter of fact we had something more, and, at the risk of being accused of post actum presci-ence, I will state that we had definite hopes of finding the tomb of one particular king, and that king Tut.ankh.Amen.

Howard Carter[1]

The survival of Tutankhamen's near-intact tomb was a lucky accident: the result of a fortunate combination of natural and man-made causes. But, contrary to public perception, its rediscovery in 1922 was a delib-erate act: the culmination of years of well-reasoned archaeological detective work. When Howard Carter started to excavate in the Valley of the Kings, Tutankhamen was a virtually unknown late 18th Dynasty pharaoh who had been omitted from Egypt's official history, yet had left enough monuments and inscriptions to confirm his existence. His 'tomb' – KV 58 – had already been discovered and published: his body had never been found.[2] Carter could not accept this. Refusing to believe that the Valley had yielded all its secrets, and unable to agree that the meagre KV 58 might have been a royal tomb, or even a secondary royal burial, Carter determined to find the missing king. To understand Carter's road to Tutankhamen we need to go back to the Valley of the Kings at the start of the 18th Dynasty.

🐆 🐆 🐆

For many centuries Egypt's kings had chosen to be buried, and to be remembered, in enormous pyramid complexes raised in the vast desert cemeteries of northern Egypt. These complexes included both the tomb where the body rested and the temple where regular offerings could be made to the dead. Then, at the start of the 18th Dynasty in approximately 1550 BC, the large-scale pyramid complex was abandoned. Kings would now build two entirely separate funerary monuments. Their mummified bodies would be buried in relative secrecy in rock-cut tombs tunnelled into the Valley of the Kings on the west bank of the Nile at the southern city of Thebes. The Theban mountain (el Qurn, or 'the horn' in modern Arabic), which rose to a sharp peak above the new necropolis, would serve as a natural pyramid, maintaining a link with the beliefs of the past for those who wished it. At the same time a highly visible memorial temple, appropriately situated on the border between the cultivated land, home of the living, and the sterile desert, home of the dead, would serve as the accessible public focus of the royal mortuary cult. Here the deceased kings would receive, until the very end of time, the offerings necessary to ensure their existence beyond death.

It is not entirely clear why the pharaohs instigated such a major

break with tradition, but it seems likely that there were several con-
tributory factors. The 18th Dynasty kings hailed from Thebes and, as
southerners, may have wished for burial close by their revered 17th
Dynasty ancestors – kings of Thebes, but not of the whole of Egypt
– who had raised small, steep-sided pyramids in the Dra Abu el-Naga
cemetery on the west bank at Thebes. Their increasing devotion to
Amen, patron deity of Thebes, almost certainly contributed towards
their decision: while the northern pyramid fields had been strongly
associated with the cult of the sun god Re of Heliopolis, the new
tombs and memorial temples belonged to one enormous sacred landscape incorporating Amen's extensive east bank Karnak temple
complex and his smaller Luxor temple. Re was certainly not forgotten
– Egypt remained polytheistic – but Amen was generally regarded as
the major state god of the 18th Dynasty. More practical considerations
– cost and security – must also have influenced the decision. While
the pyramid complexes had proved extremely expensive to build and
maintain, the new-style tombs required virtually no raw materials and
employed a far smaller workforce: scores of specialist artisans as
opposed to the tens of thousands of temporary, unskilled labourers
needed to build a pyramid. The problem of feeding and sheltering
these artisans – a logistical nightmare for the pyramid builders – was
quickly solved. By Tutankhamen's reign the royal tomb-workers,
known as the 'Servants in the Place of Truth', were full-time state
employees in receipt of a generous salary. They, and their families,
lived a self-contained life at Deir el-Medina; a purpose-built west
bank town originally built to accommodate the more transient labourers employed on the earlier 18th Dynasty tombs. Meanwhile, the
many hundreds of workers required to build the stone memorial
temples could be housed in full view of the general public: near the
temple, near the cultivated land and the water and food supplies, and
far from the precious cemetery.

Necropolis security would always be an issue in a land where the elite insisted on being buried with a vast array of valuable goods. Ineni, architect to Tuthmosis I, the first king known to have been buried in the Valley, highlights this concern when he tells us on the wall of his own tomb (TT 81) that he 'supervised the excavation of the cliff tomb of His Majesty alone, no-one seeing and no one hearing'. The Valley was the ideal site for a secret cemetery: remote and difficult for a stranger to access, admission had to be effected either via the narrow, guarded Valley entrance or by sliding down a noisy scree-covered slope. The principal weakness would always come from the tomb-workers, who had both the knowledge and the practical skills to rob the kings they had just buried. The reduction in worker numbers was therefore a major advantage; the fewer people who knew about the tombs and their contents, the better. Strict security measures were enforced: entrance to and from the Valley was controlled and metal tools were secured at the end of each shift. After the funeral the tomb doors were blocked, plastered and sealed with one or more of the official necropolis seals. No seal could prevent robbers from entering the tomb (although, as the sealing was a ritual act, it might cause the superstitious to hesitate) but any tampering would be obvious to the inspectors who regularly patrolled the cemetery looking for signs of damage. Violated tombs were quickly made superficially whole again. If thefts could not be stopped, they could at least be concealed, allowing the necropolis officials to pretend that all was well.

As a self-proclaimed devotee of Amen, Tutankhamen would have wished to be buried alongside his ancestors in either the Valley of the Kings or its offshoot, the Western Valley. This was not simply a question of conforming to 18th Dynasty tradition, although that would have been an important consideration for a king who promoted himself as a restorer of traditional royal and religious values. Cemeteries carried their own potent magic, and dead kings, now one with the gods, had powerful spirits that might benefit others. Burial among his divine ancestors would therefore help the newly deceased Tutankhamen to achieve his own afterlife. We may speculate that Tutankhamen would have wished to construct his tomb in the Western Valley, close by that of his revered grandfather, Amenhotep III (KV 22), and we may reasonably expect that work would have started on his tomb as early as possible in his reign: no king wanted to run the risk of dying without a secure home for his body. As Tutankhamen initially ruled from Amarna, a city with its own royal cemetery, this would suggest that work on his Theban tomb started during his regnal Year 2 or 3, soon after the abandonment of Amarna. As there had been a twenty-five-year hiatus in the Valley building programme, things may have got off to a slow start, but his workmen would still have had a good seven or eight years to construct his last resting place.

Whatever he may have intended, we know that Tutankhamen was not buried in a splendid royal tomb in the Western Valley. He was instead buried in a cramped, non-royal tomb cut into the floor of the main Valley (KV 62). The accepted explanation is that Tutankhamen simply died too young to realise his ambitious plans. Tradition allowed just seventy days in the embalming house before the funeral, and this was nowhere near long enough to make his unfinished tomb usable. Tutankhamen therefore had to be buried in a substitute tomb – most probably the tomb that his successor, the elderly courtier Ay, had been preparing for himself.

However, we might reasonably question the assumption that Tutankhamen's builders ran so seriously out of time as to make his chosen tomb uninhabitable. Three decades after Tutankhamen's death, the 19th Dynasty Ramesses I ruled for a mere two years, yet his architects were able to adapt his unfinished tomb (KV 16) to accommodate his burial in a suitably regal manner; Ramesses' great-grandson, Merenptah, ruled for ten years – the same reign-length as Tutankhamen – and was buried in a magnificent tomb (KV 8). It seems far more likely that Ay, inheriting the throne as an elderly man, and realising that he himself might run out of time, made a strategic swap. Just four years

after Tutankhamen's death, Ay was buried in a splendid, yet unfin-
ished, tomb in the Western Valley (KV 23), close by the tomb of
Amenhotep III. It seems reasonable to suggest that just as Tutankha-
men had been buried in Ay's intended tomb, so Ay was buried in
Tutankhamen's. It may even be that KV 23 was originally started for
Amenhotep IV, son of Amenhotep III, before he changed his name to
Akhenaten and moved his court and tomb to Amarna.

The tomb was the hidden aspect of Tutankhamen's funerary provision. The visible aspect – his memorial temple – would have been situated among the row of temples that fringed the Theban west bank
desert edge. But this temple, along with many others, vanished long
ago, its valuable stone blocks recycled in later buildings. Dozens of
dynastic blocks have been recovered from medieval housing on the
east bank, near the Luxor Temple. Some of these date to the reign of
Tutankhamen, and may have originated in his memorial temple,
although it is equally possible that they came from a separate east
bank building, the 'Mansion of Nebkheperure in Waset [Thebes]',
which we know was built by Ay as a memorial to Tutankhamen and
which has since vanished. The carved blocks show Tutankhamen in
action: processing on the river, making offerings, purifying statues
and leading his troops in campaigns against Egypt's traditional Nubian
(southern) and Asiatic (eastern) enemies.[3]

The ruined Temple of Ay and Horemheb provides a valuable clue
to the location of Tutankhamen's lost temple.[4] Situated on the west
bank, close to the remains of the memorial temple of Tuthmosis II and
the far more intact memorial temple of the 20th Dynasty king Ramesses III, it has yielded a pair of damaged, red quartzite seated colossal
statues originally carved for Tutankhamen, then inscribed by Ay and
finally usurped by Ay's successor Horemheb. Today these statues are
housed in the Cairo Museum and in the Oriental Institute, Chicago.
It is likely that Ay took these statues from Tutankhamen's temple
which, given the size and weight of the colossi, was presumably nearby:

possibly either the ruined building known today as the 'North Temple' or the equally ruined 'South Temple'. However, given the complicated history of Tutankhamen's tomb, it is tempting to suggest that the Temple of Ay and Horemheb itself may have started life as Tutankhamen's memorial temple, before being usurped by Ay. Although few foundation deposits inscribed with Ay's name have been recovered from the temple, these might well belong to a later building phase.

Tutankhamen's last resting place was a typical late 18th Dynasty non-royal rock-cut tomb, one of three (the others being KV 55 and KV 63) cut into the limestone floor of the main Valley. It was accessed via a flight of sixteen descending steps. At the bottom of the steps, a doorway opened on to a narrow, sloping passageway (measuring length 8.08 × width 1.68 × height 2m) leading to a second doorway.[5] This led into a rectangular chamber (7.85 × 3.55 × 2.68m) cut some 7.1m below the Valley floor and orientated north–south. This first chamber – a storeroom dubbed the 'Antechamber' by Carter – allowed access via a sealed doorway to a subsidiary storage chamber known as the 'Annexe' (4.35 × 2.6 × 2.55m; orientated north–south). The floor of the Annexe was almost a metre below the floor of the Antechamber. The Burial Chamber (6.37 × 4.02 × 3.63m) was separated from the Antechamber by a plastered dry stone partition wall that contained a hidden doorway. The Burial Chamber was orientated east–west, and its floor, too, was also nearly a metre lower than the floor of the Antechamber. Opening off the Burial Chamber was a subsidiary storage chamber, the 'Treasury' (4.75 × 3.8 × 2.33m; orientated north–south).

Eighteenth Dynasty royal tombs were traditionally decorated with exclusively royal texts and scenes taken from a collection of religious writings known as the *Books of the Underworld* or the *Guides to the Afterlife*. These were provided to help the king on his journey to the afterlife by recalling the night-time adventure of the sun god Re. Every day the young and vigorous Re sailed his boat across the

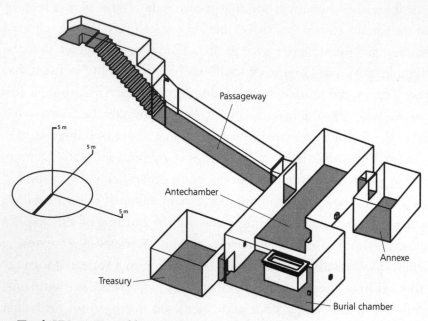

Passageway

Antechamber

Annexe

Treasury

Burial chamber

1. Tomb KV 62: Tutankhamen's last resting place.

placid sky, bringing light to Egypt. Each evening, now old and frail, Re transferred to his night boat and entered the *Duat,* the dark and hidden world of the night-time sun. If all went well, he would be reborn in the east at dawn. In Tutankhamen's small-scale tomb the passageway, Antechamber, Annexe and Treasury remained unplastered and undecorated. Only the Burial Chamber was plastered with gypsum and painted. The humidity damage suffered by a number of the grave goods suggests that this plaster may not have been fully dry when the tomb was sealed; an indication that the tomb was made ready for the king at the last minute. The decoration is similar in composition and style to the decoration in the tomb of Ay; this is hardly surprising, as the tombs are near-contemporary, and it seems likely that both were built by the courtier Maya, 'overseer of works in the place of eternity' and 'overseer of works in the west'.

𓃥 𓃥 𓃥

Soon after Tutankhamen's funeral, the Valley suffered a spate of robberies. Tutankhamen's tomb was targeted twice, in quick succession. The first robbers were able to breach the blocked and plastered doorway, make their way along the entrance passage – which was being used for extra storage – and enter the Antechamber. It is not clear how much property was stolen – did the thieves access the tomb on a regular basis, or were they caught immediately? – but it seems likely that they targeted metals, glass and high-value fat-based oils and cosmetics which would have to be stolen soon after the funeral, before they went bad. The necropolis officials who discovered the robbery made a cursory restoration of the tomb, then filled the entry passage to its ceiling with tons of white limestone chips. Sundry small objects, including items dropped by the robbers and items swept into the tomb with the stone chips, were accidentally incorporated in the fill. Finally, the outer doorway was resealed.

Stone chips may have slowed the thieves, but they could not stop them. Indeed, it seems likely that the very men who were employed to fill the passage were those who returned later to rob it. Tunnelling through the top left section of the blocked passageway, then breaching the blocked internal doors, the second band of thieves were able to access all the chambers. However, given that they could only leave via their narrow tunnel, they could only take the smaller, lighter items. Carter was to speculate that as much as 60 per cent of Tutankhamen's jewellery might have been stolen at this time, basing his estimate on the written labels attached to the abandoned boxes and chests. Again, the breach in security was detected. The tomb was restored in a somewhat haphazard fashion, the breaches in the internal doorways were resealed, the tunnel through the passageway was restored with darker-coloured chips, and the outer doorway was again made whole and sealed with the necropolis seal. So, we can assume, this pattern would have been repeated again and again until the tomb was stripped of all valuables, had nature not intervened.

The Valley of the Kings is a *wadi*, or ancient, dry riverbed. While it normally enjoys a dry environment with minimal annual rainfall, it occasionally experiences severe thunderstorms lasting just a few hours. These lead to sudden, violent and destructive flooding. After more than thirty-five years living in or near the Valley, Carter was able to recall just four of these torrential cloudbursts (in 1898, 1900, October 1916 and November 1916).[6] Writing to his mother in October 1918, he describes their effect:

> *The Valley of the Tombs of the Kings, joined by the Great Western Valley, in a few moments became little short of mountain rivers ... the torrent cutting out wide furows [sic] in the valley bed and rolling before it stones some two feet in diameter – natives returning home with their animals were unable to ford it, and thus were cut off from their homes.*[7]

On 1 November 1916 Carter had witnessed the Great Northern Ravine (separated from the Valley of the Kings by a narrow strip of land) filling up with water even though there was no rain: this was the result of a storm fifteen miles to the north-west. He noted that, although prior to the sudden influx of water the ravine was barren of plant life, by the next January it was covered in flowering plants that attracted insects. By the end of the following spring, with no further water, the plants and insects had almost entirely disappeared. The Valley and its branches, however, always remained entirely bereft of life, even after it had been saturated.

With several inches of rain falling on the high desert in minutes, the hard, dry ground cannot absorb the water generated by the storm. This water rushes down the hillside forming large streams which,

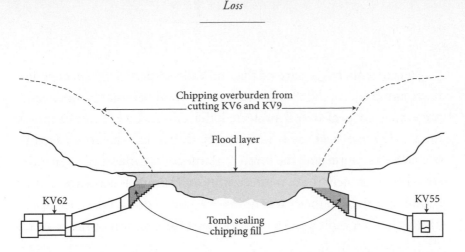

2. *Cross section of the Valley of the Kings, showing the late 18th Dynasty flood layer covering both KV 62 and KV 55.*

carrying a mass of stone, sand and rubble, invade and fill any tomb that might lie in their path. As the streams collide and mix they lose linear velocity, and the central Valley fills with a foaming lake. When the water escapes to the Nile Valley it leaves behind a hard layer of sediment incorporating mud, chalk, shale and limestone. Tombs remain packed with debris and surfaces – decorated walls, ceilings and pillars – are left wet, stained and abraded. Shale expansion and salt migration then cause further damage as the walls dry out. The statistics are sobering: all but ten of the Valley tombs have been invaded by floods; in the last 150 years, a third of all the known tombs have been re-buried under rubble and sand; two-thirds of the tombs still include flood debris.[8]

The ancient Egyptians, all too aware of the dangers of flash flooding in the Valley, attempted to protect their dead kings by digging a large drainage channel and by erecting diversionary walls near individual tombs. But all the lower-lying tombs have suffered the effects of repeated floods. Tutankhamen's tomb, cut directly into the Valley bedrock, would always be vulnerable. This vulnerability continues today as tourist paths and modern excavations have altered the Valley landscape and raised the floodwater paths. Tutankhamen's tomb occasionally admits floodwater either via its entrance or, causing more damage, through its roof.

Recent work has confirmed that the Valley experienced a devastating flood at the end of the 18th Dynasty. This flood deposited a thick sediment that concealed and protected the entrance to Tutankhamen's tomb.[9] The vanished tomb was quickly forgotten. The 20th Dynasty builders who worked on the tomb of Ramesses VI almost two centuries after Tutankhamen's death were certainly unaware of its existence, as they allowed debris from their excavations to accumulate over the entrance to his tomb, then built a series of workmen's huts on top of the mound.

Necropolis security worked well enough while the pharaohs retained their authority. The evidence from Tutankhamen's tomb suggests that there must have been many robberies and attempted robberies – that was inevitable – but that these were relatively minor affairs, easily detected and superficially put right. We must wonder how many of these breaches in necropolis security were reported to the authorities. The 19th Dynasty kings certainly thought that all was well; they abandoned all thought of hiding their tombs, and allowed their hitherto discreet doorways to become obvious, decorative features. But then, towards the end of the 19th Dynasty, the unthinkable slowly but surely started to happen. Unpredictable Nile levels led to high inflation and food shortages, and Thebes suffered occasional raids by Libyan nomads. As the increasingly corrupt civil service failed to pay the Deir el-Medina workmen there were strikes and, inevitably, a sharp increase in crime. By the late 20th Dynasty the situation had deteriorated badly, and the royal tombs were facing a serious and sustained threat from well-organised and well-informed gangs who all too often had the tacit backing of the officials responsible for guarding the tombs. Corruption now extended to the highest levels.

The reign of Ramesses XI saw Thebes in a state of civil war. The Valley had become irredeemably insecure and, on the desert edge, the memorial temples had been vandalised and stripped of their valuables. Abandoning his incomplete tomb (KV 4), Ramesses fled north. Here, denied access to his ancestral burial ground, we may reasonably assume he ordered the construction of a new, secure tomb. This tomb has yet to be discovered but, given Ramesses' obvious devotion to the god Ptah, patron deity of Memphis, it seems likely that he was buried somewhere near to Ptah's Memphite temple. Succeeding kings would follow this precedent and build tombs within the precincts of their northern temples; here the priests could guard their graves night and day.

Smendes, founder of the 21st Dynasty, ruled northern Egypt from the Delta city of Tanis, while the Theban general and High Priest of Amen Herihor, and his descendants, gradually brought the south under control. To the High Priests fell the responsibility of restoring and maintaining the plundered tombs in the Valley of the Kings. This was a time-consuming, expensive and ultimately fruitless task: it must have been very clear to everyone that as soon as the burials were made good the robberies would start again. So, the necropolis officials decided on a bold change of tactics. If the promise of hidden treasure was attracting thieves to the tombs, the well-publicised removal of that treasure should surely remove all temptation. And, as an added bonus, valuables collected from the tombs could be used to swell the sadly depleted state coffers.

The royal tombs were officially opened and emptied of their contents. The kings and their closest relations were taken from their sarcophagi and moved to undertakers' workshops within the Valley. Here they were stripped of their original bandages and jewellery, re-wrapped, labelled, and placed in plain wooden coffins. The mummies – no longer a temptation to anyone – were then stored in chambers dotted about the necropolis. From time to time these collections were inspected, moved and amalgamated, until there were two major royal caches: one housed in the family tomb of the High Priest Pinodjem II at Deir el-Bahri (DB 320) and one stored in the tomb of Amenhotep II (KV 35).

2

DISCOVERY

There are also in this city [Thebes], *they say, remarkable tombs of the early kings ... Now the priests said that in their records they find forty-seven tombs of kings; but down to the time of Ptolemy son of Lagus* [Ptolemy I], *they say, only fifteen remained, most of which had been destroyed at the time we visited...*

– Diodorus Siculus[1]

As the dynastic age ended and Egypt's official religion moved from paganism to Christianity, then from Christianity to Islam, the tombs in the Valley of the Kings remained open and unprotected. Some were simply lost; others developed a second life as chapels or houses, or were once again used as tombs. It was dimly remembered that the Valley had once been a royal cemetery; this was reflected in its name, Biban el-Moluk or 'Valley of the Doors of the Kings'. But no one knew how many tombs there were and, as all knowledge of the hieroglyphic script had been lost, no one knew who had been buried in them.

When, in 1707, Father Claude Sicard, a determined Jesuit missionary, travelled to the small and insignificant town of Luxor, he became the first European to recognise and record the true nature of the Valley and its tombs:

> *These sepulchres of Thebes are tunnelled into the rock and are of astonishing depth. Halls, rooms, all are painted from top to bottom. The variety of colours, which are almost as fresh as the day they were painted, gives an admirable effect. There are as many hieroglyphs as there are animals and objects represented, which makes us suppose that we have there the story of the lives, virtues, acts, combats and victories of the princes who are buried there, but it is impossible for us to decipher them for the present.* [2]

Others soon followed. In 1743 the Reverend Richard Pococke's *Description of the East and Some Other Countries* fascinated his readers while providing a highly inaccurate plan of the tombs that would baffle archaeologists for many years to come:

> *The vale where these grottos are, may be about one hundred yards wide. There are signs of about eighteen of them. However, it is to be remarked that Diodorus says seventeen of them only remained till the time of the Ptolemies; and I found the entrances to about that number, most of which he says were destroyed in his time, and now there are only nine that can be entered into. The hills on each side are steep rocks, and the whole place is covered with rough stones that seem to have rolled from them; the grottos are cut into the rock in a most beautiful manner in long rooms or galleries under the mountains… The galleries are mostly about ten feet wide and high; four or five of these galleries, one within another, from thirty to fifty feet long, and from ten to fifteen feet high, generally lead to a spacious room, in which is seen the tomb of the King, with his figure cut in relief on*

the lid, as I saw it on one. In the furthermost room of another, the picture of the King is painted on the stone at full length; both the sides and ceilings of the rooms are cut with hieroglyphics of birds and beasts, and some of them painted, being as fresh as if they were but just finished, though they must be above two thousand years old...[3]

In 1798 Napoleon's Commission – a band of scientists, historians and artists charged with recording Egypt ancient and modern – arrived to count a mere eleven tombs in the main Valley plus one in the Western Valley. Publication of their survey, as part of the *Description de l'Égypte* (1809–29), coincided with the culmination of Jean-François Champollion's work on the decoding of the hieroglyphic script. Suddenly, it was possible for scholars to read the texts that decorated the tomb and temple walls while the texts themselves were, for the first time, available to stay-at-home scholars via the plates of the *Description*. As her king-lists were deciphered, Egypt's lost history was restored and Egyptology became a proper, respectable subject for academic study. Museums that had once regarded Egyptian artefacts as beautiful but meaningless 'dead ends' – unlike Greek and Roman artefacts, which had always been recognised as both beautiful and relevant to the development of Western civilisation – were now increasingly interested in acquiring them.

Explorers and treasure-hunters were drawn to the Valley. These first Egyptologists had no idea that the royal mummies had already been removed from their tombs, and their hope was always that an intact royal burial would be found. Theirs was not a pure, academic curiosity: enough non-royal burials had been recovered to suggest that a royal tomb would be packed with grave-goods which could be sold at great profit to the growing number of private and institutional collectors in the west. Finding the royal tombs was not, in fact, too difficult: from 1816–17 the ex-circus strongman Giovanni Battista Belzoni used his practical engineering skills to locate eight, including the tomb of Ay. But, although they yielded occasional random artefacts, none of the tombs was intact.

The missing kings would not be discovered until the 1870s, when Ahmed el-Rassul, a member of a notorious family of tomb robbers, discovered the hidden entrance to the tomb of the High Priest Pinodjem II. As we have already seen, this tomb housed not only the Third Intermediate Period Pinodjem family burials, but an entirely separate cache of New Kingdom royal mummies. Because the royal mummies had already been stripped of all valuables, the el-Rassul brothers concentrated on the Pinodjem family grave goods. They were able to sell a series of illustrated papyri, bronze vessels, figurines and at least one mummy before their dealings attracted the attention of the Antiquities Service. On 6 July 1881 the el-Rassuls revealed the whereabouts of the tomb and Émile Brugsch, the representative of the Cairo Museum, was lowered down the shaft. To his amazement, he discovered a chamber packed with coffined and labelled mummies including the 18th Dynasty kings Ahmose, Amenhotep I, Tuthmosis I (a disputed mummy), Tuthmosis II and Tuthmosis III. A second chamber held the recently desecrated burials of the Pinodjem family.

Meanwhile, French Egyptologist Victor Loret had started to explore the Valley of the Kings. He was to discover sixteen tombs, but his most important discovery, in 1898, was the tomb of Amenhotep II (KV 35). Lying in the tomb passageway he found an anonymous male mummy stuck to a model boat. Within the Burial Chamber he found the king himself, stripped of all valuables and re-wrapped, but lying in his original quartzite sarcophagus. A sealed side chamber yielded three unwrapped, unconfined and unlabelled New Kingdom mummies lying side by side, each with a hole in the head and a damaged abdomen, while a second side chamber held nine plain coffins bearing royal names including those of the 18th Dynasty Tuthmosis IV and Amenhotep III.

Within just seventeen years, almost all the 18th Dynasty kings had been rediscovered. Still missing were Hatshepsut, Akhenaten, Smenkhkare, Tutankhamen, Ay and Horemheb. Ay, however, had an open tomb in the Western Valley, while Akhenaten had an open tomb at Amarna. Hatshepsut's pillaged tomb would be identified in 1903 (KV 20); Horemheb's equally pillaged tomb in 1908 (KV 57). By 1910 only Smenkhkare and Tutankhamen lacked both a mummy and a tomb. Excavators searching for an intact 18th Dynasty royal tomb were effectively looking for these two relatively unknown characters.

The 19th Dynasty Ramesside kings were arrivistes, a military family from the north who, in order to justify their right to rule, consistently emphasised their links with Egypt's earlier kings. The temples that the commoner-born kings Seti I and Ramesses II built at Abydos therefore included King Lists: lines of 'ancestor' pharaohs inscribed in chronological order. These lists omitted Akhenaten, Smenkhkare, Tutankhamen and Ay, passing directly from the well-respected Amenhotep III to the equally well-respected Horemheb. Excluded from Egypt's official history, Akhenaten and his immediate successors became non-kings: their reigns, totalling maybe thirty years, had never officially happened. Modern observers find this blatant falsification of history difficult to accept. To a people who accepted that the written word might have magical properties, however, it made perfect sense. History could and indeed must be corrected to reflect events as they should have been.

Fortunately, the missing kings had left enough textual and archaeological evidence to confirm the existence of the 'Amarna Period' – the period when Egypt was ruled from the city of Amarna – and Egyptologists were in general agreement that the omitted reigns slotted into the late 18th Dynasty as follows:

- Amenhotep III: ruling from Thebes and Memphis
- Akhenaten (initially known as Amenhotep IV): ruling first from Thebes, then from Amarna
- Akhenaten with Smenkhkare as co-regent: ruling from Amarna
- Smenkhkare: ruling from Amarna
- Tutankhamen: ruling initially from Amarna, then from Thebes and Memphis
- Ay: ruling from Thebes and Memphis
- Horemheb: ruling from Thebes and Memphis
- Ramesses I: first king of the 19th Dynasty

The exact sequence of events surrounding the death of Akhenaten was, however, hazy, and the relationship between Akhenaten, Smenkhkare and Tutankhamen was uncertain, although the succession following the death of Tutankhamen was clear. As his immediate successor, Smenkhkare was generally assumed to have been Akhenaten's son. Egyptologist Percy Newberry, influenced by the florid Amarna art-style, felt able to draw a very different conclusion. Here he describes a round-topped limestone stela, a votive dedicated by the soldier Pasi, carved with an image of two kings, seated side by side on a couch. One king wears the double crown of Upper and Lower Egypt, the other wears the blue crown:

> *The two royal personages here are undoubtedly Akhenaten and his co-regent Semenekhkare [sic]. The intimate relations between the Pharaoh and the boy as shown by the scene on this stela recall the relationship between the Emperor Hadrian and the youth Antinous.*[4]

In fact Newberry was letting his imagination run away with him. It is not possible to determine who the two 'kings' are, as the cartouches which would have recorded their names are empty. While one is almost universally recognised as Akhenaten, the other has been variously identified as Smenkhkare, Nefertiti or Amenhotep III. Whatever their relationship, Smenkhkare was closely associated with Akhenaten as his co-regent. Like Akhenaten, he had ruled and died at Amarna and, while he was occasionally mentioned outside that city, he had almost certainly been buried in the Amarna royal tomb. It was therefore highly unlikely that his tomb would be discovered at Thebes.

Writing in 1917, for a non-specialist readership, the Reverend James Baikie, author of many popular books on Egypt and the Near East, told all that was known of Smenkhkare and Tutankhamen:

> [Akhenaten]… While he had six daughters, he had no son to succeed him. He had, indeed, married some of his daughters to powerful nobles, and towards the end of his reign he associated with himself on the throne the husband of Mery-aten, his eldest daughter, a noble named Smenkhara [sic]…
>
> His successor, Smenkhkara, enjoyed only a brief lease of power, and practically nothing is known of his reign. In turn he was succeeded by Tutankhaten who had married Akhenaten's third daughter Ank-s-en-pa-aten…
>
> Tutankhamen seems to have made some attempt to regain a little of the old ascendancy in Syria; but no details are known of an effort which can scarcely have been very successful. The Great Eighteenth Dynasty dribbled miserably to a close in the person of the Divine Father Ay…[5]

Five years later, E. Wallis Budge, Keeper of Egyptology at the British Museum, was able to summarise Tutankhamen's life and reign in just six sentences:

> Our knowledge of the life and times of this king is small. His reign cannot have lasted more than six years; but he is extremely important

as showing that during his reign the famous heresy of the disc wor-shippers came to an end. He married a daughter of Amenhotep IV, now better know perhaps as Akhenaten... Tutankhamen succeeded to the throne of Egypt through his marriage with the daughter of Amenhotep IV, but very soon after he began to reign he saw that the cult of the Aten was doomed and he promptly eliminated the name of Aten from his own name and from that of his wife, and moved his capital from Tall-al-Amarnah back to Thebes. Here he at once pro-ceeded to undo the evil which his father-in-law had perpetuated in the city. In a very short time the city at Akhuenaten (Tall-al-Amar-nah) was deserted by the inhabitants, and fell into ruin, and the old cult of Amen was set upon a firmer basis in Egypt than before, if possible, by Tutankhamen. [6]

Tutankhamen was understood to have been Akhenaten's son-in-law. However, while he, too, had lived at Amarna, many of his monu-ments and texts had been discovered at Thebes. There had been a handful of finds at Memphis, Abydos and Gurob, and his name had even been mentioned outside Egypt, in Nubia and Palestine. Tut-ankhamen, unlike Smenkhkare, was not purely an Amarna king. The 'Restoration Stela' – a large carved stone slab originally erected to stand before the third Pylon, or gateway, of the Karnak temple – con-firmed this. Its thirty lines of text told how Tutankhamen worked to restore Egypt and her traditional gods after the tribulations of the Amarna Period:

The good ruler; who does things beneficial to his Father and all the gods, he has made that which was in ruins to flourish as a monument of eternal age; he has suppressed wrongdoing throughout the Two Lands; Truth is established, [he causes] falsehood to be the abomina-tion of the land... Now when His Majesty arose as king, the temples of the gods and goddesses, beginning from Elephantine [down] to the marshes of the Delta, had fallen into neglect, their shrines had fallen into desolation and become tracts overgrown with weeds, their sanctuaries were as if they had never been, their halls were a trodden path. The land was in confusion, the gods forsook this land. If an [army? was] sent to Djahy to widen the frontiers of Egypt, it met with no success at all. If one prayed to a god to ask things of him, [in no wise] did he come. If one made supplication to a goddess in like manner, in no wise did she come. Their hearts were weak of themselves (with anger); they destroyed what had been done.

After some days had passed by this, [His Majesty appeared] on the throne of his father; he ruled the countries of Horus, the Black Land and the Red Land were under his dominion, and every land was in obeisance to his might. Behold His Majesty was in his palace… Then His Majesty took counsel with his heart, searching out every excellent occasion, seeking what was beneficial to his father Amun… And His Majesty has made monuments for the gods, [fashioning] their statues of real fine-gold, the best of foreign lands, building anew their sanctuaries as monuments of eternal age, they being endowed with property for ever, establishing for them divine gifts as a lasting daily sacrifice, and supplying them with food-offerings upon earth. He has added to what was in former time, he has [surpassed that] done since the time of the ancestors, he has inducted priests and prophets, children of the notables of their towns, each the son of a noted man, and one whose name is known; he has multiplied their [wealth?] with gold, silver, bronze and copper, without limit of [all things?], he has filled their storehouses with slaves, men and women, the fruit of His Majesty's plundering. All the [possessions?] of the temples are doubled, trebled and quadrupled with silver, gold, lapis-lazuli, turquoise, all rare costly stones, royal linen, white cloth, fine linen, olive oil…[7]

It was highly unlikely that this self-proclaimed traditionalist would have been buried anywhere but the Valley of the Kings or the Western

Valley. The logical conclusion was that Tutankhamen had somehow evaded removal by the necropolis restorers, and was still resting in his Theban tomb. But where was his tomb?

🐆 🐆 🐆

There were plenty of Egyptologists eager to search for the missing king, but Antiquities Service regulations, devised to protect Egypt's heritage from naked plundering, stipulated that only one would be allowed to work in the Valley at a time. Theodore Monroe Davis, a retired and extremely wealthy American lawyer fuelled by a burning obsession to find an intact royal tomb, was the chosen one. He had been granted the coveted Valley concession in 1902, and was to retain it for twelve years. This rather curious choice of excavator makes perfect sense when the practicalities of the arrangement are considered. Davis, who had neither the skills nor the inclination to excavate alone, paid for Antiquities Service excavations conducted by three successive, highly competent Inspectors: first Carter, then James Quibell and finally Arthur Weigall.

Quibell was funded by Davis when, on 5 February 1905, he discovered the most intact Valley tomb yet. KV 46 housed the double burial of Yuya and Thuya, parents-in-law to Amenhotep III. Their tomb was cut into the south-east branch of the main Valley. A man-sized hole in the blocked doorway indicated that the burial had been disturbed in antiquity, but Yuya and Thuya still lay in their undecorated tomb, surrounded by a remarkable collection of grave goods. Davis could barely contain his excitement as he entered the burial chamber with the elderly Gaston Maspero, Director General of the Egyptian Antiquities Service, and Weigall, Quibell's successor as Inspector:

Though we had nothing but our bare hands, we managed to take
down the upper layers of stones, and then Monsieur Maspero and I

put our heads and candles into the chamber, which enabled us to get a glimpse of shining gold covering some form of furniture, though we could not identify it. This stimulated us to make the entry without further enlarging the opening. I managed to get over the wall and found myself in the sepulchral chamber. With considerable difficulty we helped Monsieur Maspero safely to scale the obstruction, and then Mr Weigall made his entry. The chamber was as dark as dark could be and extremely hot... We held up our candles, but they gave so little light and so dazzled our eyes that we could see nothing except the glint of gold.

As Davis leaned forward to read the name of the tomb owner, 'Iouiya' (or Yuya), triumph almost turned to disaster:

...Monsieur Maspero cried out 'Be careful!' and pulled my hands back. In a moment we realised that, had my candle touched the bitumen, which I came dangerously near doing, the coffin would have been in a blaze. As the entire contents of the tomb were inflammable, and directly opposite the coffin was a corridor leading to the open air and making a draught, we undoubtedly should have lost our lives, as the only escape was by the corridor, which would have necessitated climbing over the stone wall barring the doorway. This would have retarded our exit for at least ten minutes.[8]

Weigall, a more fluent commentator, was equally struck by the enormity of the occasion:

Imagine entering a town house which had been closed for the summer: imagine the stuffy room, the stiff, silent appearance of the furniture, the feeling that some ghostly occupants of the vacant chairs have just been disturbed, the desire to throw open the windows to let life into the room once more. That was perhaps the first sensation as we stood, really dumbfounded, and stared around at the relics of the life of over three thousand years ago, all of which were as new almost as when they graced the palace of Prince Yuaa. Three arm-chairs were perhaps the first objects to attract the attention: beautiful carved wooden chairs, decorated with gold. Belonging to one of these was a pillow made of down and covered with linen. It was so perfectly preserved that one might have sat upon it or tossed it from this chair to that without doing it injury. Here were fine alabaster vases, and in one of these we were startled to find a liquid, like honey or syrup, still unsolidified by time. Boxes of exquisite workmanship stood in various parts of the room, some resting on delicately wrought legs. Now the eye was directed to a wicker trunk fitted with trays and partitions, and ventilated with little apertures, since the scents were doubtless strong. Two most comfortable beds were to be observed, fitted with springy string mattresses and decorated with charming designs in gold. There in the far corner, placed upon the top of a number of large white jars, stood the light chariot which Yuaa had owned in his lifetime. In all directions stood objects gleaming with gold undulled by a speck of dust, and one looked from one article to another with the feeling that the entire human conception of Time was wrong. These were the things of yesterday, of a year or so ago... [9]

Word of the spectacular discovery spread and, in a foretaste of things to come, Weigall's work – the official recording of the tomb contents – was interrupted that afternoon by a stream of titled visitors including the Duke of Connaught, the Duke of Devonshire and the Crown Prince of Norway. The next day the Empress Eugénie, widow of Napoleon III, arrived for a private tour. Despite these interruptions, the tomb was emptied in just ten days. Although Maspero offered Davis a share of the artefacts, Davis waived any claim, preferring to keep the assemblage intact. Today Yuya and Thuya and their grave goods are displayed in Cairo Museum. During the riots that ended the Mubarak regime in early 2011, several items from their burial assemblage were damaged and some were reported stolen. As I write, the lost artefacts are gradually being recovered by the Museum authorities.

Yuya and Thuya came from the Middle Egyptian city of Akhmim. Although non-royal, they had the closest of links with the royal family. Among his string of impressive titles, Yuya was 'God's Father': a title often translated as 'king's father-in-law'.[10] That he was indeed the father of Tiy, consort to Amenhotep III, is confirmed by ceremonial scarab, published during that king's regnal Year 1 or 2:

> ...*Amenhotep ruler of Thebes, given life, and the king's principal wife Tiy, may she live. The name of her father is Yuya and the name of her mother is Thuya; she is the wife of a mighty king...*

It is interesting that, while Thuya repeatedly uses the title 'Royal Mother of the Chief Wife of the King' on her burial equipment, Yuya makes absolutely no reference to his daughter. If it was not for the ceremonial scarab, we might think, quite wrongly, that Tiy was the daughter of Thuya's (non-existent) first husband. The fact that Tiy's brother, Anen, also neglects to mention the far from trivial fact that his sister is queen of Egypt suggests that men did not consider it proper to boast of links through female family members to the king. This has wide-reaching implications for our understanding of Tutankhamen's family. We can never assume, just because an individual does not claim a relationship with the king, that such a relationship does not exist.

While he worked in close association with the Inspectors of the Antiquities Service Davis's fieldwork, although horribly hasty by modern standards, was acceptable. But in late 1905 the overworked Weigall determined to stop excavating for Davis, and encouraged him to employ the freelance Egyptologist Edward Ayrton to dig on his behalf. Weigall would continue to inspect Davis's work, and would take charge of any major find, but in the meantime, as he did not to be on site every day, he was freed to attend to his many other duties.

Ayrton was probably a competent archaeologist: he had trained with the acknowledged fieldwork expert Flinders Petrie, and so should have known how to conduct an excavation correctly. But, as a twenty-two-year-old with no real authority, he found it impossible to resist his millionaire employer's demand for rapid results at the expense of scientific accuracy, conservation and recording. It is therefore very unfortunate that, on 6 January 1907, Davis's new team stumbled across a uniquely complex late 18th Dynasty cache in tomb KV 55.[11] Today it is recognised that KV 55 may have provided the key to unlocking the complexities of the Amarna royal family. To Davis, however, it was simply another disappointing tomb to be cleared as part of his ongoing quest for an intact royal burial.

There was nothing that anyone could do to stop Davis dismantling, and essentially destroying, the burial. By 28 January KV 55 had been misidentified as the tomb of Queen Tiy, mother of Akhenaten. It had been (to a very limited extent) photographed and emptied, unplanned; the eclectic mix of grave goods packed into boxes – 'everything that is to be moved is out of the tomb' – and sent on their way by steamer to the Cairo Museum. Not all the grave goods found their way to Cairo, however. KV 55 had been robbed immediately after its discovery, and the Luxor dealers were soon doing a brisk trade in small antiquities bearing Akhenaten's name. Howard Carter was able to help Davis trace and retrieve some of the stolen pieces but, as their provenance was now compromised, they were excluded from the official 'catalogue of the objects discovered' compiled by Georges Daressy. These pieces went to the United States as part of Davis's private collection; this was eventually sold at auction, and dispersed.[12] Objects retained by Davis, or given away as gifts by him, were also excluded from the official catalogue, as were some objects which were noted by those present at the tomb opening, but which have not been seen since; presumably these too were stolen, and never recovered.

Ayrton drowned in a hunting accident in Ceylon in 1914, and so could not contribute to the developing debate over his most important find. His fuller archaeological report was never published, and is now lost. Davis's report, which was published in 1910, was universally agreed to be woefully inaccurate. As Weigall later explained, with an understandable touch of bitterness:

My Davis paid for the publication of the annual volume; and we all united to give him the honour and glory of the discoveries, the work being deemed worthy of every encouragement in spite of the fact that its promoter was himself an amateur, and that the greatest tact had to be used in order to impose proper supervision on his work and check his enthusiastic but quite untrained interference in what he very naturally regarded as his own affair. [13]

Philologist Sir Alan Gardiner was more direct in his criticism:

The history of excavation Egypt presents, side by side with much splendid work, an almost continuous series of disasters. The greatest disaster of all is when the results have remained completely unpublished. But it is also a disaster when the publication is incomplete or inaccurate. This is unfortunately what has happened with Theodore M. Davis' volume entitled The Tomb of Queen Tiyi, London 1910. Egyptologists owe so much to the extraordinarily kind and generous Maecenas to whom the said volume is due that it would be unjustified and ungrateful to judge it too censoriously. Who knows what difficulties or obstacles may have prevented the all too early defunct

E. Ayrton and his patron from producing a more satisfactory record? Still, the fact remains that the book, though containing a catalogue by G. Daressy of the objects found, gives no plan and wholly inadequate explanations, and that the accounts given by the various contributors show ambiguities and discrepancies which we cannot but deplore.[14]

This sorry history makes it impossible to compile a complete inventory of the tomb contents, or to reconstruct an accurate and complete tomb plan. It is therefore fortunate that the artist and travel writer Walter Tyndale was present to witness events as they unfolded. His description of Ayrton's face on the day of the discovery, which 'bore the expression of a gentle angler who, having landed a big fish, joins his companions who have done no more than lose their tackle' is inspired. As for the locals:

Ayrton, let him do his work ever so quietly, could not stop a thousand native tongues from wagging; and wag they did, to great purpose, one fine morning. The very air seemed thick with news! News that Ayrton was knee-deep in gold and precious stones, feverishly filling petroleum tins, pickle pots and cans from Chicago with the spoil, was the very least that one's imagination could conjure up…Needless to say the archaeological value of the find did not interest them in the least. That everyone connected with these excavations is doing it simply for the plunder is rooted in the native mind which neither proof nor argument can disturb. That the share of the spoil which 'Mistrr Davis' or 'Mistrr Eirton' would get would allow them to retire, sip coffee and play backgammon for the rest of their lives, was what exercised their minds, and the possibility caused a great deal of secret resentment…[15]

KV 55 was an incomplete, single-chambered corridor tomb cut into the floor of the main Valley. Ayrton's brief report mentions

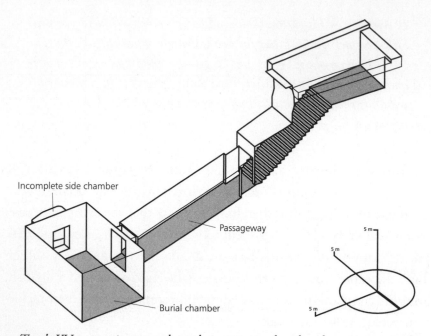

Incomplete side chamber

Passageway

Burial chamber

5 m

5 m

5 m

3. Tomb KV 55: a private tomb used as a storage chamber, home to a secondary Amarna burial.

digging through 'chippings which at this depth were cemented together by the action of water'; this suggests that KV 55 was protected by the same layer of late 18th Dynasty flood debris that covered Tutankhamen's tomb.[16] A rough flight of steps led down to a blocked doorway, which Davis neglected to photograph before he had it dismantled; Weigall tells us that the remains of an original wall of plastered limestone blocks lay beneath a second and more loosely constructed wall.[17] Sealings found within the tomb suggested that the tomb had initially been closed during Tutankhamen's reign: the layer of flood debris suggested that the re-entry and re-sealing occurred no later than the early part of Horemheb's reign.

The entrance opened into a descending passageway, partially filled with stone and blocked by a large wooden panel, one of the four sides of a gilded funerary shrine with bronze fittings. The panel was in poor condition and could not be moved without treatment: rather than wait, the over-eager excavators constructed a plank bridge which would allow them to cross to the burial chamber beyond. This proved to be an unfinished and undecorated room whose seemingly random collection of grave goods – the remainder of the shrine, a cosmetic box, alabaster jars, mud bricks, a decayed funerary pall, faience objects and beads which had once been strung together to form jewellery – were, according to Weigall, 'roughly arranged'. A coffin with a dislodged lid lay on the floor, while a niche in the south wall – probably an unfinished chamber – held a set of human-headed canopic jars (jars designed to hold the preserved entrails of the deceased). Clearly, this was by no means a primary burial. It was a secondary burial, or re-burial, incorporating artefacts prepared for several Amarna royals, some of which had been adapted for use by someone other than their original owner.

Davis's companion, Mrs Emma B. Andrews, entered the chamber after the passageway had been cleared, and was struck by the sheer quantity of gold on display:

> *1907, Jan 19… I went down to the burial chamber and it is now almost easy of access; and saw the poor Queen as she lies now just a bit outside her magnificent coffin, with the vulture crown on her head. All the woodwork of the shrine, doors etc. is heavily overlaid with gold foil and I seemed to be walking on gold, and even the Arab working inside had some of it sticking in his woolly hair.* [18]

Mrs Andrews's 'vulture crown' had a missing leg and, like so many objects in the tomb, a confusing history. It had started life as a gold pectoral or collar designed to rest on the mummy's chest; it is not clear whether it had simply been displaced, perhaps when the coffin fell to the ground, or whether it had been deliberately re-used as a headdress. The funerary bricks – magical bricks intended to ensure the rebirth of the deceased – bore Akhenaten's titles with his cartouche erased, and almost certainly came from his Amarna burial. The funerary shrine, however, had been commissioned by Akhenaten as part of his mother's burial equipment. Akhenaten's image had subsequently been deleted, although Tiy still remained to worship beneath the Aten's rays. Vases inscribed with the name of Amenhotep III, husband of Tiy, may also have formed a part of the queen's funerary equipment.

The four alabaster canopic jars had originally been carved with the name of their owner, but this inscription had then been ground away, leaving the cartouches of the Aten and Akhenaten intact. Next the cartouches had been chiselled away, leaving the anonymous jars suitable for re-use by either a man or a woman. Egyptologists are fairly certain that these jars were originally made for Akhenaten's favoured secondary queen, Kiya.[19] The near-identical jar lids are beautifully carved female heads dressed in the Nubian-style bobbed wigs worn by the Amarna royal women. Holes in the forehead indicate where the uraei (the protective cobras worn on the brow) should be; it would appear that these were a late addition to the lids. The delicate lids do not sit well on their rather heavy bases, and this suggests that they may not be the original stoppers.[20] On the basis of the wigs and the facial features, which have been compared to images found at Amarna, it seems likely that they are female, and that they represent either Kiya or the eldest Amarna princess, Meritaten; others have suggested that they may be Tutankhamen or Tiy (Daressy) or Akhenaten (Maspero and Weigall). Three of these jars have been subjected to chemical analysis. Two contained a 'hard, compact, black, pitch-like mass surrounding a well-defined centrally-situated zone of different material, which was of a brown colour and friable nature'; this brown and friable material was almost certainly the remains of the viscera. The third jar yielded the same compact black mass, but the viscera had been removed some time after its discovery.[21]

The elaborate inlaid *rishi* or feathered-style anthropoid coffin (the earliest coffin of this type to be found in the Valley) lay on the ground with its lid displaced and its mummy partially revealed. The five bands of hieroglyphs that decorated the coffin exterior, and the twelve lines of text on the foot-end, showed obvious signs of mutilation, and the cartouche which would have named the coffin's owner was empty. The coffin's face had been torn away, and further, accidental, damage had been caused by a rock that had fallen from the ceiling, splitting the coffin lid. Davis assumed that the coffin had originally rested on a lion-legged bed, and that this had rotted and collapsed when water entered the tomb, causing the coffin to fall. There is good evidence to suggest that floodwater did indeed run along the ceiling and drip into the tomb, damaging much of what lay below. But no diagnostic pieces of the 'bed' survive; it may therefore be that the coffin, which always lay on the ground, was simply disturbed by the intruder (either a robber or necropolis official), who tore away its golden face and – perhaps – stole the golden mummy mask that lay beneath the coffin lid.

The fragile coffin disintegrated as it was removed from the tomb, leaving the excavators with a collection of glass and semi-precious stone inlays and gold. By 1915 conservators in the Cairo Museum had restored the coffin lid, but the base remained a collection of fragments stored in two boxes; by 1931 these boxes had vanished, and were presumed lost or stolen.[22] They eventually found their way, via Switzerland, into the collection of the State Museum of Egyptian Art in Munich, where the lower part of the coffin was restored and mounted on a Plexiglas shell. The coffin base, together with some gold foil from the inside and outside of the coffin, was returned to Cairo Museum in January 2002.

Ayrton tells us that the mummy within the coffin was 'wrapped in flexible gold plates', Davis that it 'was covered with pure gold sheets, called gold foil, but nearly all so thick that, when taken in the hands, they would stand alone without bending'.[23] It seems likely that these large, flat gold sheets were part of the coffin lining, rather than a separate mummy cover, and the fact that Daressy excluded them from his catalogue suggests that he, too, regarded them as integral to the coffin. These gold sheets are today housed in Cairo Museum; they are inscribed but, as they have been repeatedly folded and badly creased, are almost impossible to read. A further six uninscribed sheets of gold foil, which appear to have fallen off the underside of the lid (five pieces) and the exterior of the base (one decorated piece), were given to Davis by Maspero; today these are in the collections of the Metropolitan Museum, New York.

Weigall's description of the mummy adds another layer of complexity to an already confused situation:

> *…when we removed the lid of the coffin we found a band or ribbon of thin gold which had evidently passed round the body. When we had gathered up the bones and fragments and dust we found another similar band which had evidently passed down the back of the mummy. These bands, as I remember them, were about two inches wide and were inscribed with the titles of Akhenaten, but the cartouche was in each case cut out, so that there was simply an oval hole in the band, wherever it occurred.* [24]

These inscribed gold ribbons were obviously very different in appearance to the flat gold sheets, yet Weigall is apparently the only witness to have seen them. He tells us that they were sent to Cairo, where he again saw them in the Museum workshop. However, they were omitted from the Daressy catalogue, and Weigall rather sadly concludes: '…I am now not sure whether they are still somewhere in the Cairo Museum, or whether they have disappeared.' Grafton Elliot Smith subsequently mentioned the ribbons in his report on the KV 55 human remains, but there is no indication that he actually saw them with his own eyes:

From the circumstances under which the coffin and the human remains were found, in association with many inscribed objects bearing the name of Khouniatonou [Akhenaten], which also appeared not only on the coffin itself but also on the gold band encircling the mummy, there can no longer be any doubt that the body found in this tomb was that of the heretic king or was believed to be his corpse by the embalmers. [25]

It is probable that the gold which Weigall saw in Cairo was not in fact the remains of (non-existent) ribbon-like mummy bands, but the remains of the six gold foil bracelets which, everyone agrees, were found adhering to the mummy's skeletal arms. These bracelets were sent to the museum in a box of bones, and were stolen from Smith's desk on the day that they were unpacked. The gold 'ribbons' that Weigall saw in the tomb were probably a part of the coffin.

The quality of the coffin confirms that it was made for an elite, almost certainly royal, owner. Some experts have argued, on stylistic grounds, that it must have been made for (but not necessarily used by) Akhenaten, towards the beginning of his reign when he was still Amenhotep IV. Others, studying both the coffin's style and its surviving inscriptions, have felt able to identify two distinct manufacturing stages, with the coffin originally built for a woman who could be described as the 'beloved of Waenre [Akhenaten]', then modified, with alterations to the texts and the addition of a false beard and uraeus, for use by a royal man. This suggestion is supported by the mutilated hieroglyphs, which James Allen has reconstructed to read:

[Wife and greatly beloved of] the King of Upper and Lower Egypt, living in order, Lord of the Two Lands [Neferkheperure Waenre: Akhenaten], the perfect little one of the living disk, who shall be alive continuously forever, [Kiya]. [26]

The text on the exterior foot-end is more intact, but again shows evidence of alteration:

... I shall breathe the sweet breath which comes forth from your mouth and shall behold thy beauty daily. [My] prayer is that [I] may hear thy sweet voices of the north wind, that [my] flesh may grow young with life through thy love, that thou mayest give me your hands bearing thy spirit and I receive it and live by it, and that thou mayest call upon my name eternally, and it shall not fail from thy mouth ...[27]

Finally – and almost certainly while in use – the coffin was vandalised, its face and uraeus ripped away and its cartouches erased. Ominously, the mummy was damp:

Presently, we cleared the mummy from the coffin, and found that it was a smallish person, with a delicate head and hands. The mouth was partly open, showing a perfect set of upper and lower teeth. The body was enclosed in mummy-cloth of fine texture, but all of the cloth covering the body was of a very dark colour. Naturally it ought to be a much brighter colour. Rather suspecting injury from the evident dampness, I gently touched one of the front teeth (3,000 years old) and alas! it fell into dust, thereby showing that the mummy could not be preserved. We then cleared the entire mummy ...[28]

No photographs were taken at the unwrapping, so once again we are reliant on eye-witness accounts; accounts which vary wildly. Davis, for example, tells us that the hands were clasped, while Ayrton reports that the left arm was bent with the hand resting on the breast and the right arm was fully extended along the thigh. Tyndale, who had been told that the mummy was female, remembered:

Her dried up face, sunken cheeks, and thin, leathery-looking lips, exposing a few teeth, were in ghastly contrast to the golden diadem which encircled her head and the gold necklace that partially hid her sunken throat. Her body was wrapped in thin gold plate, but this being broken and torn made it yet more horrible to look at. An uncomfortable feeling that it was unchivalrous to stare at the poor creature when she was looking so far from her best brought me back to her effigy on the mummy-case with a mental apology that I regretted having taken her unawares, and would in future only think of her as she appeared in all her glory. [29]

This atmospheric description may owe something to Tyndale's artistic imagination: others tell us that the exposed head was bare of flesh, and that the face had been crushed by a rockfall. If Tyndale is correct, his account suggests that there was originally more flesh on the mummy than Davis would have us believe. However, the fact that Davis could not immediately determine the mummy's gender suggests that some parts, at least, had rotted away.

The golden shrine had unambiguously been a part of Tiy's burial equipment, and the canopic jars were obviously female. The positioning of the mummy's arms, according to Ayrton, also suggested a female burial. It is therefore not too surprising that Davis immediately assumed that he had discovered Queen Tiy. This would have been a great find for him. In the days before the discovery and public display of the Berlin bust of Nefertiti, it was Tiy who was regarded as the most intriguing, most glamorous, and most important of the 18th Dynasty queens. Davis sought to prove his own identification by calling on the services of a local doctor, Dr Pollock, and an American obstetrician who was spending the winter in Luxor. He tells us that the two pronounced the remains female on the basis of the wide pelvis. The accuracy of Davis's report is, however, open to some doubt, as Weigall (who did not believe the body to be female) confirms: 'I saw Dr Pollock in Luxor the other day, who denies that he ever thought that

it was a woman, and says he and the other doctor could not be sure.'
[30] Davis never wavered in his conviction that he had discovered Tiy,
and it was as *The Tomb of Queen Tiyi* that he published the tomb.

Davis did not feel that the bones had more to offer, and it was left
to Weigall to pursue the matter. Several months after their unwrapping, having soaked the bones in paraffin wax to strengthen them, he
sent them to Cairo Museum to be examined by Smith. Smith had been
expecting the bones of an elderly woman. Opening the bone box, he
found instead the bones of a man of about twenty-five years of age.

Although he had a string of spectacular discoveries to his name, Davis
was becoming disillusioned with his inability to find an intact royal
burial. Had he but realised it, his team had actually discovered three
crucial clues to Tutankhamen's whereabouts:

Clue 1: During his 1905–6 excavation season Ayrton found a simple
faience cup 'under a rock'. The cup bore Tutankhamen's name and
was, perhaps, part of swag dropped by the robbers who raided his
tomb soon after the funeral.

Clue 2: On 21 December 1907 the team discovered a stone-lined pit (KV
54) housing a collection of large storage vessels. The jars were opened,
and then quickly forgotten. Herbert Winlock, of the Metropolitan
Museum of Art, New York, was present to record the sorry story:

> *Sometime early in January 1908 I spent two or three days with
> Edward Ayrton, to see his work for Mr Davis in the Valley of the
> Kings. When I got to the house the front 'lawn' had about a dozen
> gigantic white pots lying on it where the men had placed them when
> they brought them back from the work. At that time Ayrton had*

finished a dig up in the Valley of the Kings just east of the tomb of Ramesses XI [KV 18: now believed to be the tomb of Ramesses X]. He had quite a job on his hands to find something to amuse Sir Eldon Gorst, the British diplomatic agent who was to be Mr Davis' self-invited guest soon. Sir Eldon had written a very strange little note, which I saw, saying to Mr Davis that he had heard that the latter's men found a royal tomb every winter and requesting, as he intended to be in the Valley of the Kings in a few days, that all discoveries be postponed until his arrival... Davis had found the jewelry [sic] of Queen Tawosret in another tomb, but that was not sufficiently spectacular, and as he had opened up one of the great pots and found a charming little yellow mask in it, everybody thought they were going to find many more objects in the other jars ... That evening I walked back over the hills to the Davis house in the Valley, and I have still got a picture in the back of my head of what things looked like. What in the morning had been fairly neat rows of pots were tumbled in every direction, with little bundles of natron and broken pottery all over the ground. The little mask which had been taken as a harbinger of something better to come had brought forth nothing and poor Ayrton was a very sick and tired person after the undeserved tongue-lashing he had had all that afternoon. [31]

Among the material discovered in the jars were seal impressions bearing Tutankhamen's name, linen bundles of natron salt, floral funerary collars (which Davis tore apart in order to demonstrate their strength), and the miniature gold mummy mask mentioned by Winlock. The Antiquities Service was not interested in this valueless jumble and, while the small gold mask was sent to Cairo Museum, the other finds went the Metropolitan Museum with a different small mask (probably from KV 51); a well-meaning but ill-recorded substitution which was to cause much confusion to future generations of scholars.[32] Many years later, Winlock identified the jar contents as the remnants of the embalming materials and funerary feast of Tutankhamen. He believed that these objects, which had ritual significance and so could not be simply thrown away, had been buried in an unfinished tomb near the main tomb. This idea was subsequently refined so that the cache became the material cleared from the passageway of Tutankhamen's tomb after the first robbery, immediately before the passageway was filled with stone chips. Thus it included items which were deliberately left in the passageway of Tutankhamen's tomb plus, perhaps, odd items dropped by the robbers. Finally, following the 2004 discovery of KV 63, a New Kingdom cache tomb yielding embalming materials, broken pots and floral collars, it has been suggested that the pit may have been a separate original and untouched part of Tutankhamen's funerary provision.[33]

Clue 3: In 1909 the team discovered the 'Chariot Tomb': a small, undecorated chamber (KV 58) which yielded an uninscribed alabaster figurine and the gold foil from a chariot harness inscribed with the names of Tutankhamen and his successor Ay, whose name is given both as a commoner and a king.

Convincing himself that 'the Valley of the Tombs is now exhausted', Davis published the Chariot Tomb as the long-lost, and rather disappointing, tomb of Tutankhamen.[34] His book betrays a somewhat split personality. Its title – *The Tombs of Harmhabi and Touatânkhamanou* – leaves no room for doubt over the nature of the find. However, the chapter describing the artefacts is more cautiously titled 'Catalogue of the Objects Found in an Unknown Tomb, supposed to be Touatânkhamanou's'. Contributing to Davis's publication, Sir Gaston Maspero suggested that the Chariot Tomb was not the original tomb of Tutankhamen, but a re-burial:

Such are the few facts that we know about Touatânkhamanou's life and reign. If he had children by his queen Ankhounamanou or by another wife, they have left no trace of their existence on the monuments; when he died, Aiya replaced him on the throne, and buried him. I suppose that his tomb was in the Western Valley, somewhere between or near Amenothes III [Amenhotep III] and Aiya [Ay]: when the reaction against Atonou [the Aten] and his followers was complete, his mummy and its furniture was taken to a hiding place... and there Davis found what remained of it after so many transfers and plunders. But this also is mere hypothesis, the truth of which we have no means of proving or disproving as yet.[35]

Few were convinced by Davis's argument. Howard Carter, a former excavation partner of Davis, realised that the 'Chariot Tomb' was not a tomb, royal or otherwise, but a storage chamber. He believed that Tutankhamen still lay in the Valley, waiting to be found. But, while Davis still held the sole concession to excavate, he could only stand by and watch.

4. *Scrap of gold foil from a chariot harness, recovered from KV 58. Tutankhamen is shown smiting a stereotypical enemy, while his consort Ankhesenamen stands behind him and his successor, Ay, stands before him.*

Carter's career had seen a meteoric rise and a sudden, catastrophic fall. In 1891, aged just seventeen and with no formal education, he had travelled from Norfolk, England, to work as a draughtsman with Percy Newberry. He learned his craft recording the decorated walls of the rapidly deteriorating Middle Kingdom rock-cut tombs at Beni Hasan and el-Bersha. A valuable five-month secondment with Flinders Petrie at Amarna had allowed him to learn the art of scientific excavation from its master. Petrie, who was to become known as the 'father of Egyptian archaeology', was one of the first to recognise that artefacts could not simply be snatched greedily from the ground, and his methods were to have a profound effect on Carter's own working practices. Carter completed his training by working as a draughtsman for Édouard Naville at the Deir el-Bahri memorial temple of Hatshepsut. Here he took full responsibility for copying the scenes on the temple walls, and the magnificent publication of the temple includes work by both Howard Carter and his elder brother Vernet, who spent a season working at Deir el-Bahri.

In 1899 Carter was appointed Chief Inspector of Antiquities for southern (Upper) Egypt. Based at Luxor, he assumed responsibility for the 500-mile stretch of southern sites including the Theban monuments and the Valley of the Kings. During his tenure Carter fitted iron doors to protect the more important Valley tombs, and installed electric light in six of them. He also built a large donkey park to accommodate the ever-increasing numbers of tourists visiting the Valley. Then, after five very successful years, Carter swapped positions with the northern Inspector, Quibell, and moved to Cairo. Initially, things went well. Then, on the afternoon of 8 January 1905, came the 'Sakkara Affair': a group of drunken Frenchmen forced their way into the Sakkara Serapeum (the burial place of the divine Apis bulls), manhandling the native inspectors and guards. Carter, summoned to the fracas, gave his men permission to defend themselves against the French. Weigall, who was taking tea with Carter that afternoon, explained events in a letter to his wife, Hortense:

> *Fifteen French tourists had tried to get into one of the tombs with only 11 tickets, and had finally beaten the guards and burst the door open ... Carter arrived on the scene, and after some words ordered the guards – now reinforced – to eject them. Result: a serious fight in which sticks and chairs were used and two guards and two tourists rendered unconscious. When I saw the place afterwards it was a pool of blood.*[36]

For an early twentieth-century Englishman to encourage 'natives' to assault Frenchmen was, to say the least, politically naive. As the dispute escalated into a full-scale diplomatic battle, the British Consul-General, Lord Cromer, asked Carter to apologise to the French Consul. Carter refused: a refusal that many found hard to understand, as the apology was considered a very little thing (no one expected him to mean it) and his refusal to bend in any way childish and unhelpful. Maspero, himself French, was infuriated by his employee's inability to compromise. He was eventually able to resolve the matter without the apology, but he retaliated by restricting Carter's authority, and transferring him to the dull Delta backwater of Tanta. Hurt, and angered by what he saw as a lack of official support, Carter resigned from the Antiquities Service on 21 October 1905.

Carter spent a few months living in Cairo, then returned to Luxor to spend three years scraping a precarious living as an artist working for archaeological missions who, in the absence of colour photography, needed a good watercolour record of their finds. Most memorably, he painted some of the contents of the tomb of Yuya and Thuya for Davis, being paid £15 for each of the fourteen plates featured in the publication. At the same time he acted as an up-market tourist guide, and sold paintings and antiquities to wealthy visitors who might want a unique souvenir of their Egyptian holiday.

In 1909 Maspero introduced Carter to George Herbert, 5th Earl of Carnarvon, with the suggestion that they might work profitably together. Carnarvon, like Davis, was a wealthy amateur with a passion for Egyptology. He, too, wanted to make a spectacular discovery, and he, too, needed a professional colleague who would allow him to overcome the amateur status that was causing the authorities, in the person of Weigall, to refuse him permission to excavate the more important Theban sites. Weigall, who had been forced to work alongside the slapdash Davis, firmly believed that wealthy amateurs such as Carnarvon (or Davis, or Robert Mond, an equally wealthy amateur who had worked with Weigall in the Theban necropolis) should not be allowed to buy their way on to an archaeological excavation, where they might do irreparable damage.

Carter became Carnarvon's employee, the bond between them one of mutual convenience and a shared goal. Contemporary accounts, and their own correspondence, show that this formal working relationship soon matured into a firm friendship. The normally introverted Carter got on extremely well with his new patron and, indeed, with the whole Herbert family, and he became a frequent visitor to Highclere, the Carnarvon family's Berkshire estate. With Carter and Carnarvon working as a team, Weigall felt able to allocate more promising sites. They were rewarded by a steady stream of unspectacular, but archaeologically satisfying, results which allowed Carter to polish his skills as an excavator. In 1912 the team moved to northern Egypt, and the less immediately appealing sites of the Delta. There was a brief excavation at the snake-infested site of Sakha (ancient Xois), followed by a longer season at the town mound of Tell el-Balamun (ancient Pa-iu-en-Amen), where Carter discovered some silver Graeco-Roman jewellery, hidden in a pot. After that minor excitement there was a return to the familiar comforts, and sunnier climate, of Thebes.

In 1914 Davis gave up the concession to excavate in the Valley of the Kings and Carnarvon seized his chance. Many people thought that he was wasting his time:

Sir Gaston Maspero, Director of the Antiquities department, who signed our concession, agreed with Mr Davis that the site was exhausted, and told us frankly that he did not consider that it would repay further investigation. We remembered, however, that nearly a hundred years earlier Belzoni had made a similar claim, and refused to be convinced. We had made a thorough investigation of the site, and were quite sure that there were areas, covered by the dumps of previous excavators, which had never been properly examined. [37]

A temporary agreement allowing Carter to perform some work in February 1915 was superseded by official permission signed on 18 April 1915, which confirmed that 'the work of excavation shall be carried out at the expense, risk and peril of the Earl of Carnarvon by Mr Howard Carter; the latter should be constantly present during excavation'. [38] The days when an excavator might reasonably expect to receive half of any finds were, however, long gone, and Article 8 stated that 'mummies of the Kings, of Princes, and of High Priests, together with their coffins and sarcophagi, shall remain the property of the Antiquities Service'. More ominously, Articles 9 and 10 stipulated:

9: Tombs which are discovered intact, together with all objects they may contain, shall be handed over to the Museum whole and without division.

10: In the case of tombs which have already been searched, the Antiquities Service shall, over and above the mummies and sarcophagi intended in Article 8, reserve for themselves all objects of capital importance from the point of view of history and archaeology, and shall share the remainder with the Permittee.

This new, tough approach – an approach which does not appear unduly tough today – sparked intense resentment among Western excavators, most of whom relied on funding from museums, institutions and private individuals who expected to be rewarded for their generosity with a share of the finds. There was a strong feeling that, without this reward, there would be no financial contribution. It would be the end of excavation in Egypt, and perhaps of Egyptology as a whole. Meanwhile, the Great War prevented any intensive excavation. Carter spent his war years doing unspecified intelligence work in Cairo, and his leave conducting useful but essentially small-scale field-work in Luxor. It was not until 1 December 1917 that he finally started work in the Valley of the Kings.

Carter and Carnarvon had determined to find Tutankhamen's tomb, which, for perfectly sound archaeological and historical reasons, they believed was situated in the Valley. But the Valley was an ill-documented mess; there was no official record of who had already excavated or where, and the vast spoil heaps left by earlier excavators made it difficult to reconstruct its excavation history. The only way to be certain that there were no lost tombs was to clear the Valley floor down to its bedrock. Carter realised that this was 'a rather desperate undertaking', but he felt that there was no other option.[39] It proved to be slow, dull work: not only did the rubble have to be cleared from the Valley, it had to be inspected, then dumped responsibly. And, of course, the earlier spoil heaps also had to be removed, inspected and dumped. In an article written for *The Times* on 11 December 1922, Carnarvon estimated that they had moved something approaching 150,000–200,000 tons of rubbish, concentrating on a triangle between the tombs of Ramesses II, Merenptah and Ramesses VI.

Results were so meagre that Carnarvon started to have serious doubts over the wisdom of pouring time, energy and money into a potentially fruitless mission. Maybe they should abandon the Valley, and look for a more fertile site? By most people's standards, Carnarvon

was an extremely rich man. In addition to his inherited wealth and
properties, his marriage to Almina Wombwell, the natural daughter of
the extraordinarily wealthy Alfred de Rothschild, had brought a
£500,000 dowry plus an annual income of £12,000 and the repayment
of his outstanding gaming and personal debts.[40] It was effectively Rothschild money that financed his Egyptian adventure, and that would
continue to fund it, via Almina, after his death. He was not, however, a
man of infinite resources and nor was he a dedicated Egyptologist. He
enjoyed a wide range of expensive interests, including photography,
horse racing, yachting and the newfangled automobiles, and it is possible that he was simply growing slightly bored with his slow-moving
new hobby. As a gambler, he understood the importance of not throwing good money after bad.

Carter, who was definitely not a wealthy man, disagreed. He felt
that they should carry on until the entire Valley had been inspected.
It is even rumoured, though he makes no mention of this in his publication, that he offered to pay the costs of a final season himself.
Could this have been a genuine offer – could he really have afforded
to pay for a short season? Perhaps. While it has been estimated that
Carnarvon's Egyptian adventure had already cost him something in
the region of £35,000,[41] local labour was cheap, and a few weeks' work
would probably have cost no more than a few hundred pounds.
Weigall gives us some idea of the relevant costs when he tells us that
in 1905 'the total cost to Mr Davis of the season's work which produced one of the greatest finds ever made in Egypt [the tomb of Yuya
and Thuya] was about £80'.[42] Carnarvon's associated social activities
– transport, hotels, dressing, dining and entertaining – would have
cost far more than the work itself.

Carnarvon agreed to one last gamble. Carter would be given time
to clear the part of the Valley, a heap of rubble and ancient workmen's
huts beneath the entrance to the tomb of Ramesses VI (KV 9), that
had so far been left untouched because excavations in this area would

disrupt the flow of tourists intent on visiting the tomb above. In fact Carter had already started to remove these huts in 1917 and, like Davis, had come very close to finding Tutankhamen, stopping within a metre or so of the lost tomb. In order to cause minimum disruption, and to allow Carter to remove the footpath if necessary, the 1922–3 season would start unusually early. Carter arrived in Luxor on 28 October, full of determination:

> *This was to be our final season in the Valley. Six full seasons we had excavated there, and season after season had drawn a blank; we had worked for months at a stretch and found nothing, and only an excavator knows how desperately depressing that can be; we had almost made up our minds that we were beaten, and were preparing to leave The Valley and try our luck elsewhere; and then – hardly had we set hoe to ground in our last despairing effort than we made a discovery that far exceeded our wildest dreams. Surely, never before in the whole history of excavation has a full digging season been compressed within the space of five days.* [43]

On 1 November 1922 Carter's workmen, led by the highly experienced foreman Reis Ahmed Gerigar, cleared away the rubbish below Ramesses' tomb. They then cut through a 3ft layer of what Carter somewhat loosely describes as 'soil' or, in his diary 'heavy rubbish'.[44] Three days later – while Carter was temporarily absent from the site – they discovered the first of a flight of sixteen stone steps. These led down to a small blocked and plastered doorway stamped with a range of oval seal impressions including the distinctive seal of the necropolis: a jackal crouching above nine bound captives. None of the seal impressions included a name.

A small portion of plaster had fallen away from the upper section of the doorway, revealing a heavy wooden lintel. This point of weakness allowed Carter to make a small hole. Inserting an electric torch he peered into a passage packed with stones and rubbish. Clearly he had made a significant discovery, although whether it was a tomb or a cache, intact or robbed and resealed, was not yet clear; 'anything, literally anything, might lie beyond that passage, and it needed all my self-control to keep from breaking down the doorway and investigating there and then'.[45] On 6 November Carter crossed the river to the Luxor telegram office, where he composed a coded message (here decoded) for his patron:

AT LAST HAVE MADE WONDERFUL DISCOVERY IN THE VALLEY STOP A MAGNIFICENT TOMB WITH SEALS INTACT STOP RE-COVERED SAME FOR YOUR ARRIVAL STOP CONGRATULATIONS ENDS

3

RECOVERY

In December 1922 Pierre Lacau, Head of the Egyptian Antiquities Service, wrote formally to Lord Carnarvon. An edited version of his letter, translated from the French, was reproduced in *The Times* on 14 December 1922:

All my colleagues are greatly impressed, not only by the extraordinary results obtained, but also by the method by which your work has been carried out. They wish unanimously to associate themselves with their President [Lacau himself] in the expression to you of all their congratulations and thanks. You have attached your name to one of the greatest discoveries made not only in Egypt, but in all the domains of archaeology.

As regards your collaborator, Mr Howard Carter, who has conducted the work during so many years, it is for him the finest crowning of a career and the most astonishing reward that any archaeologist could have. Such a reward is truly merited, for he has afforded a fine example of method and patience, the rarest virtue in an excavator. May he often be emulated.

I would add that the entire committee have been particularly struck and touched by the conditions of complete disinterestedness in which the work was undertaken. This is an example of the ideal excavation which should be realized in the future. You have proved to the great astonishment of others that it is possible to accept in the interests of high science conditions of disinterested excavation. Also Egypt and our science owe you full acknowledgement. That of Egypt has so far manifested itself only by press articles which are intended to be disagreeable both to you and to me. That, however, is of no importance. The Sovereign and the Council of Ministers fully appreciate the true aspect, and Egyptian opinion when it understands (it now has all the details before it) will thank you, I am sure, in a proper manner.

The First Season: 1922–3

In order to protect the anonymous tomb and its unknown contents, Carter re-buried the stairwell and rolled large flint boulders on top. He then resigned himself to a tense wait. On 18 November 1922 he left Luxor for Cairo, where he met Carnarvon and his daughter, Lady Evelyn Herbert. He returned to Luxor on the 21st, and Carnarvon followed two days later. With the assistance of Carter's friend, retired engineer and architect Arthur Callender, the clearing of the lower stairwell was completed by the afternoon of 24 November. The fill from the lower part of the stairwell yielded a mixture of objects, including large quantities of broken pottery, a scarab of Tuthmosis III and fragments of boxes inscribed with the names of Amenhotep III, Akhenaten, Neferneferu-aten and Meritaten, and Tutankhamen. This was curious. Why were so many 18th Dynasty royal names associated with this one tomb? Carter persuaded himself that he had discovered a late 18th Dynasty cache, a tomb similar in design and use, perhaps, to the nearby KV 55.

With the doorway fully exposed, a different seal-type was revealed. Now it was possible to read a name: Tutankhamen. Tutankhamen, then, or his officials, had sealed this tomb. His seals were intact and ancient, and it was clear there had been no recent breach of security. But it was equally clear that the upper left corner of the door showed signs of tampering: the tomb had been opened and re-sealed at least twice in antiquity and, although it might be reasonably supposed that no one would bother to re-seal an empty tomb, it was by no means certain that Carter had discovered an unplundered cache or burial.

The doorway blocking – limestone masonry covered in gypsum plaster – was dismantled on 25 November, revealing a descending passageway packed to the ceiling with light-coloured rubble and limestone chips. Here, again, were the unmistakable signs of robbery: a tunnel cut through the upper left corner of the fill, directly aligned with the breach in the outer door, had itself been filled with dark rubble. Two days were spent clearing the passageway, and checking its fill. Again, this revealed a curious assortment of finds, including pottery fragments, jar seals, broken and intact alabaster vessels and the water skins abandoned by the ancient workmen who plastered the inner tomb door. Meanwhile the practical Callender was busy constructing a wooden grille to protect the now-exposed tomb.

By 26 November Carter and Carnarvon – plus Lady Evelyn, Callender and a small group of workmen – again found themselves standing in front of a blocked and plastered doorway bearing the seal of the necropolis and the seal of Tutankhamen. Again, there was unmistakable evidence of tampering and re-sealing in the upper left corner of the door. Carter – who was to class this as 'the day of days, the most wonderful that I have ever lived, and certainly one whose like I can never hope to see again' – was about to discover just how much damage the ancient robbers had wrought. It seems only right to leave the exact moment of discovery to him:

The decisive moment had arrived. With trembling hands I made a tiny breach in the upper left hand corner. Darkness and blank space, as far as an iron testing-rod could reach, showed that whatever lay beyond was empty, and not filled like the passage we had just cleared. Candle tests were applied as a precaution against possible foul gasses, and then, widening the hole a little, I inserted the candle and peered in, Lord Carnarvon, Lady Evelyn and Callender standing anxiously beside me to hear the verdict. At first I could see nothing, the hot air escaping from the chamber causing the candle flame to flicker, but presently, as my eyes grew accustomed to the light, details of the room within emerged slowly from the mist, strange animals, statues and gold – everywhere the glint of gold. For the moment – an eternity it must have seemed to the others standing by – I was struck dumb with amazement, and when Lord Carnarvon, unable to stand the suspense any longer, inquired anxiously, 'Can you see anything?' it was all I could do to get out the words 'Yes, wonderful things.' Then, widening the hole a little further, so that we both could see, we inserted an electric torch.[1]

The following day the doorway was officially opened and a power line was connected to the Valley supply. The harsh electric light confirmed what Carter's flickering candle had suggested. The Antechamber was crammed with a vast assortment of goods: dismantled chariots, three golden beds carved to resemble exotic animals, and numerous chests, boxes, vessels and packages all, presumably, filled with treasures. All of the larger objects, and many of the smaller ones, bore the name of Tutankhamen. There was, however, no sign of a sarcophagus or coffin. The southern wall was living rock, but a small, once-sealed doorway in the western wall, which had been breached by robbers and not repaired, offered the possibility of more treasures beyond. The northern wall, guarded by two imposing statues of the king himself, was even more promising: an obvious partition wall, it housed the blocked and plastered entrance to a chamber, or multiple chambers.

However, a very obvious hole, just large enough to admit a boy or a slightly built man, had been restored and resealed by the necropolis officials. It was therefore by no means certain that Tutankhamen still rested within what was now clearly his tomb.

All doubt was removed when, shortly after the official opening of the Antechamber, Carter, Carnarvon and Lady Evelyn re-opened the robber's hole and crawled into what proved to be the Burial Chamber beyond. Curiosity satisfied, they then retreated, reblocking the hole and concealing the modern plaster behind a carefully placed basket lid, which is clearly visible in contemporary photographs. Although it has been suggested that they did this on 26 November, immediately after the 'wonderful things' moment, it seems far more likely that they waited until the evening of the 27th, when the inner doorway had been unblocked. By waiting, they would have made less mess at the doorway and would have had less trouble progressing through the artefact-packed Antechamber; their actions would therefore have been less obvious.[2]

There is no official record of this nocturnal adventure but Lady Evelyn told her half-uncle, Mervyn Herbert, about it immediately prior to the official opening of the Burial Chamber. Herbert, sworn to secrecy, recorded their conversation in his journal and concluded, rather optimistically: 'The only others who know anything about it are the workmen, none of whom would ever breathe a word to a soul about it.'[3] In fact, the unofficial inspection was a widely known 'secret'. The chemist and conservator Alfred Lucas certainly knew all about it: he spotted the modern plasterwork as soon as he saw it:

> Of the door leading into the burial chamber, it is stated that 'close examination revealed the fact that a small breach had been made near the bottom ... and that the hole made had subsequently been filled up and re-sealed'. A considerable amount of mystery was made about this robber's hole. When I first saw the tomb about December

20th the hole was hidden by the basketwork tray, or lid, and some rushes taken from the floor that Mr Carter had placed before it … Lord Carnarvon, his daughter and Mr Carter certainly entered the burial chamber and also entered the store chamber, which latter had no door, before the formal opening. Whether Mr Callender, who was present at the time, also entered the burial chamber, I am not sure, but he was a very big man and I once heard a remark that made me think that the hole was too small to admit him.

The question of the hole and its condition when found, whether open or closed, is a matter of no archaeological importance, and, by itself, is hardly worth mentioning… [4]

Opening the sealed chamber privately, without inviting the Antiquities Service to attend, was both discourteous and a breach of Carnarvon's permission to excavate. It would certainly not be considered acceptable behaviour on any excavation today. However, given that Carnarvon was paying for the excavation, that he was responsible for guarding the tomb and its contents, and that he fully expected to retain a portion of its artefacts, his curiosity is perhaps understandable. Carter had a more personal reason for wanting to know exactly what lay behind the partition wall. In 1898 he had discovered the 'Tomb of the Horse', so called because his horse had quite literally stumbled over it. Excavating in 1900, and uncovering what appeared to be a large and unviolated tomb, he planned a grand opening of the sealed 'burial chamber', inviting, amongst other illustrious guests, the British Consul General, Lord Cromer. Unfortunately, when the chamber was opened it held just three wooden boats and some pots. Archaeologically the Tomb of the Horse is very interesting – it also yielded a wooden statue which suggests that it may have been part of the mortuary provision of the Middle Kingdom pharaoh Nebhepetre Montuhotep II – but the visitors did not trouble to hide their disappointment. Carter never forgot this humiliation.

However much we may sympathise with Carter and Carnarvon's motives, the furtive inspection was bad archaeology for which there can be no real excuse. The opening of the sealed Chamber should have been fully documented, and nothing in the Antechamber should have been disturbed before it had been fully recorded. Now, not only was the position of the basket in front of the robber's hole falsified in the official photographs, some of the Chamber contents had been displaced. Lucas was confident that he could identify an artefact that had been taken from the Burial Chamber on that first clandestine visit, and then restored in a slightly different place:

> *This perfume box was not found in the sarcophagus, as stated by Mr Carter, but either outside, or inside, the outermost shrine, and I think inside. I saw it at Mr Carter's house before the official opening of the burial chamber, and evidently it was found when Lord Carnarvon and Mr Carter first penetrated into the burial chamber.* [5]

There is no reason to doubt the veracity of Lucas's statement: he is writing as Carter's friend and colleague, and he is clearly not over-concerned about the incursion into the chamber. His account leaves two lingering questions. Just how accurate is the official record of the Burial Chamber contents? And, perhaps more importantly, was anything else taken from the chamber?

The official opening was followed by a series of open days for the great and the good. Already, the excavation was taking on the air of an elite jamboree, as the report in the *Illustrated London News* of 16 December shows:

> *The official opening of the tomb, or funeral chambers, of king Tut-ankhamen, found by the Earl of Carnarvon and Mr Howard Carter in the Valley of the Kings, near Luxor, took place on November 29. Before the opening, Lord Carnarvon's daughter, Lady Evelyn Herbert,*

entertained a large party for luncheon in the valley, among the guests being Lady Allenby and the governor of Kena Province, Abdel Aziz Bey Yehia, who had given invaluable assistance on guarding the treasures.

The accompanying photograph shows a formal dining table improbably set out in the Valley. As enterprising locals started to hawk Tutankhamen-themed Christmas cards, *The Times* prepared to break the news to the world. The article, written with Carter's help in the Valley of the Kings and sent to Luxor by runner, was published in London on 30 November 1922:

From the manner in which its contents were disposed it is evident that this cache had not remained untouched since it was buried. There seems no doubt that this wonderful collection of objects formed part of the funeral paraphernalia of King Tutankhamen, whose cartouche is seen everywhere, in both its forms, and that they were moved from the tombs where they were originally placed, and in order to preserve them from thieves were transferred for safety to these chambers.

The sealing and blocking of the doors and passages which have so far been opened suggest that metal robbers had attacked these chambers and that inspectors of Rameses [sic] IX had reason to enter to reclose them. From the famous Abbot and other papyri it is known that these Royal tombs suffered at the hands of robbers. But, whatever the chambers may have contained originally, their contents today are sufficient cause for sensation in the Egyptological world. They considerably increase our knowledge of Ancient Egyptian history and art, and experts who were present at today's opening consider that the discovery will probably rank as the most important of modern times...

What adds interest to this discovery is that there is still yet a third sealed chamber, which, significantly, the two figures of the king discovered are guarding, and which may possibly turn out to be the

*actual tomb of King Tutankhamen, with members of the heretic's
family buried with him. Until the vast amount of material in the
other chambers has been completely removed it will be impossible to
ascertain the contents of this third chamber.*

The Times was quite right. The packed Antechamber would have
to be cleared before the Burial Chamber could be officially opened.
Fortunately Carter had a proper understanding of archaeology's greatest paradox – that the excavator who clears a site necessarily destroys
it – and he knew that he had to work slowly and methodically in order
to preserve the original layout of the chambers in his records. Every
single object would have to be recorded *in situ* – numbered, photographed, marked on the tomb plan, described and drawn – before
being removed to a conservation lab for immediate treatment and
further photography. Then, everything would have to be packed
securely for the long journey to Cairo. Further conservation may even
be required in Cairo, before the artefacts could be put on display. This
was clearly not a task that any excavator, no matter how determined,
could tackle alone. He would have to seek professional assistance, and
supplies, and for that he would have to go to Cairo.

Security had to be Carter's top priority. A metal gate would have to
be fitted to protect the tomb, as the wooden gate constructed by Callender was simply not strong enough to deter robbers. Meanwhile
Carter's absence from the Valley meant that the electricity supply
would have to be disconnected, the entrance to the tomb blocked with
heavy timber baulks, the stairway re-buried under an estimated 1,700
tons of sand, rock and rubble, and the whole site put under guard. This
time-consuming procedure would have to be followed every time the
tomb was closed down, and reversed every time it was re-opened, as an
essential protection not just against thieves, but against the floods that
had the potential to sweep into the tomb and destroy everything.

As Carter boarded the train for Cairo, Carnarvon set sail for

England. Interviewed by *The Times* special correspondent in Marseilles on 16 December, he was persuaded to reveal his plans:

> 'We are resigned to the necessity of waiting,' Lord Carnarvon said.
> 'The wall barring the way to the inner chamber cannot be touched
> without serious risk to the valuable antiquities scattered in indescrib-
> able confusion in the outer chamber. The work of packing and
> removing them will require the greatest care and delicacy in han-
> dling. The majority of them are wonderfully well preserved, but after
> being buried for three thousand years everything is very dry and
> fragile. We have not dared to touch anything. There is danger that
> the inlaying of the boxes may be displaced and that the fabrics may
> crumble under the touch. They must all be treated with a preserva-
> tive preparation before they are touched. That will be a question for
> expert chemists.' Lord Carnarvon added that he intends to return to
> Luxor at the end of January in order that he may personally supervise
> the clearing of the outer chamber.

Back in London, Carnarvon entertained King George and Queen
Mary with an account of his adventures. More importantly, he opened
formal negotiations with *The Times*. Tutankhamen was likely to prove
a drain on Carnarvon's resources for a long time to come. Of course,
he fully expected to receive a share of the artefacts from the tomb, and
these could be sold to defray expenses. The sums involved were likely
to be huge: on 2 December the *Daily Express* valued the grave goods
at £3,000,000; on 4 December the *New York Times* suggested
$15,000,000. Nevertheless, it seemed sensible to capitalise on Tut-
ankhamen's obvious commercial value, and negotiate an exclusive
deal. Tutankhamen had already entered Western popular culture, and
others were making money from the discovery. In America, inevitably,
questions were even being asked over the ownership of his name.
Could Tutankhamen, or Tut, or Tut-Tut possibly be copyrighted?
Although he suspected that the *Daily Mail* might pay more,

Carnarvon preferred to deal with the more upmarket *Times*. On 9 January 1923 he signed a contract:

> *The Earl hereby appoints* The Times *as sole agent for the sale through-out the world to newspapers, magazines and other publications of all news articles, interviews and photographs (other than cinematograph and coloured photographs both of which are excluded from this Agreement) relating to the present and future exploration work conducted by the Earl and his agents in the Valley of the Tombs of the Kings* ...[6]

Carnarvon was to receive £5,000 on signature of the agreement, plus 75 per cent of net profits above this initial payment. From this point onwards, the most important and accurate account of events in the Valley would be provided, not by learned journals, but by a British national newspaper. Ambitious plans to release a film of work in the Valley never came to fruition, although the Goldwyn Picture Company did express a great deal of interest in an outline film script prepared by the Earl himself. This would have included documentary footage of the actual discovery plus reconstructions by actors.

Financially, *The Times* deal was a sensible move. Practically, too, it made sense, as it would restrict the number of journalists disrupting work within the tomb. But it was a move that alienated the world's press, many of whom had representatives ready and waiting for news in the Valley. To a man, the excluded journalists were furious. With Reuters (represented by V. Williams), the *Daily Express* (H.V. Morton), the *Daily Mail* (Weigall) and the *Morning Post* and *New York Times* (both A. H. Bradstreet) taking the lead, they formed an anti-*Times* alliance. Refusing to leave Luxor, yet denied any form of official story, they used what the excavators considered to be underhand means to obtain information, and printed whatever they could. The Egyptian journalists, who faced the prospect of being excluded from a discovery in their own country, were particularly incensed and, in an age of growing nationalism, it was not long before the question of tomb-ownership was being raised. What right did foreigners have to disturb, and profit from, Egypt's dead kings?

In dire need of assistance, Carter appealed, by telegram, to Albert M. Lythgoe, Head of the Department of Egyptian Art at the Metropolitan Museum, New York. The response was immediate and enthusiastic:

Carter to Lythgoe, Metropolitan Museum, New York, 7th December 1922
[D]iscovery colossal and need every assistance could you consider loan of Burton in recording in time being costs to us immediate reply would oblige every regards Carter.

Lythgoe to Carter, 7th December 1922
Only too delighted to assist in every possible way. Please call upon Burton and any other members of our staff. Am cabling Burton to that effect. Lythgoe.[7]

Carter's team would vary from season to season, but at its core were Callender and the government chemist Lucas, plus, on loan from the Metropolitan Museum, the archaeologist and conservator Arthur Mace and the photographer Harry Burton. Burton was particularly welcome, as it had proved impossible to take decent photographs inside the dark tomb and, given the potential fire risk, no one wanted to risk experimenting with flashlight. His images and occasional short films are still proving their worth today as, even though some were undoubtedly deliberately posed for the press, they offer a helpful eye-witness supplement to Carter's written records. Architect Walter Hauser and artist Lindsley Foote Hall, also borrowed from the Metropolitan Museum, were to plan the tomb while Gardiner was to work on any texts and inscriptions. Additional, occasional, team members included Percy Newberry, who worked on the botanical specimens while his wife, Essie, assisted with the textiles, and James Henry Breastead, founder of the Oriental Institute at Chicago.

Acting Sergeant Richard Adamson was almost certainly not a member of the team, despite his claim to have guarded the tomb night and day for seven years, sleeping on a camp bed in the Burial Chamber and playing loud music on his portable gramophone to frighten away thieves. Adamson did not tell his remarkable story until the death of his wife, and the deaths of all the core team members, in 1966. He quickly became a popular public speaker, presenting a slide show of images published in books and magazines. He collaborated with author Barry Wynne in the writing of *Behind the Mask of Tutankhamen* (1972) and, as 'the last surviving member of the Tutankhamen expedition', was interviewed by the *Daily Mail* in August 1980. However, Adamson is excluded from all official and unofficial accounts of the discovery: he is never mentioned by any tomb visitor or journalist, and is not included in any of the many hundreds of photographs. There is compelling evidence – his marriage certificate and the birth certificates of his three children – to suggest that Adamson was not in Egypt at the times that he claimed.[8]

Carter returned to Luxor with enormous quantities of material including three and a half miles of cotton wool and several thousand light bulbs. The tomb was re-opened on 16 December 1922 and a steel security gate was fitted on the 17th. The Valley now became Carter's workshop, as KV 55 was converted into a photographic darkroom, KV 15 (Seti II) became a combined laboratory and store, and KV 4 (Ramesses XI) became the essential 'luncheon tomb'. Finally, the task of clearing the Antechamber could begin. This was difficult: the chamber had been packed with a multitude of objects which, in a conventional, far larger, royal tomb, would probably have been distributed between several storerooms. It had then been robbed and restored, in a somewhat haphazard fashion, twice. With everything jumbled together, and objects precariously balanced on other objects, there was no space to manoeuvre; even to enter the room was difficult, as the team were forced to step over the 'wishing cup', a semi-translucent calcite goblet with lotus flower handles supporting kneeling figures signifying eternity, which lay in the doorway. Carter likened the clearance to playing a 'gigantic game of spillikins'; a popular parlour game which required players to use physical and mental dexterity in extracting sticks from a heap, without disturbing the other sticks. In fact, as he later came to realise:

> *There was a certain amount of confusion, it was true, but it was orderly confusion, and had it not been for the evidence of plundering afforded by the tunnel and the re-sealed doorways, one might have imagined at first view that there never had been any plundering, and that the confusion was due to Oriental carelessness at the time of the funeral.* [9]

The team worked their way around the room in an anti-clockwise direction, starting to the right of the doorway (working towards the north-east corner) and ending with the dismantled chariots which lay to the left of the door. The work was painfully slow and nerve-racking, as the team fought to prevent the artefacts from crumbling beneath their touch. Each chest or bundle, safely extracted from the heap in the tomb, then had to undergo its own mini-excavation in the conservation lab. Just one of the boxes yielded contents that agreed with its original label; all the others contained a mixture of artefacts stuffed in any old how by the restorers.

The first artefact to be taken for treatment – a beautiful chest, known today as the 'Painted Box' – provides a perfect example of the problems encountered by the conservators. The wooden chest had been plastered and painted over its entire outer surface with traditional scenes of hunting in the desert (lid) and fierce battles featuring

5. The 'Painted Box': a beautiful artefact in its own right, which housed a jumble of garments.

Tutankhamen triumphant in his chariot, vanquishing his Syrian enemies (body). There were a few chips in the plaster and a few gaps in the joints, but at first sight the chest appeared to be in good condition. It was therefore cleaned, patches of discoloration were treated with benzine, and the whole was sprayed with celluloid solution. However, after three weeks in the dry atmosphere of the conservation tomb, the wood began to shrink and the painted plaster to buckle. The chest was therefore treated with melted paraffin wax, which penetrated the plaster, effectively gluing it back in place. Inside the box was a curious and ill-assorted mess of decaying objects which Mace, in his diary entry for 10 January 1923, described as 'a hay pie, jumbled up anyhow'. The pie included a pair of woven sandals, three pairs of leather sandals, at least seven beaded and finely decorated robes including an imitation leopardskin cloak, two bags or caps, two faience collars, loincloths, rolls of cloth and bandages, a glove and a golden headrest. Many of the robes were beyond redemption: 'a mass of decayed cloth, much of it the consistency of soot, spangled throughout with rosettes and sequins of gold and silver'.[10] Some were obviously children's garments, causing Mace to speculate, for the first time, that Tutankhamen may have succeeded to his throne as a boy. It took Mace three weeks to empty this one chest, picking out fragments of material piece by piece and photographing each stage of the operation.

On the afternoon of Friday 16 February the doorway to the Burial Chamber was dismantled in the presence of an invited audience of archaeologists and government officials.[11] Spotlighted by two lamps, focused on the wall, Carnarvon started proceedings with a brief but impressive speech, thanking all those who had assisted in the work so far. Mervyn Herbert tells us that his brother was unusually nervous, 'like a naughty schoolboy', in case anyone should realise that the wall had already been breached.[12] Standing on a specially designed wooden platform, Carter too made a speech, which was, according to Herbert, less impressive than Carnarvon's. Then, having stripped to his trousers and vest, he located the wooden lintel at the top of the doorway and applied his crowbar, working, for reasons of safety, from the top downwards. Mace took the blocks from the wall and handed them to Callender, who passed them along a chain of workmen to be stacked outside the tomb. The pack of reporters, who spent the afternoon glumly sitting on the tomb parapet listening to events within, was deliberately fed misinformation by the workmen: first eight mummies had been found, then four, then an enormous cat statue. Inevitably, some of this misinformation made its way into print.

After about fifteen minutes Carter had made a hole large enough to insert an electric torch; this revealed what appeared to be a wall of solid gold. Soon after, he was able to push a mattress through the hole, to protect the golden wall from falling masonry. After two hours the party was at last able, three at a time, to squeeze through the hole and drop down into the Burial Chamber. Carter recorded his impressions of this first official visit to the Chamber:

It was, beyond any question, the sepulchral chamber in which we stood, for there, towering above us, was one of the great gilt shrines beneath which kings were laid. So enormous was the structure (17 feet by 11 feet, and 9 feet high, we found afterwards) that it filled within a little the entire area of the chamber, a space of some two feet only separating it from the walls on all four sides, while its roof, with cornice top and torus moulding, reached almost to the ceiling. From top to bottom it was overlaid with gold, and upon its sides there were inlaid panels of brilliant blue faience, in which were represented, repeated over and over, the magic symbols which would ensure its strength and safety. [13]

The enormous and very fragile gilt shrine was fitted, on its eastern face, with double folding doors which were closed and bolted, but not sealed. Eagerly, Carter drew back the ebony bolts and swung open the doors to reveal a second golden shrine, covered with a delicate linen pall appliquéd with gilded bronze flowers. This shrine was bolted top and bottom and sealed with two seals: the necropolis seal of the jackal and nine bound captives, and Tutankhamen's own necropolis seal. Finally, here was proof that the ancient robbers had failed to penetrate to the heart of Tutankhamen's burial.

The narrow space between the outermost shrine and the chamber walls yielded an assortment of artefacts which seem to modern eyes bafflingly random, but which had been deliberately chosen by the undertakers for their ritual significance: two calcite lamps, a wooden goose, two boxes, two wine jars, an unidentifiable 'ritual object', eleven magical oars, a double shrine, two 'Anubis fetishes' (an animal skin, filled with embalming fluid, suspended on a pole), gilded wooden hieroglyphic symbols meaning 'to awake' and a funerary bouquet. Hidden from view in the painted walls, four niches held the magical bricks that would assist Tutankhamen in his rebirth. Opening off the Burial Chamber an open doorway revealed yet another room

6. Carter (left), Carnarvon and the partially dismantled, plastered and sealed wall to the Burial Chamber.

packed with objects including a gleaming golden canopic shrine, an object of such significance and beauty that it brought a lump to the normally undemonstrative Carter's throat. This 'Treasury' would be boarded up and left untouched until 1927. Amazed by what they had seen, the weary visitors left the tomb after 5 p.m. and, in true British style, went for tea. *The Times* broke the news to the waiting world:

> *Today, between the hours of 1 and 3 in the afternoon, the culminating moment in the discovery of Tutankhamen's tomb took place, when Lord Carnarvon and Mr Howard Carter opened the inner sealed doorway … The process of opening this doorway bearing the Royal insignia and guarded by protective statues of the King had taken several hours of careful manipulation under intensive heat. It finally ended in a wonderful revelation, for before the spectators was the resplendent mausoleum of the King, a spacious, beautifully decorated chamber, completely occupied by an immense shrine covered with gold inlaid with brilliant blue faience.*

The next couple of days were taken up with private viewings, and private luncheons, for Egyptologists and distinguished visitors; among the latter were Queen Élisabeth of the Belgians and her son Prince Léopold. This was to be the first of several royal visits and the queen, an enthusiastic amateur Egyptologist, became something of a nuisance to the archaeologists as she interrupted their work. It was a nuisance, too, when the portly General Sir John Maxwell got stuck in the still-small hole in the Burial Chamber wall. Mervyn Herbert's diary records, with some sympathy, that it took four men pushing and pulling to free him 'with a noise like a champagne cork and with injury to what he wrongly described as his chest'. There would always be an uncomfortable tension between the scientific work of the excavators, who very much saw the tomb as their own private laboratory, and the exploitation of the tomb as a public spectacle by the authorities and, on occasion, the archaeologists themselves. The Valley had become the ultimate elite tourist attraction, with Carnarvon and Lady Evelyn acting as guides; anyone who could claim even the slightest acquaintance with any member of the team felt free to turn up, uninvited but with a letter of introduction, for a personal tour which would inevitably bring all work to a standstill.

The general public was condemned to loiter with the journalists beyond the tomb perimeter wall. This was not, perhaps, as bad as it seems, as every object removed from the tomb had to pass before their gaze en route for the sanctuary of the conservation tomb. This endless parade of grave goods – the constant anticipation that something exciting might at any moment appear – ensured that interest in the tomb increased rather than decreased. Luxor was swamped with visitors – the more enterprising hotels set up tents in their gardens where tourists could sleep, for one uncomfortable night only, on narrow cot beds – and the expedition lived in near-siege conditions:

> *The tomb drew like a magnet. From a very early hour in the morning the pilgrimage began. Visitors arrived on donkeys, in sand-carts, and in two-horse cabs, and proceeded to make themselves at home in The Valley for the day. Round the top of the upper level of the tomb there was a low wall, and here they each staked out a claim and established themselves, waiting for something to happen. Sometimes it did, more often it did not, but it seemed to make no difference to their patience. There they would sit the whole morning, reading, talking, writing, photographing the tomb and each other, quite satisfied if at the end they could get a glimpse of anything ...*[14]

Those unable to visit Egypt, wrote: the volume of post received by the Luxor post office first doubled, then tripled, and the telegraph office was overwhelmed by the sheer number of journalistic dispatches. Carter was bombarded with correspondence from all over the world, from well-wishers, beggars, schoolchildren, scholars, people wanting to buy, or sell, antiquities, people offering money for public lectures, and what might be loosely termed 'eccentrics', including those who believed themselves to be reincarnated Egyptians. All wanted a reply from the celebrity archaeologist.

Conditions within the tomb were hot, humid and extremely stressful. A serious, never explained quarrel between Carter and Carnarvon, which ended dramatically with Carter briefly banning Carnarvon from his house, was a sign that the team needed a break from the tomb, from the press, from the public and from each other. On 26 February 1923 the tomb was closed; the next day the laboratories were shut and the team dispersed. While Carter typically chose to hide himself away in his Luxor house, Lucas went to Cairo and Callender to Armant. Mace accompanied Carnarvon and Lady Evelyn as they sailed southwards to spend a few peaceful days at Aswan. It was on this trip that Carnarvon was bitten on the cheek by a mosquito, an everyday occurrence on the Nile. But soon after his return to Luxor, he sliced the scab off the bite while shaving. Here, accounts of the tragedy vary. Most state that Carnarvon treated the wound immediately with iodine (already an invalid, he travelled with a well-stocked medical chest); a few that he allowed the wound to bleed freely, and inadvertently allowed an 'unspeakably filthy' fly to settle on it.[15] The wound quickly became infected, and Carnarvon started to feel unwell. A few days' bed rest – insisted upon by Lady Evelyn – soon had him feeling fit again, but then there came a sudden relapse. Unwilling to admit just how ill he felt, Carnarvon travelled to Cairo to start discussing the division of finds with the Antiquities Service. Here his condition deteriorated rapidly. Blood poisoning set in, and pneumonia followed. Lady Carnarvon flew to Cairo with her husband's personal doctor, Dr Johnson, and Lord Porchester, Carnarvon's heir, sailed from India. At 1.45 a.m. on 5 April 1923, Carnarvon died. His body was embalmed in Egypt and then returned to England for burial on Beacon Hill, part of the Highclere estate.

Carter, who had travelled to Cairo to support Lady Evelyn through-out her father's illness, and had remained to assist Lady Carnarvon with the funeral arrangements, returned to Luxor to wind down the excavation. The finds were packed into crates, and transported along the Décauville railway (a tramway allowing open carts to be pushed along a temporary track) to the river. This was not quite the slick opera-tion that it sounds; there was not enough track to cover the distance from the Valley to the river, and so it had to be dismantled and reposi-tioned as the train of carts progressed. At the river, the crates were loaded on to a steamer. When the ship arrived in Cairo on 21 May, Carter was ready to meet it. It took just three days for the artefacts to be unloaded, transported to the museum, unpacked and put on display.

The Second Season: 1923–4

The Concession to work in the Valley expired with Carnarvon's death. However, the Antiquities Service were keen that the clearance of the tomb should continue, and they were unwilling to finance it them-selves. Work therefore started as planned in October 1923, with Lady Carnarvon allowed to finish her husband's work, but not to conduct any further excavations in the Valley. In addition to his other duties, Carter now assumed Carnarvon's role of liaising with the authorities and the press: a development which those who remembered the infa-mous 'Sakkara affair' had reason to view with some foreboding. Carter was a man of many talents, but diplomacy was not one of them.

From the very beginning of the season, there were problems. Carter provides us with an unusually tactful and essentially unin-formative summary of events that would lead to the closure of the tomb, and threaten the security of its remaining contents:

Gradually troubles began to arise. Newspapers were competing for 'copy', tourists were leaving no efforts untried to obtain permits to visit the tomb: endless jealousies were let loose; days which should have been devoted to scientific work were wasted in negotiations too often futile, whilst the claims of archaeology were thrust into the background. But this is no place for weighing the merits of a controversy now ended, and it would serve no good purpose to relate in detail the long series of unpleasant incidents which harassed our work. We are all of us human. No man is wise at all times – perhaps least of all the archaeologist who finds his efforts to carry out an all-absorbing task frustrated by a thousand pin-pricks and irritations without end. It is not for me to affix the blame for what occurred, nor yet to bear responsibility for a dispute in which at one moment the interests of archaeology in Egypt seemed menaced. [16]

Carter believed that time-wasting visitor numbers should be controlled by banning informal visits, while implementing a series of planned open days. After a great deal of negotiation, and repeated journeys between Luxor and Cairo, the matter was to a certain extent settled. The Antiquities Service would issue visitor permits which would limit the number of tourists demanding access to the tomb. In theory this should have worked, but in practice the Service issued permits to more or less anyone who applied for them, while Carter was prone to break his own rule, finding it difficult to refuse admission to prominent Egyptian families or important diplomatic parties. The problem of press access was more difficult. Carter suggested that it could be resolved quite simply by 'employing' Arthur Merton, correspondent of *The Times*, as an official member of the excavation team. Merton would issue daily reports which *The Times* would receive in time for the evening edition and the Egyptian newspapers would receive the next day. Thus, he hoped, news from the Valley would break more or less simultaneously in London and Cairo, and other newspapers could take their information from the published bulletins. Naturally enough, the representatives of Reuters and the *Morning Post* lobbied tirelessly against Carter's appointment of Merton, while the Egyptian press, and growing numbers of Egyptian nationalists, continued their campaign against colonialist archaeology.

Petty differences over press and public access to the tomb were extremely trying, but they were a symptom rather than a cause. Carter had become caught up in a political situation which he could do nothing to resolve. The British Protectorate was coming to an end and Egypt was becoming a modern, independent state. Fuad I had proclaimed himself king in 1922; a new constitution had been announced in 1923; there were to be general elections in 1924. The Antiquities Service was still run by a Frenchman, Pierre Lacau, but the politically astute Lacau was no longer prepared to be seen indulging foreign excavators in what many were beginning to regard as the exploitation of Egypt's heritage. Soon, a new rule was imposed: an Inspector of the Antiquities Service must always be present to oversee work at the site. Then, on 1 December 1923, came the demand that Carter submit a formal list of all members of his excavation staff for the approval of the Antiquities Service. Today this is standard procedure; the Antiquities Service has the right to veto anyone whom they deem unfit to work on any archaeological site. But in the 1920s it was seen as an unprecedented impertinence, and a less than subtle attack on the newly appointed press spokesman, Merton. Carter attempted to argue, but there was no room for negotiation. Lacau stood firm: '… the Government no longer discusses, but informs you of its decision'.

Meanwhile, work continued amid all the distractions. Carter had removed the two guardian statues from the Antechamber, and had completely demolished the partition wall separating it from the Burial Chamber. Even with the wall missing, the team were forced to work in uncomfortably cramped conditions as they struggled to dismantle the unwieldy, heavy and extremely fragile shrines, which fitted so neatly into the Burial Chamber that, without ruling out the possibility that they were merely the inner shrines of a far larger set, they seem to have been purpose-designed for the space. As Carter recollected: 'we bumped our heads, nipped our fingers, we had to squeeze in and out like weasels and work in all kinds of embarrassing positions'.[17] It soon became apparent that the ancient carpenters, too, had struggled in the restricted space. Despite a plethora of instructions scratched or painted on to the shrine components, the shrines had not been properly assembled. There were dents and gaping cracks, carpenter's debris was left on the floor and, most surprising of all, the shrine doors were misaligned so that they faced east, not west. This unusual arrangement was probably adopted to take advantage of the extra space offered by the Treasury; we can only wonder at the effect it would have had on Tutankhamen's spirit as he set off on his final journey moving away from, rather than towards, the setting sun.

The doors of the second shrine had been opened to reveal a third, sealed, golden shrine. On 3 January 1924, in the presence of a small group of scholars, this shrine was opened to reveal a fourth shrine whose doors were shut but not sealed. Inside this fourth shrine was a large quartzite sarcophagus:

> It was certainly a thrilling moment, as we gazed upon the spectacle enhanced by the striking contrast – the glitter of metal – of the gold shrines shielding it. Especially striking were the outstretched hand and wing of a goddess sculptured on one end of the sarcophagus, as if to ward off an intruder. It symbolised an idea beautiful in conception, and, indeed, seemed an eloquent illustration of the perfect faith and tender solicitude for the well-being of their loved one, that animated the people who dwelt in that land over thirty centuries ago.[18]

This moment of beauty and quiet triumph was soured by two

7. Protecting one of the two guardian statues that stood before the entrance to the Burial Chamber, prior to moving it.

malicious complaints sent to Lacau, one claiming that a representative of *The Times* had been allowed to watch the proceedings, and the other that there had been no Inspector of the Antiquities Service present when the shrine doors were opened. Both were easily proved false – Rex Engelbach, Chief Inspector of the Antiquities Service, had attended the opening and could confirm that events were conducted with the utmost propriety – but they left a nasty taste. On 10 January Lacau wrote a stiff letter to Carter, making it clear that the tomb and its entire contents were regarded as Egyptian property. By now, whatever good relationship had once existed between Carter and Lacau had entirely evaporated. Carter believed that Lacau was attempting to frustrate valuable research being conducted to the highest standard to the benefit of Egypt and Egyptology, while at the same time refusing to acknowledge any rights that the Carnarvon family might have over the work that they were financing. He also thought that Lacau in particular, and the Antiquities Service in general, were behaving in a needlessly offensive manner when they should be supporting the rights of Egyptologists against the demands of politicians. Lacau's thoughts are less well documented, but he seems to have believed quite simply that Carter and his team were arrogantly exploiting Egyptian property over which, as non-Egyptians, they had no moral authority.

After another month of hard labour all four shrines had been dismantled, their side panels propped against the wall of the Burial Chamber and their roofs stored in the Antechamber. It was now time to open the sarcophagus, but a crack running across the centre of the lid threatened to make this a difficult operation. Angle irons were positioned alongside the lid and a pulley system was introduced so that it might be raised in one piece. Carter had invited seventeen Egyptologists to attend the raising, which was planned for 12 February. The day before, however, the Ministry of Public Works sent an objection, stipulating that only fifteen guests would be allowed in the tomb. The matter was resolved amicably and, as planned, in front of an audience of Egyptian dignitaries, Antiquity Service officials, and Egyptologists, the granite lid was slowly hoisted upwards to hover over its quartzite base. A shrouded figure lay within. Carter and Mace drew back the two fragile linen sheets and:

… as the last was removed a gasp of wonderment escaped our lips, so gorgeous was the sight that met our eyes: a golden effigy of the young boy king, of most magnificent workmanship, filled the whole of the interior of the sarcophagus. This was the lid of a wonderful anthropoid coffin… [19]

The next day the tomb was to be opened to the press, and then 'the Ladies', the long-suffering wives and families of the archaeologists, were to be allowed a private viewing of the sarcophagus and its contents. But late on the evening of 12 February, the government sent a telegram. The press visit might go ahead, but the ladies could not be admitted to the tomb as they did not hold an official permit. This directive came from the Minister for Public Works, Morcos Bey Hanna, via his Under-Secretary, Mohammed Zaghlul Pasha. Lacau, who found the decision incomprehensible and wrote to Carter to tell him so, was blamed by many for not preventing it. However, it is perhaps not so incomprehensible. The nationalist Morcos Bey Hanna had no reason to accommodate the British: they had, after all, imprisoned him for treason, and attempted to have him hanged, the previous year.

Furious, the team – Carter, Mace, Lythgoe, Breasted, Gardiner and Newberry – held urgent discussions in the Winter Palace Hotel. These ended with Carter issuing a blunt statement:

Owing to impossible restrictions and discourtesies on the part of the Public Works Department and its Antiquities Service, all my collaborators in protest have refused to work any further upon the scientific investigations of the discovery of the tomb of Tut.ankh. amen.

I therefore am obliged to make known to the public that, immediately after the press viewing of the tomb this morning, between 10 am and noon, the tomb will be closed, and no further work can be carried out.

Now, at last, the journalists had something to write about. As they composed their headlines, 'Locked out at Luxor', the tomb was abandoned exactly as it stood, with the sarcophagus lid still precariously suspended in mid-air. Carter felt that he, his team and Lady Carnarvon had been grievously offended. The Antiquities Service, however, viewed his closure of the tomb as a childish over-reaction to an essentially trivial matter. More importantly, they saw it as a direct contravention of Lady Carnarvon's permission to clear the tomb. On 20 February 1924 her concession was formally withdrawn; on the 22nd, officials of the Antiquities Service confiscated the tomb and, as Carter had refused to hand over his keys, employed workmen to cut the padlocks off the tomb gates. As Carter commenced legal action, the response of his colleagues was muted. Those who worked on the tomb supported him, but those who excavated away from Thebes were reluctant to become involved in an essentially local dispute that might escalate and threaten their own work.

It was not in Carter's nature to concede easily. Months of negotiations followed, complicated by the fact that Carter had a long-standing commitment to lecture in America and Canada; a commitment that he could not break, as he now had no other source of income.

The Third Season: 1924–5

Carter returned to Egypt on 15 December 1924. He found himself dealing with a very different regime. On 19 November the British Sirdar (commander in chief of the Egyptian army), Sir Lee Stack, had been assassinated. This had led to the fall of the nationalist government and the imposition of stricter British controls. Saad Zaghlul Pasha had resigned, and had been replaced as prime minister by Ahmed Ziwar Pasha, an old acquaintance of Carter. Meeting accidentally in the Continental Hotel in Cairo, the two were able to start unofficial discussions over the future of the tomb. A series of official meetings followed and, eventually, an agreement was reached. Lady Carnarvon would continue to pay for the work on the tomb and its artefacts, but the Carnarvon estate would waive all rights to the tomb and *The Times* would lose its press monopoly. The question of compensation would rumble on until 1930, when the estate was offered £35,867 13s 8d as full recompense for their costs. Lady Carnarvon had promised to pay a quarter of this to Carter, but in the event she paid him £8,012 up front, with a further £546 2s 9d paid later that year. The Metropolitan Museum, whose costs have been estimated in the region of £8,000, received nothing.

From late January 1925 onwards, the shortened season of work proceeded with an unaccustomed calmness. Nothing was taken out of the tomb. Instead, the team concentrated on the artefacts already awaiting study in the conservation lab. This vital work – fascinating to the Egyptologists – was not in any way newsworthy. With no daily display of grave goods leaving the tomb, and no political infighting, the pack of reporters quickly dispersed. After two successful months, nineteen cases of antiquities were sent by steamer to Cairo Museum, and Carter and Callender travelled north by motor car – Carter had become a great motoring enthusiast – to supervise their unpacking.

The Fourth Season: 1925–6

Work re-started on 11 October 1925, with attention firmly focused on the Burial Chamber. Carter intended to extract Tutankhamen from his sarcophagus before the winter tourist season got under way, as an influx of visitors would only hinder operations. However, recovering the mummy proved far more difficult than anyone had anticipated. It was not immediately apparent, but Tutankhamen had been interred in a nest of three close-fitting anthropoid (human-shaped) coffins, which had been placed on a low bier and wedged into the rectangular sarcophagus. There was very little room to manoeuvre, the coffins were extremely fragile, and the combined weight of the coffins and mummy was an extraordinary ton and a quarter.

The first task was to raise the lid of the outer coffin. This had been fastened to its base by a system of silver pins securing ten silver tongues that slotted into sockets in the base. On 13 October the pins were removed and, using its original silver handles, the lid was hoisted away. This exposed a second gilded wooden coffin covered with a decaying linen shroud and disintegrating garlands of lotus flowers and cornflowers woven with olive and willow leaves.

This second anthropoid coffin was more fragile than the first; it showed signs of damp, and some of its inlay was falling away. With only a centimetre of space separating it from the base of the outer coffin (Carter could not put even his little finger between the two), it was sensible to extract the combined coffins from the deep sarcophagus before attempting to raise the second lid. Steel pins were inserted into the original sockets in the outer coffin base, and the lifting apparatus was used to raise the nested coffins above the sarcophagus. Wooden planks were quickly placed over the top of the sarcophagus, and the outer coffin base was lowered on to this improvised table. Unfortunately, although the second coffin lid had been fixed to its base using the same tongue and socket system as the outer coffin, it had not been provided with handles. There was therefore no easy way of lifting it. After two days of deliberation, the pins holding the tongues were extended as far as the outer coffin base would allow, wires were attached to the pins, and, in what appears almost a counter-intuitive move, the second coffin was held still while the outer coffin base was lowered, leaving the second coffin dangling somewhat precariously from the hoist. The empty outer coffin was placed in the sarcophagus for storage, and the entire second coffin was lowered on to a wooden tray placed over the open sarcophagus.

The lid of the second coffin was lifted, with considerable difficulty, on 23 October, revealing a third anthropoid coffin, with a red-brown linen sheet carefully tucked around it so as to leave the face exposed. Unlike the previous two, this third coffin was made of beaten sheet gold. It was now obvious why the weight of the coffin assemblage had barely diminished as the outer coffins were removed.

Gold it may have been, but this innermost coffin was far from gleaming:

> *… the ultimate details of the ornamentation were hidden by a black lustrous coating due to liquid unguents that had evidently been profusely poured over the coffin. As a result this unparalleled monument was not only disfigured – as it afterwards proved, only temporarily – but was stuck fast to the interior of the second coffin, the consolidated liquid filling up the space between the second and third coffins almost to the level of the lid of the third.* [20]

The innermost coffin, still lying in the base of the second, was transferred to the Antechamber, where there was more room to move. Here the base of the second coffin was coated with hot paraffin wax, which would, as it cooled, hold its delicate inlays firmly in position. Finally, the gold pins holding the third lid in place were extracted, using long screwdrivers adapted for the purpose. The lid was raised to reveal Tutankhamen's mummy, his head and shoulders covered by a golden funerary mask:

> *Before us, occupying the whole interior of the golden coffin, was an impressive, neat and carefully made mummy, over which had been poured anointing unguents ... in great quantity – consolidated and blackened by age. In contradiction to the general dark and sombre effect, due to these unguents, was a brilliant, one might say magnificent, burnished gold mask or similitude of the king, covering his head and shoulders, which, like the feet, had been intentionally avoided when using the unguents. [21]*

The resin-based unguents, which were still tacky in places, were a part of the funerary ritual: Carter estimated that maybe two bucketfuls had been poured over the king, carefully missing the face and feet. The unguents had glued the king's bandaged face into his funerary mask, and both his mask and his body into his innermost coffin, which was itself still glued into the second coffin base. Once Tutankhamen had been extracted, Carter took a calculated gamble:

> *...the interior of the golden coffin had to be completely lined with thick plates of zinc, which would not melt under temperatures of 968° Fahrenheit (520° C). The coffins were then reversed upon trestles, the outer one being protected against undue heat and fire by several blankets saturated and kept wet with water. Our next procedure was to place under the hollow of the gold coffin several Primus paraffin lamps burning at full blast. The heat from the lamps had to be regulated so as to keep the temperature well within the melting-point of zinc. It should be noted here that the coating of wax upon the surface of the second coffin acted as a pyrometer – while it remained unmelted under the wet blanketing there was manifestly no fear of injury.*
>
> *Although the temperature arrived at was some 932° Fahrenheit*

(500° C), it took several hours before any real effect was noticeable. The moment signs of movement became apparent, the lamps were turned out, and the coffins left suspended upon the trestles, when, after an hour, they began to fall apart …

As for the mask:

In the same manner that the outside of the golden coffin was covered with a viscid mass, so was the interior, to which still adhered the gold mask. This mask had also been protected by being bound with a folded wet blanket continually fed with water, its face padded with wet wadding. As it had necessarily been subjected to the full power of the heat collected in the interior of the coffin, it was freed and lifted away with comparative ease …[22]

With the pieces separated, the unguent could be removed with the help of cleaning solvents and a blast lamp. It was now apparent that the mask was made of gold sheets beaten together, the surface of the mask being 18.4 carat gold, the headdress 22.5 carats and the underlying mask 23 carats. There were solder-lines around the edges of the face and forehead, and rivets visible at the base of the throat, while the beard was a separate piece, made of gold inlaid with faience. The mask wore the *nemes* headdress: a headcloth covering the head and nape of the neck, with large flaps of cloth decending behind each ear to the shoulder. This was inlaid with stripes of blue glass, and bore the protective vulture and cobra on the brow. Texts inscribed on the back of the mask were taken from the *Book of the Dead*.

On 31 December 1925, the innermost coffin and the funerary mask journeyed north by train, escorted by Carter, Lucas and an armed guard. For maximum security, the train was shunted directly into the Museum gardens. The rest of the season was then dedicated to conserving the coffins and the jewellery.

The Fifth Season: 1926–7

Work started with the restoration of the mummy to the granite sarcophagus. With Tutankhamen secure, attention turned to the Treasury. This room, too, had been robbed, with many of its chests showing the unmissable evidence of broken seals. However, it appeared to have suffered less disturbance, or maybe to have been better restored, than the other chambers. Here were a host of highly symbolic artefacts including a large shrine topped with the jackal-figure of the funerary god Anubis, a large and curious golden cow's head representing a form of the goddess Hathor, and a fleet of boats that would allow the dead king to sail to Abydos, the cult centre of Osiris. Most astonishing of all was the object that had caught Carter's eye four years earlier: the magnificent canopic shrine provided to house Tutankhamen's preserved entrails:

> *Facing the doorway, on the farther side, stood the most beautiful monument that I have ever seen – so lovely that it made one gasp with wonder and admiration. The central portion of it consisted of a large shrine-shaped chest, completely overlaid with gold and surmounted by a cornice of sacred cobras. Surrounding this, free-standing, were statues of the four tutelary goddesses of the dead – gracious figures with outstretched protective arms, so natural and lifelike in their pose, so pitiful and compassionate the expressions upon their faces, that one felt it almost sacrilege to look at them. One guarded the shrine on each of its four sides, but whereas the figures at the front and back kept their gaze firmly fixed upon their charge, an additional note of touching realism was imparted by the other two, for their heads were turned sideways, looking over their shoulders towards the entrance, as though to watch against surprise. There is a simple grandeur about this monument that made an irresistible appeal to the imagination, and I am not ashamed to confess that it brought a lump to my throat.* [23]

The Annexe was the last chamber to be cleared. This was the chamber most affected by the robberies, and unlike the 'orderly confusion' of the Antechamber, its restoration appeared to have been effected by the ancient equivalent of sweeping everything under the bed. There was not a single inch of floor space for Carter and his team to stand, and the tower of grave goods reached a height, in some places, of 1.8m:

> ... *a jumble of every kind of funerary chattels, tumbled any way one upon the other, almost defying description. Bedsteads, chairs, stools, footstools, hassocks, gameboards, baskets of fruits, every kind of alabaster vessel and pottery wine-jars, boxes of funerary figures, toys, shields, bows and arrows, and other missiles, all topsy-turvy. Caskets thrown over, their contents spilled; in fact, everything in confusion.*[24]

The fact that the floor of the Annexe was almost a metre below the floor of the Antechamber simply compounded Carter's problems: the first objects had to be moved by team members dangling head-first from the doorway, supported by a rope sling which passed under the armpits, and was held by three or four men standing in the Antechamber. Once it became possible to actually stand in the room, Carter realised that the Annexe had originally been used to store food, wine, oils and perfumes, plus some miscellaneous furniture which more properly belonged in the over-filled Antechamber. Work proceeded slowly and methodically, following tried and tested patterns, until the final piece was removed from the Annexe on 15 December. Attention then switched to the conservation lab and to the large shrines, which were still stacked in pieces in the Antechamber.

The Final Seasons: 1928–30

The 1928–9 season was a peaceful one, although the team was plagued with illnesses. The 1929–30 season proved more tricky. With the work almost ended, Lady Carnarvon had given up her concession and, from 1930 onwards, all costs were met by the Egyptian government. This caused problems for Carter, who, as a foreigner with no official position, suddenly found himself locked out of the tomb and the lab. His knee-jerk response – to argue that the steel gates, locks and keys actually belonged to Lady Carnarvon rather than to the Antiquities Service – did little to help resolve the issue. Finally it was agreed that the keys would be held by a local Antiquities Service Inspector, who would arrive every day to unlock the tombs.

The last piece of shrine was removed from Tutankhamen's tomb in November 1930. Conservation work continued for another year, and it was not until February 1932 that the last consignment of grave goods was sent to Cairo. Carter's long labour was finally over and he was free to turn his attention to the academic publication of his work.

Carter never did finish the publication of Tutankhamen's tomb. This may explain why he never received any official recognition for his life's work. What few academic honours he did receive came from abroad. In 1924 he received an honorary science doctorate from Yale, and that same year he became a corresponding member of the Royal Academy of History in Madrid. He received a decoration from the King of Egypt in 1926, and a decoration from the King of Belgium in 1932. Given that he lived in an age when prominent British archaeologists and Egyptologists were routinely rewarded with knighthoods – Sirs Flinders Petrie, Leonard Woolley, Max Mallowan, Mortimer Wheeler and Alan Gardiner were either contemporaries, or near-contemporaries – he might reasonably have expected something similar. His lack of a patron, lack of a supporting institution and, perhaps, lack of breeding did not help his cause, but it may simply be that his

8. Tutankhamen's 'wishing cup': a calcite vessel in the form of a lotus.

own complex personality was to blame. Opinion among his contemporaries seems to have been more or less equally divided over whether Carter was simply shy and insecure about his lack of formal education, or an overbearingly arrogant boor.

Carter died in London on 2 March 1939. After an unimpressive, ill-attended funeral he was buried in a nondescript grave in Putney Vale Cemetery. A simple headstone commemorated 'Howard Carter, Archaeologist and Egyptologist, 1874–1939'.[25] His grave was then more or less forgotten so that when, in 1991, archaeologist Paul Bahn arrived to pay his respects to perhaps the most famous archaeologist in history, the stone surround was broken and it was barely possible to read the epitaph. Bahn wrote an article for *Archaeology* magazine in the United States, suggesting that something should be done to restore the grave for the seventieth anniversary of the discovery of Tutankhamen's tomb, and readers started to send in cheques.[26] Inevitably, *The Times* picked up the story. When the British Museum stepped in to commission a new gravestone, the cheques were returned to the generous American readers. Today his grave bears a more splendid stone, dedicated to 'Howard Carter, Egyptologist, Discoverer of the tomb of Tutankhamen 1922. Born 9 May 1874, Died, 2 March 1939.' There are two quotations from hieroglyphic texts. 'Oh night, spread thy wings over me as the imperishable stars', a version of the hymn to the sky goddess Nut, which is inscribed inside many New Kingdom coffins, is on the foot of the surround. The headstone bears an abbreviated form of the prayer engraved on Tutankhamen's 'wishing cup':

May your spirit live, may you spend millions of years, you who love Thebes, sitting with your face to the north wind, your eyes beholding happiness.

4

INVENTORY

First they saw three magnificent State couches, all gilt, with exquisite carving and heads of Typhon [Seth], Hathor and lion … Two life-sized bituminized statues of the king, with gold work holding a golden stick and mace, faced each other, the handsome features, the feet, and the hands, delicately carved, with eyes of glass and head-dress richly studded with gems. There were also four chariots, the sides of which were encrusted with semi-precious stones and rich gold decoration. These were dismantled, with a charioteer's apron of leopard's skin hanging over the seat … There were some remarkable wreaths, still looking evergreen, and one of the boxes contained rolls of papyri, which are expected to render a mass of information.

The Times[1]

The box of papyri – Tutankhamen's library – caused great excitement. As the linguist charged with decoding the tomb's texts, Gardiner outlined its importance for readers of *The Times*:

My own predilections lead me to be particularly interested in the box of papyri which has been found. It is possible – it is even probable – that the papyri will turn out to be no more than 'Books of the Dead' as they are called, such as were buried with practically every king and person of note, and which consisted of incantations ensuring the dead king's welfare in the other world. On the other hand, these documents may throw some light on the change from the religion of the heretics back to the old traditional religion, and that would be extremely interesting.[2]

Unfortunately, the library proved to be a less than exciting box of discoloured linen rolls. The *Daily Mail,* no great friend to Carter, dismissed them as 'simply folded table napkins'; they have since been tentatively identified as Tutankhamen's loincloths. Much to everyone's great surprise, the tomb yielded no original or personal writings and, although there were extracts from the standard funerary texts engraved on some of the grave goods, there was just one badly decayed and essentially uninformative scrap of papyrus recovered from the mummy itself. Gardiner was far less optimistic when he next shared his thoughts with *The Times*:

What students of Egyptian history and philology long for is not a corrupt, garbled version of ancient funerary spells such as a papyrus of the 'Book of the Dead' belonging to this period would undoubtedly present, but rather a series of letters, journals, or archives of some sort that could throw light upon the stirring times in which King Tutankhamen lived, or upon his conversion from the Aten heresy back to the faith of his forefathers.

The hope that any such documents will emerge is, we must admit, but a very faint one. Probably in the end the claim of the new tomb to be the greatest discovery ever made in Egypt will rest mainly on the great quantity of objects found and their amazingly high artistic quality. The historical harvest will be of less importance.[3]

It was natural that Gardiner felt some disappointment. Technology and material culture, no matter how beautiful, would never excite a linguist, while a library of scrolls, or even a simple family tree, would have given a welcome boost to the understanding of the complex history of the late 18th Dynasty royal family. However, Gardiner was wrong in his supposition that Tutankhamen's mute grave goods would be valued primarily for their artistic quality. As Egyptology has developed into a science rather than a language-based discipline, items that in his day were essentially ornate dead ends are starting to yield an unexpected harvest. It is now recognised that every artefact, no matter how superficially mundane, has a story to tell. This phenomenon is particularly well illustrated by a consideration of the textiles recovered from the tomb.

𓃿 𓃿 𓃿

Ancient Egyptian clothing was almost invariably made from linen, a product of the flax plant which flourished in the fertile fields of the Nile Valley. Wool was available but rarely used; cotton was not available during the 18th Dynasty. Tutankhamen was therefore buried with vast quantities of linen, including garments, rolls of cloth, sheets and bandages. There were painted linen components included in his chariots, and miniature linen cloaks tied neatly around the necks of many of the funerary figurines, some of which bore labels indicating that the linen at least dated to the reign of Akhenaten. It is impossible to estimate how much cloth was originally included in Tutankhamen's burial. Their unique and somewhat wasteful funerary practices meant that the Egyptians had an insatiable demand for cloth, and linen – expensive, portable, difficult to identify and easy to sell – would have been one of the prime targets of the robbers who ransacked his tomb.

Those textiles that survived the robbery were simply stuffed, crumpled and unfolded, into any old chest or box. When recovered from these containers, they were in a highly fragile condition, with some far better preserved than others:

> One of the disappointments of the tomb was the very bad state of preservation of practically all the textile fabrics. These, most of which had been white originally, varied in colour when found from light yellowish brown, to very dark brown, almost black, and were generally in very poor condition, the darker the colour the worse the condition; the best preserved were fragile and tender, and the worst had become a mass of black powder.[4]

An unfortunate combination of circumstances, including sealing the tomb while the plaster and mortar were still wet, moisture percolating through the innermost wall and, maybe, the decomposition of the fruits and liquids included among the grave goods, had caused a damp, slightly humid atmosphere within the tomb. There was evidence of a brown fungus on the walls and on some of the objects, and a 'peculiar pink film' had been deposited everywhere. Lucas, the team chemist, suggested that the 'pink film' may have been caused by the deterioration of a ferrous compound within the stone and plaster, which was drawn to the surface by capillary action, then oxidised to iron oxide. He was, however, uncertain why the colour of the deposit varied, appearing scarlet on calcite and pink on limestone and plaster. A story which Carter tells as a footnote may be relevant here (while serving as a reminder that the tomb was at all times a magnet for enterprising thieves):

> Latterly, I witnessed a very interesting demonstration of a somewhat similar effect. My magazine wherein masses of materials were stored was set on fire by thieves to cover a theft they had perpetrated. They set fire to a heap of hemp sacks and large rolls of brown paper that were stored in the magazine (an ancient Egyptian rock-cut tomb chamber closed by a heavy modern wooden door). The fire was

detected, from smoke issuing from the cracks of the door, within about an hour of ignition; in fact, in time to prevent any great harm being done, further than charring the sacks and brown paper, which had only smouldered owing to insufficient air in the chamber. Having extinguished the fire and removed the charred sacking and paper, I found, upon inspection, a light amber brown sticky (? resinous) deposit from the smoke all over the walls, ceiling and floor of the chamber, as well as on all the exposed materials stored therein: an effect, except for the colour and nature of the film, exactly as met with in the tomb of Tut-ankh-amen.[5]

The textiles were not, of course, the only artefacts to have suffered in the microclimate of the tomb. We are accustomed to seeing the best of Tutankhamen's grave goods displayed in Cairo Museum after extensive cleaning, conservation and, in some cases, reconstruction, but this is not necessarily the condition in which they were found. Leaving aside the ubiquitous but harmless 'pink film', much of the wood had warped, and much of the glue had dissolved, so that many objects simply fell apart as they were moved. Objects made from a combination of materials – a chest, for example, might typically be made of wooden planks veneered with ivory, ebony and gold, or might be coated with painted plaster – posed a particular challenge to the conservators, as the individual components warped and deteriorated at different rates and this caused them to separate. At the opposite extreme, some of the grave goods had to be dismantled by the excavators: the shrines, for example, could not be removed intact from the Burial Chamber, and the three animal-headed couches had to be taken apart so that they might fit through the tomb door. It would be difficult to over-estimate the importance of the immediate, on-site conservation work, but Carter believed that, without it, less than one tenth of the artefacts would have survived to reach Cairo. As it was, he estimated that less than 0.25 per cent of the artefacts were lost.

The care taken over the preservation of the delicate spangled linen pall discovered within the outermost shrine in the Burial Chamber is a shining example of Carter's innovative approach to conservation. The pall, brown with age and already tearing under its own weight, hung on a wooden frame immediately above, and blocking access to, the second shrine. After much thought, a plan was developed. First, with Carter and Mace crawling along planks placed across the outer shrine, the hundreds of gilded bronze flowers were removed. Some could simply be lifted off the linen; others had to be cut away with scissors. This greatly reduced the weight of the cloth, and allowed it to be wound on to a giant, purpose-made wooden roller. Experimentation by Dr Alexander Scott, director of scientific research at the British Museum, led to the fabric being strengthened with a mixture of duroprene (a chlorinated rubber compound dissolved in an organic solvent) and xylol.[6] Unfortunately, during the 1924 Antiquities Service lockout, the pall was left unattended in the conservation tomb, and was ruined beyond redemption.

Tutankhamen's wardrobe included sleeved and sleeveless robes, kilts, sashes, gloves, headdresses, sandals, and what Carter coyly describes as 'shirts and undergarments'.[7] Although contemporary images show the New Kingdom elite dressed in conservative white (undyed) clothes, Tutankhamen's garments were lavishly embellished, and demonstrated techniques of tapestry weave, dyeing, bleaching, fringing, appliqué, embroidery (including chain stitch and buttonhole stitch), heavy beading and the application of sequin-like spangles and cartouches which unfortunately caused the tunics to tear. Some of the robes were so elaborate that they were initially identified – purely on the basis of early twentieth-century cultural expectations – as women's clothes. Others were so small that they had obviously been made for a child. There were some curious inconsistencies: Tutankhamen had almost 150 loincloths but no more than ten tunics, yet these garments were worn as sets, one tunic with one loincloth.[8]

9. Tutankhamen's 'mannequin'.

A curious omission was Tutankhamen's crown or crowns. In fact no royal crown has ever been recovered from any context, and this suggests that crowns may not have been considered the personal property of individual kings. Lest there should be any doubt over his status, Tutankhamen was buried with three crooks and two flails, the symbols of his earthly kingship. He was also buried with a curious figure discovered by Carter in the Antechamber. This wooden, plastered and painted life-sized model of the king is dressed in a simple white robe resembling a tight modern T-shirt. It wears a crown with a uraeus, yet lacks arms and legs. Under normal circumstances it would be considered extremely bad luck to include an incomplete or otherwise mutilated figure of an owner in his tomb, as this might cause the deceased to be reborn with the same mutilation. It therefore seems likely that the figure had a specific purpose. Carter identified it as a mannequin, used to model Tutankhamen's robes and jewellery, and the *New York*

Times advanced this theory: 'like a modern woman's dress dummy, called, I believe, by dressmakers an Arabella or tailor's mannequin used for trying on and fitting garments'.[8] Here was a thrilling, direct connection between the ancient tomb and the modern, Tut-inspired clothes that were all the rage in the West.

The textiles were recorded, treated, and then transferred to Cairo where, all but forgotten, they continued to deteriorate so that today the vibrant colours recorded by Carter have dimmed.[10] They were never published, although there were occasional, tantalisingly brief, mentions in Carter's own popular books, in the *Illustrated London News* (August 1929) and in *Embroidery* (December 1932). As with all the other artefact types, the intention was that a specialist volume would eventually be produced. Now, after decades of neglect, Tut-ankhamen's wardrobe is finally being reconstructed and studied by a dedicated team of textile historians led by Gillian Vogelsang-East-wood at the Textile Research Centre, Leiden University.[11] Their results have the potential to provide information not only about the com-mercially important Egyptian textile industry, and about 18th Dynasty clothing and fashion in general, but about Tutankhamen himself.

Tomb walls and statuary suggest that the elite Egyptians favoured stylish but impractical clothing, with the women hobbling around in skin-tight white sheaths, the men dressed in skimpy kilts and the children of both sexes naked. This is directly contradicted by the archaeological evidence, recovered from Tutankhamen's tomb and elsewhere, which shows that they actually wore comfortable, loose-fitting tunic-style garments that they draped and tied around the body. Even allowing for this loose fit, his reconstructed clothing indi-cates that Tutankhamen's vital statistics were unusual for a man of his height. His mummy, measured during the autopsy, was approximately 167.5 cm in length (almost 5ft 6ins); his chest, measured from his near life-sized mannequin, was approximately 80 cm (31 inches); his waist, estimated by measuring his belts, sashes and the mannequin, measured approximately 75 cm (29 inches); his hips, measured from his loincloths, a disproportionately large 108–110 cm (perhaps as wide as 43 inches).[10] This is the same, rather feminine body-shape – a narrow waist and wide hips – that we see, greatly exaggerated, on Akhenaten's formal art work. It suggests that the pear-shape was a family trait – possibly, even, the symptom of some hereditary illness – and that Akhenaten may, as Egyptologists have long suspected, have provided his own artistic inspiration.

Tutankhamen's tomb is not the Egyptian equivalent of a shipwreck, or of Pompeii, or of any other disaster where death came in an instant, preserving the unaudited evidence of life actually lived. It is a frozen rite: a collection of artefacts deliberately selected because they had meaning for either the king or those who buried him. Taken as a whole, the collection is capable of stirring emotion in the most experienced of Egyptological breasts:

If tradition and priestly practice governed ancient Egyptian burial ceremonial, as the contents of Tut-ankh-Amen's tomb suggest, their rituals left room for a personal side which confronted the grief of the mourners, while it aimed at encouraging the dead on their journey through the dangers of the Underworld. This human sentiment has not been concealed by the mysterious symbolism of a complex creed. It dawns on the observer gradually as he pursues his investigations. The impression of a personal sorrow is perhaps more distinctly conveyed to us from what we learn of the tomb of Tut-ankh-Amen than by most other discoveries. It meets us as an emotion which we are accustomed to deem comparatively modern in origin. The tiny wreath on the stately coffin, the beautiful alabaster wishing cup with its touching inscription, the treasured reed with its suggestive memories

*– cut by the young king himself by the lake-side – these, and other
objects, help to convey the message – the message of the living mourning the dead.*[13]

In order to make sense of Tutankhamen's tomb, we have to understand how he came to be buried in a warehouse full of goods. Was this
simply a convenient means of disposing of the unwanted, and maybe
even unlucky, possessions of a deceased king? Was it a fairly meaningless following of long-established tradition: Tutankhamen was buried
this way simply because kings had always been buried this way? Did
Tutankhamen actually intend to use his property after death? Did his
plans for the provisioning of his own tomb reconcile him to the inevitability of his own death? The answer is probably a combination of all
of these, and more.

Official religion is of surprisingly little help here. The theology
that Tutankhamen promoted as the living representative of the gods
in Egypt taught that a dead king who experienced the correct rituals
would be reborn to become one with those gods. Funerary texts –
writings for the tomb designed to help the deceased achieve an appropriate afterlife – show that this belief stretched as least as far back as
the Old Kingdom pyramids, built more than 1,000 years before Tutankhamen's birth. It would continue more or less unbroken to the end
of the dynastic age. A dead king, having passed through a series of
ordeals, was more or less guaranteed to achieve an afterlife away from
the tomb. He might twinkle in the night sky as an unborn star, or
descend to the underworld to become one with Osiris, king of the
underworld, or ascend into the sky to sail in the solar boat of the sun
god Re. In theory, then, a dead king had little need of extensive grave
goods, as he would not be lingering to enjoy them.

Egypt's elite were less fortunate. Throughout the Old Kingdom (*c.*
2686–2125 BC) they, too, expected to live beyond death, but they did
not expect to leave the tomb. As the tomb would be their home until

the end of eternity, and as the dead had the same basic requirements as the living, they needed to cram in as many goods as possible. More and more items were packed away – food, drink, clothing, toys, games, toiletries, even toilets – until it was realised that the situation was hopeless. No tomb would ever be large enough, and no family ever rich enough, to provide sufficient grave goods. The elite now started to rely on magical provisions: these might be offerings left by visitors to the tomb, small-scale models, or scenes carved and painted on the tomb walls. Given the correct rituals, all three could supply an eternal sustenance.

This situation underwent a profound change at the end of the Old Kingdom, when Osiris opened his kingdom to anyone who could afford the proper rituals. As a minimum these included a mummified body, a properly conducted funeral, and an appropriate set of funerary texts. The elite, who could afford all these things, had a reasonable expectation that one of their three spirits, the *akh* (the immortality of the deceased), would embark on the perilous journey to the next life. Their other two spirts, the *ba* (the soul or personality of the deceased) and the *ka* (the spiritual essence, or life-force, of the deceased), would remain closer to the corpse, sustained by the offerings left by the living. The illiterate poor, the vast majority of the population, could afford none of the necessary rituals. As we are unable to read their words, we are unable to understand what, if anything, they believed would happen after death.

There was now no need for anyone to invest in extensive grave goods. Nevertheless, the elite never quite lost the habit of packing for their final journey and kings, too, persisted with the tradition. As Tutankhamen's is the only New Kingdom royal tomb to survive substantially intact, it is not possible to state exactly what, or how much, others took with them. It is tempting to assume that a more 'successful', longer-lived king would have had his far larger tomb crammed to the ceiling with immensely valuable objects, so that, for example, the tombs of Amenhotep III (the New Kingdom's wealthiest king) or

Ramesses II (the New Kingdom's longest-lived king) would have been veritable treasure troves. This is, however, an illogical assumption. It may be that Tutankhamen was provided with a fairly standard set of grave goods and that, were we able to examine the untouched tomb of Amenhotep III or Ramesses II, we would find pretty much the same assemblage – a carefully calculated mixture of ritual and personal objects, new and old – more aesthetically displayed in its spacious surrounds.

It is, however, clear that Tutankhamen's tomb was not big enough for the goods it was to hold. This was a question of size, rather than quantity. The funerary shrines and the quartzite sarcophagus – designed for a more spacious tomb? – were quite simply too large to pass down the entrance steps and through the first doorway, and the workmen were forced to cut away the last six steps of the entrance stairway and the door lintel and jambs. The damaged areas were later restored in stone, wood and plaster. Carter's men would have to perform a similar operation when they extracted the shrine panels from the tomb.

This evidence – the small tomb and the jumbled and mis-sized grave goods – has led to the popular supposition that Tutankhamen's burial was a 'cut price and makeshift affair'; 'fast and careless … with a rag-bag mix of whatever new, old and adaptable funerary equipment was readily to hand'.[14] This has in turn been cited as evidence that Tutankhamen was unloved at his death; that he may even have been murdered by whoever arranged his funeral. Again, there is little logicality in this assumption, and we have no means of knowing how atypical Tutankhamen's burial really was.

Our scanty knowledge of Theban funerary rituals is largely derived from non-royal sources. These show the coffined mummy travelling to the cemetery on a sledge dragged across the desert sands. A series of ceremonies was performed at the tomb entrance, the most important being the 'Opening of the Mouth', a ceremony designed to animate the eyes, ears, nose and mouth and, in so doing, convert inanimate images into beings heavy with the possibility of coming alive. The mourners ate a last meal with the deceased, then sealed the tomb. The last person to leave swept the ground behind him, so that his footprints would not disturb the harmony of the tomb. As night-time fell, the spirit prepared to embark on the long journey to the afterlife, a journey that would invariably involve some form of test. Ultimately, with all trials overcome, the righteous king would be united with the gods.

Confirmation of this basic ritual may be gained from the painted walls of Tutankhamen's Burial Chamber, where the artists depicted the more important of the funerary rites. The east wall shows Tutankhamen's funeral. The king, in an anthropoid coffin which looks nothing like his real coffin, is dragged to the cemetery on a wooden sledge pulled by men dressed in white. Included among them are the shaven-headed viziers of Upper and Lower Egypt. The North wall has three scenes which are intended to be read from right to left. The first shows Ay, Tutankhamen's successor, as he dons the leopardskin of a priest to perform the Opening of the Mouth ceremony on the mummy. Ay appears young and fit: a good example of royal propaganda in action, as he must have been well into his sixties by the time of Tutankhamen's death. The middle scene shows Tutankhamen, a man rather than a bandaged mummy, being welcomed to his afterlife by the goddess Nut. Finally we see Tutankhamen and his *ka* spirit, embracing the god Osiris. The South wall is the partition wall which houses the tomb doorway, and so was partially destroyed when the burial chamber was opened. Here we are shown Tutankhamen as he is greeted by the funerary deities Hathor, Anubis and Isis. Behind Isis once sat three gods of the underworld. The West wall presents a scene from the funerary text known as the *Book of the Hidden Chamber which is in the Underworld* (more popularly known today as the *Amduat*). As the solar boat sails through the night-time terrors of the underworld, twelve baboons, the gods of the twelve hours of night, provide their support.

All three of his coffins, and his funerary mask, depict Tutankhamen as one with the king of the dead, Osiris. The myth of Osiris had a particular relevance to Egypt's kings, for Osiris, too, had ruled Egypt before being murdered and dismembered by his jealous brother Seth. His sister-wife Isis was able to use her potent magic to restore him to a semblance of life, but the resurrected Osiris could no longer live in Egypt. As he journeyed into the west, to rule the land of the dead, his son Horus inherited his throne and ruled the land of the living.

Osiris invariably appears as a neatly bandaged being whose crossed arms hold the crook and flail which symbolise royalty, and whose unwrapped head is fitted with a curled beard and elaborate, composite crown. In his bandaged body we can find a neat explanation for the similarly bandaged mummies who occupied Egypt's elite tombs. To modern eyes, Osiris is an uncompromising and uncomfortable reminder of the inevitability of death. But to the ancients he was a life-affirming god of rejuvenation, agriculture and the inundation, whose occasionally erect penis served as a reminder of his original role as a fertility god. Osiris beds – seeded and watered Osiris-shaped troughs – were placed in New Kingdom tombs so that they might germinate and serve as a living symbol of resurrection. One of these beds was discovered in Tutankhamen's Treasury, filled with Nile silt and seeds.

Love and respect were not merely shown to the sovereign during his lifetime, but were continued to his memory after his death; and the manner in which his funeral obsequies were celebrated tended to show that, though their benefactor was no more, they retained a grateful sense of his goodness, and admiration for his virtues. And what, says the historian [Diodorus], can convey a greater testimony

of sincerity, free from all colour of dissimulation, when the person who conferred it no longer lives to witness the honour done to his memory?[16]

It is always difficult to force ancient Egyptian artefacts into modern systems of classification – ritual, practical, decorative, sentimental, etc. – as it is very apparent that, in a land where the most mundane of objects might be capable of multiple interpretations, and even colour might carry ritual significance, many artefacts simply defy classification. Writing equipment, for example, had a very obvious practical use, yet it was possible that the deceased might become the scribe of the sun god. How, then, do we classify Tutankhamen's fifteen writing palettes and associated paraphernalia –are they practical, or ritual? Headrests were supremely practical artefacts designed to allow a good night's sleep (however unlikely that might seem to those of us accustomed to soft pillows). However, night was a time of extreme danger, a time when evil spirits might invade the dreams of the just, and the decoration on Tutankhamen's ivory headrest – the god Shu and the twin lions of the eastern and western horizons – offered a protection to the king when he was at his most vulnerable. Tutankhamen's four game boards might have simply have been provided as a distraction, to allow him while away the long hours. But board games were a means of communicating with other worlds, and Tutankhamen's games may have provided him with some reassurance that he would indeed achieve his afterlife.

Bearing these caveats in mind, it is possible to divide Tutankhamen's grave goods into two broad categories. Some were practical objects which the dead king might use in his afterlife. Others were sacred or magical objects provided to help the funerary rites become effective. Shrines, amulets and magic bricks fall neatly into the latter category: they may have some decorative appeal, but they have no real practical use. Coffins and canopic jars have a more obvious practical application as boxes to store body parts, but they too may be classed as ritual objects, as their primary function is to assist the deceased. While a few ritual objects were found in the Antechamber, most were discovered in the Treasury and the Burial Chamber where, lying close to the mummy, they could best perform their sacred function. This distribution was immediately clear to Carter, who classified the contents of the Treasury as:

> ... *objects many, both of mystic and of absorbing interest, but mostly of purely funerary nature and of intense religious character ... It is obvious that this collection of objects placed within this room formed part of one great recondite idea, and that each of them has a mystical potency of some kind.*[16]

That these two rooms suffered least from the attention of the robbers may be no coincidence; the ritual objects would have been less marketable than the practical, everyday objects that filled the Antechamber and Annexe, and there are clear signs that the robbers selected their loot with some care, rejecting large and unwieldy objects, and anything made of gold leaf rather than solid gold.

Included among the ritual objects are a large number of images of the king. These range from the two life-sized guardian statues to gilded statuettes housed in wooden shrines. These small figures show the king striding forward (three statues), harpooning (two statues), and precariously balanced on the back of a leopard (two statues), and may be ranked alongside the twenty-eight statuettes of twenty-five different gods recovered from the Treasury. Also included in this category are Tutankhamen's *shabti*, or servant, figures. These figures were included in the tomb so that they might work for the tomb owner in the afterlife when, animated by a magic spell, they would perform any menial labour that Osiris might allocate. Tutankhamen had 413 *shabtis*: a labourer for every day of the year plus thirty-six overseers (one for each ten-day week) and twelve supervisors (one for each month). These servants came complete with a range of miniature tools – baskets, picks, hoes and yokes – which would help them to toil efficiently in the fields. Taking *shabtis* to the grave was far from unusual; the elite often included them in their burial equipment. Tutankhamen, however, did not really expect to perform manual labour in his afterlife; he expected to become an undying star, or a god. Yet he could not be certain of this and, perhaps more importantly, he had no wish to tempt fate by challenging a long-established funerary tradition.[17] This reluctance to abandon the *shabti* – which had clearly come to represent more than its original purpose – is even seen at Amarna where both Akhenaten and Nefertiti, who almost certainly did not expect to enter a conventional Osirian afterlife, were provided with servant figures.

Inscriptions show that some of Tutankhamen's *shabtis* were dedicated by the courtiers Maya and Nakhtmin, who presumably wished to be associated for eternity with their newly divine king. This is not unusual; the tomb of Yuya and Thuya included an elaborate throne or chair dedicated by their most prominent granddaughter, Princess Sitamen. However, we have no idea how the system worked.

Given our own association of flowers with funerals, it is tempting to imagine Tutankhamen's funerary wreaths being donated by wellwishers, although this is probably an assumption too far. The Egyptians, like us, associated flowers with funerals, and several of the rewrapped royal mummies were provided with garlands by their restorers. Tutankhamen had flowers incorporated within his coffins: a wreath adorning the uraeus of the second coffin, a pectoral garland lying on the chest of the second coffin and a floral collar lying on the third coffin. None of these were well preserved – like the bandages, they had become hard and brittle – but Percy Newberry was able to determine that they were flowers which bloomed from the middle of March to the end of April.[18] Assuming that Tutankhamen spent the usual seventy days in the embalming house, this would suggest that he died in January or February.

Not all of Tutankhamen's grave goods were new: some had clearly been used – presumably by him – and some bore the earlier form of his name, Tutankhaten, rather than Tutankhamen, indicating that they were made within the first few years of his reign. Along with the childhood clothing there were earrings, which, during the 18th Dynasty, were worn by children and women but not by adult men. The rather large piercings in Tutankhamen's empty ears were presumably the legacy of a childhood spent wearing wide ear studs.[19] Perhaps the most personal item of all was the empty box whose label Carter translates as 'The King's side lock (?) as a boy'; the side-lock being the long plait of hair worn by children on the side of their otherwise bald heads.[20] It is tempting to speculate that these items were included in the tomb for sentimental reasons: many people find it immensely comforting to have their own property around them at times of stress. Alternatively, it may simply be that all items discarded by a king – including his hair – were routinely saved for inclusion in his burial.

Sentimental attachment may also explain the presence of what Carter categorised as 'heirlooms': artefacts inscribed with the names of deceased royal family members, including Tuthmosis III, Amenhotep III, Tiy, Akhenaten, Nefertiti, Meritaten and 'Neferneferuaten'. It is not always clear whether these are genuine heirlooms, or simply old artefacts somehow acquired and re-used by Tutankhamen. What are we to make, for example, of faience bangles, recovered from the Annexe, inscribed with the names of Akhenaten and Neferneferuaten? That Tutankhamen did 'borrow' from others is made clear by those pieces of jewellery whose cartouches have been altered to give Tutankhamen's name. Other pieces – such as the pectoral ornament displaying a beetle (kheper) pushing the sun disc (re), which forms a rebus reading 'Neb-kheperu-re' (Tutankhamen) – were clearly made for him.

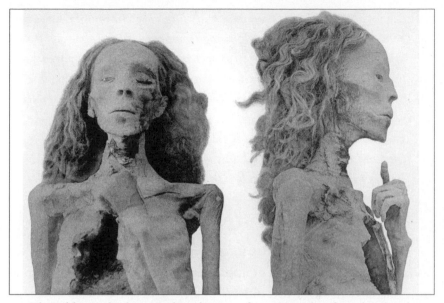

10. The 'Elder Lady' discovered in the Amenhotep II cache of royal mummies and believed by many to be Tiy, consort of Amenhotep III and mother of Akhenaten.

The most intriguing of the 'heirlooms' was discovered in the Treasury. At first sight it was nothing spectacular: a small, wooden anthropoid coffin which had been coated in resin, bound with linen strips and sealed with the necropolis seal. Inside this, however, was a second coffin, and inside this second coffin a third coffin plus, wrapped in a piece of linen, a solid gold statuette of a squatting king wearing the blue crown. This figure, which was designed to be worn as a pendant, has been identified on stylistic grounds as either Amenhotep III or Tutankhamen himself. Within the third coffin was a fourth miniature coffin, anointed and sealed, which bore the name and titles of Tiy, consort of Amenhotep III, and inside this coffin was a plait of hair, carefully folded in a linen cloth. Scientific analysis indicated that this hair matched the still abundant hair on the head of the 'Elder Lady' (KV 35EL), one of the three unwrapped mummies discovered in a side chamber of the tomb of Amenhotep II:

...a small, middle-aged woman with long, brown, wavy, lustrous hair, parted in the centre and falling down both sides of the head on to the shoulders. Its ends are converted into numerous apparently natural curls. Her teeth are well-worn but otherwise healthy. The sternum is completely ankylosed. She has no grey hair. She has small pointed features. The right arm is placed vertically-extended at the side and the palm of the hand is placed flat upon the right thigh. The left hand was tightly clenched, but with the thumb fully extended; it is placed in front of the manubrium sterni, the forearm being sharply flexed at the brachium.[21]

For a time it was unquestioningly accepted that the Elder Lady must be Tiy, even though, at apparently no more than forty years of age, she was perhaps less elderly than might have been expected. However, doubts then started to arise over the accuracy of the analytical technique and this, along with the somewhat late realisation that a name on a box cannot by itself prove the ownership or origin of anything within that box, meant that the identity of the Elder Lady was not as cut and dried as was once supposed.[22] In 2010 scientists working for the Egyptian Antiquities Service under the leadership of Dr Zahi Hawass used genetic analysis to identify KV 35EL as the grandmother of Tutankhamen and the daughter of Yuya and Thuya: an identification which has been generally accepted.[23]

No amount of sentimental attachment can sensibly explain why a significant number of Tutankhamen's most intimate grave goods – his middle coffin, mummy bands, canopic chest and miniature canopic coffins – were originally made for someone else. Their re-use is made obvious by their style – the facial features resemble neither Tutankhamen's death mask nor his innermost and outermost coffins, but do resemble the coffin found in KV 55 – and by their inscriptions, which betray signs of alteration. Style makes it equally obvious that this equipment belongs to the late Amarna period. These are not the long-lost grave goods of the pyramid kings, they are grave goods prepared for a person or people known to Tutankhamen: a member of his family. Most experts now accept that they were originally made for 'Neferneferuaten', an enigmatic individual or individuals of unknown gender who has been variously equated with Nefertiti, her eldest daughter Meritamen and Tutankhamen's immediate predecessor, Smenkhkare.

These were essential items. A king might be interred without food, clothing or childhood memorabilia, but would need his coffin and his canopic jars to help him achieve a full rebirth. Why then did Neferneferuaten not need this equipment? It may simply be that these were unwanted spares, unused by Neferneferuaten and subsequently retrieved from the royal workshop. But it seems far more likely that Tutankhamen, or those who buried him, 'borrowed' them either directly from Neferneferuaten's own tomb or more indirectly from KV 55, which, as we have already seen, contained a series of items gleaned from various Amarna burials. KV 55 confirms that Tutankhamen was not squeamish about re-opening tombs, moving mummies and recycling funerary artefacts. Indeed, the evidence provided by the two royal caches, although somewhat later in date, suggests that re-using the grave goods of the ancestors was a standard, if not well-advertised, procedure. This would certainly explain why tomb robbery was ranked among the most serious of Egyptian crimes, punishable by an unpleasant death by impaling. Not only were tomb robbers denying the dead their chance of eternal life, they were stealing valuable state assets.

We may guess how Tutankhamen acquired Neferneferuaten's goods. Why he needed them is a different matter. We might have expected that all Tutankhamen's coffins and canopic equipment were made early in his reign and stored in a place of safety – the royal work-shop perhaps, or his memorial temple – until required. Tutankhamen, however, was not a typical king. Might his craftsmen have waited until their king reached maturity, uncertain not only about his eventual size but also about his eventual religious beliefs? Could this delay explain why he lacked essential items? Or could it simply be that he could not afford a full set of grave goods? Alternatively, was Ay responsible? Tutankhamen may have planned his own burial, but there was nothing that he could do to ensure that his plans were implemented. In the absence of a son who might be presumed to have a father's best interest at heart, he was dependent on Ay's goodwill. Contrary to much published fiction, there is no evidence to suggest that Ay was in any way Tutankhamen's enemy. However, Ay was an elderly man who might reasonably have feared dying before his own royal funerary preparations were complete. Usurping Tutankhamen's grave goods, and substituting items taken from the handy KV 55 cache, may well have seemed a prudent idea.

Tutankhamen's sarcophagus was in far from pristine condition when he was interred. It wasn't even one piece; the body was carved from a single block of yellow quartzite, while the sloping lid was carved from red granite which had been painted yellow in a crude attempt to match the base. The lid was decorated with a winged sun disc at the head end, and three vertical lines of hieroglyphic funerary text. The base, which also bore hieroglyphic texts, was protected by four funerary goddesses carved in raised relief, one at each corner. Isis (north-west), Nephthys (south-west), Serket (south-east) and Neith (north-east) stood with their winged arms outstretched so that they completely encircle the sarcophagus, embracing and protecting Tutankhamen. Their role as the four female guardians of the dead was an ancient one, already well established by the Old Kingdom. However, it is clear that the base has undergone extensive alteration, and that the four goddesses originally had human arms rather than feathered wings. This suggests that they were conceived as mortals, possibly queens, and that they only became divine following the change in official religious beliefs in the earlier part of Tutankhamen's reign. A parallel may be drawn with Akhenaten's badly damaged sarcophagus, fragments of which have been recovered from the royal tomb at Amarna. Akhenaten's mythless religion denied the existence of the traditional deities, and his sarcophagus was protected by four images of his consort, Nefertiti, standing at its corners. Nefertiti's status in this context is debatable; is she protecting her husband's coffin in her role as a dutiful wife, or is she a living goddess? Either way, this parallel suggests that Tutankhamen's sarcophagus, if indeed it was originally intended for him, might have borne four protective images of his consort, Ankhesenamen.[24]

Texts and illustrations from Thebes and Amarna confirm that Ankhesenamen, formerly known as Ankhesenpaaten, was the third of the six surviving daughters born to Akhenaten and his consort Nefertiti. At Amarna she appeared regularly as a little girl in 'informal' family groups with her parents and sisters. Here, like all the princesses, she had a curious, elongated, egg-shaped head; the egg being a potent symbol of creation which served to link Akhenaten's semidivine family with his god. As she was born before the end of Akhenaten's Year 7, and probably a year or two before that, Ankhesenamen would have been approximately six years older than Tutankhamen. Assuming that they married as he became king, he is likely to have been eight years old; she would have been fourteen.

Following Tutankhamen's ascent to the throne, Ankhesenamen, her head restored to normal proportions, became a vigorous and conspicuous queen in the tradition of her mother Nefertiti and her grandmother Tiy. She appears on a number of Tutankhamen's monuments, while a statue of the goddess Mut, recovered from the Luxor temple, has what art-experts have identified as Ankhesenamen's face (Plate 10). Within his tomb, Ankhesenamen features on several of her husband's grave goods. On the front panel of the back of the 'Golden Throne' for example, one of Tutankhamen's four thrones, we see what Carter describes as:

> ... *one of the halls of the palace, a room decorated with flower-garlanded pillars, frieze of uraei (royal cobras), and dado of conventional 'recessed' panelling. Through a hole in the roof the sun shoots down life-giving protective rays. The king himself sits in an unconventional attitude upon a cushioned throne, his arm thrown carelessly across its back. Before him stands the girlish figure of the queen, putting, apparently, the last touches to his toilet: in one hand she holds a small jar of scent or ointment, and with the other she gently anoints his shoulder or adds a touch of perfume to his collar. A simple homely little composition, but how instinct with life and feeling it is, and with what a sense of movement!*[25]

This throne was recovered, wrapped in linen, from beneath the hippopotamus bed in the Antechamber. This may not, however, have been its original location; Carter believed that it was placed there by the 18th Dynasty restorers.[26] Standing just over a metre tall, it is a wooden chair with a solid, slightly sloping back panel, arms, openwork side panels and four legs carved to resemble lion legs. Two carved lion heads stand proud of the top of the two front legs. Originally these legs would have been connected by a carving representing the 'unification of the two lands', but this was torn away by the ancient tomb robbers. The chair was covered in gold and silver foil and inlaid with colourful stones, glass and faience.

As most ancient Egyptians squatted on the floor, or sat on low stools, chairs were a luxury item, indicative not only of wealth, but also of power. They therefore made a very suitable place to display

11. Tutankhamen's 'Golden Throne'.

official propaganda. This piece clearly has its artistic roots in Amarna theology, although a serious attempt has been made to adapt it to the new orthodoxy. The two side panels display winged uraei wearing the double crown of Upper and Lower Egypt; on these panels, Tutankhamen's name is given as 'Tutankhaten'. The centre back panel shows the scene described by Carter. Ankhesenamen is standing to anoint her husband, who sits in an elaborate chair. Above the royal couple an Amarna sun disc shines, its long rays ending in small, human-style hands. Rather than a 'simple homely little composition', Ankhesenamen is here playing the role of Weret-Hekau, 'great of magic', a goddess strongly linked to the king's coronation and crowns.[27] It is clear that this scene has been altered; the royal headdresses, for example, interrupt the sun's rays and are presumably late additions. The names of the royal couple are given in their later, Amen-based form, but they appear to have been altered from the earlier,

Aten-based form. It would appear that this piece was made soon after the king's accession (or even made for a different king?) and then rather roughly adapted to suit Tutankhamen's needs.

The 'Little Golden Shrine', also discovered in the Antechamber near the hippopotamus bed, was decorated with yet more pleasing domestic scenes:

> ...depicting, in delightfully naive fashion a number of episodes in the daily life of king and queen. In all these scenes the dominant note is that of friendly relationship between the husband and wife, the unselfconscious friendliness that marks the Tell el Amarna school.[28]

Carter is again forgetting the cardinal rule that no royal art was ever commissioned for its decorative value. Art, like writing, was a means of reinforcing truth or, if necessary, a means of correcting history and creating truth. No piece of official Egyptian art can ever be taken at face value no matter how informal it may seem, and it is only in the scribbled graffiti, and the occasional incidental figures that appear in private tombs, that we can glimpse real life being lived. Looking again at the shrine, we see that it represents *Per-Wer*, the shrine of the vulture goddess Nekhbet. It is essentially a double-doored wooden box (measuring 50.5 × 26.5 × 32 cm) with a sloping roof, mounted on a sledge. Inside the shrine Carter discovered the ebony pedestal for a now vanished statuette, parts of a corselet, and a beaded necklace bearing an amulet of Weret-Hekau, who appears as a human-headed snake to suckle the miniature Tutankhamen and prepare him for his coronation. Weret-Hekau was just one of several goddesses, Hathor, Isis and Neith included, who might assume the role of king's mother and, in so doing, impart the right to rule via their milk. She personified the magic of the royal crowns and, as she might also serve as the uraeus, she might be considered an aspect of the cobra goddess Wadjet.

The box had been plastered, then covered in thick gold foil.

12. Tutankhamen and Ankhesenamen featured on the 'Little Golden Shrine'.

Eighteen scenes carved into the foil show Ankhesenamen assuming a priestly role before her seated husband. She pours liquid into his ceremonial goblet and, in so doing, assumes the role of Weret-Hekau. In other scenes she mirrors the traditional postures of the goddess Maat, divine personification of truth (*maat*) and constant companion to the king, as she squats at Tutankhamen's feet to receive the water which he pours into her cupped hands, or passes him an arrow to shoot in the marshes. The apparently simple, intimate scenes should probably be read as confirmation of the queen's role in supporting her husband in his royal duties. More specifically, it seems that she is preparing him for his coronation and for his participation in the New Year ceremonies. Ankhesenamen serves as the earthly representative of Maat, or of the goddess Hathor/Sekhmet, while Tutankhamen is presented as the son of Ptah and Sekhmet, the son of Amen and Mut, and the image of Re.[29] Here on the Little Golden Shrine we have confirmation, if confirmation is needed, of the uniquely important role played by Ankhesenamen throughout Tutankhamen's reign and, perhaps, beyond it.

5

AUTOPSY

To most investigators, and especially to those absorbed in archaeological research, there are moments when their work becomes of transcending interest, and it was now our good fortune to pass through one of those rare and wonderful periods. The time that immediately followed we shall ever recall with the profoundest satisfaction. After years of toil – of excavating, conserving and recording – we were to see, with the eye of reality, that which we had hitherto beheld only in imagination.

Howard Carter[1]

Of the many thousands of artefacts within Tutankhamen's tomb, the king's mummy should have been considered the ultimate artefact. Yet, perhaps because it fell into an uncomfortable no-man's-land between object and human remains, it received curiously little attention from the excavation team. Carter, usually so meticulous in preserving the most trivial of details, seems to have been happy to leave the recording

13. The north wall of his Burial Chamber shows the mummified Tutankhamen undergoing the 'Opening of the Mouth ceremony' conducted by Ay (right), the human-form Tutankhamen being welcomed by the goddess Nut (middle), and Tutankhamen and his ka-spirit being embraced by the king of the dead, Osiris.

of the autopsy to others more suitably qualified. The anatomist Douglas Derry, the first to examine Tutankhamen's body, published a brief summary of his work as an appendix to Carter's second popular Tutankhamen book (1927) but, at Carter's request, this was written to be 'comprehensible to the layman and the man in the street.' [2] His longer and more scientific report remained unpublished and forgotten until, in 1972, dental surgeon F. Filce Leek reconstructed the results of the original autopsy and published *The Human Remains from the Tomb of Tut'ankhamūn*.

Artificial mummification was a practical response to the desire to preserve the corpse for ever. This desire for preservation was itself a response to the unique Egyptian belief that only those with a lifelike body could hope to live beyond death, as that body would provide a vital bridge between the spirit of the deceased and the offerings provided by the living. Today, even though the Egyptians are not the only people to have attempted the artificial preservation of the corpse, mummification has become the defining ancient Egyptian ritual, and the bandaged mummy the defining Egyptian artefact.

Mummification was both a practical science and a religious rite. To create a proper mummy – a bandaged, inert Osiris carrying the potential for life – both elements had to be present. No mummy, no matter how neat its bandages, could hope to be restored to life if it had not undergone the correct rituals in the undertaker's workshop. While the ritual aspects of the process are almost entirely lost, we have a reasonable understanding of the bloody and violent practicalities of mummification, derived from modern experimentation (which, naturally, has its limitations), the scientific investigation and occasional unwrapping of ancient mummies, and the works of the Classical authors who were happy to record all they could of what they regarded as a quite frankly bizarre practice. Herodotus' down-to-earth description has proved most useful here and, although it is unlikely that he ever paid a visit to an undertaker's workshop when he visited Egypt in the fifth century BC, his account agrees in many respects with modern observations:

> *The most perfect process is as follows: as much as possible of the brain is extracted through the nostrils with an iron hook, and what the hook cannot reach is rinsed out with drugs; next the flank is laid open with a flint knife and the whole contents of the abdomen removed; the cavity is then thoroughly cleansed and washed out, first with palm wine and again with an infusion of pounded spices. After that it is filled with pure bruised myrrh, cassia, and every other aromatic substance with the exception of frankincense, and sewn up again, after which the body is placed in natron, covered entirely over, for seventy days – never longer. When this period, which must not be exceeded, is over, the body is washed and wrapped from head to foot in linen cut into strips and smeared on the underside with gum,*

which is commonly used by the Egyptians instead of glue. In this
condition the body is given back to the family, who have a wooden
case made shaped like the human figure, into which it is put. [3]

Carter had read Herodotus; he even quoted his writings on mummification in his diary. He therefore had a good, basic understanding of the processes that Tutankhamen's body would have undergone and, even before the mummy was revealed, could reconstruct events immediately following the king's death with a fair degree of accuracy.

Egypt is a hot, fly-infested country. Assuming that he died in Egypt, Tutankhamen would have been taken to the undertaker's workshop (more realistically, the undertaker's tent) as quickly as possible, before putrefaction could set in. Undertakers traditionally operated on the edge of the desert, partway between the land of the living and the land of the dead. Thus their workshops, often accessed by boat, served as a ritually significant first stage in the journey to the afterlife while maintaining a healthy distance from the settlements. As a king Tutankhamen would probably have had his own dedicated workshop; he may even have been embalmed within the grounds of his memorial temple. Here he would have been stripped, laid on a gently sloping embalming table, and washed in natron solution; a naturally occurring mixture of sodium carbonate decahydrate and sodium bicarbonate used both as soap and a preservative.

The brain, its function unknown, was discarded at the start of the mummification process. This was usually achieved by breaking the ethmoid bone (the bone separating the nasal cavity from the skull cavity), poking a long-handled spoon up a nostril, and whisking vigorously until the brain became sufficiently liquid to trickle down the nose. The empty skull cavity would then be part-filled with resin. The heart, in contrast, was regarded as the essential organ of reasoning. As such it would be required in the afterlife, when it would testify before Osiris. It was therefore left in place and, if accidentally removed, immediately sewn back; though not always in its original location.

Next an incision would be made in Tutankhamen's left flank, and his entrails – stomach, intestine, lungs and liver – drawn out. This was a messy but vital part of the proceedings: as all non-vegetarian cooks know, these organs would decay rapidly if left inside the body. The insistence on extracting the organs through a relatively small and inconveniently placed hole – rather than through the major Y-shaped incision used in modern autopsies – hints either at a reluctance to damage the corpse, or at an adherence to a particular ritual. The dead Tutankhamen would need his internal organs. Preserved in natron, they were encased in miniature anthropomorphic coffins labelled with the names of the protective Sons of Horus: the human-headed Imseti (guardian of the liver), baboon-headed Hapy (guardian of the lungs), dog-headed Duamutef (guardian of the stomach) and falcon-headed Qebehsenuef (guardian of the intestines). The four coffins were wrapped in linen, coated in unguents, and stored in hollows carved into the base of a calcite canopic chest. The hollows were plugged with royal heads carved from calcite. The canopic chest was then placed in a gilded shrine guarded by figures of the protective goddesses Isis, Nephthys, Serket and Neith. During the funeral this canopic shrine would be placed close by the mummy, in the Treasury.

Back in the embalmer's workshop, Tutankhamen's finger and toe nails would have been tied in place and his corpse would have been packed inside and out with natron salt.[4] He would then have been left for up to forty days, until entirely dry. His desiccated body, which would be both lighter in weight and darker in colour, would have been washed, oiled and packed with resin-impregnated linen to restore its shape. Wrapping would have been a long and complicated process, as the undertakers employed a mixture of bandages, linen pads and sheets to impart a lifelike appearance to the corpse, and a mixture of charms and amulets, distributed within the bandage layers, to ensure its protection. With the body desiccated and somewhat stiff, and the limbs difficult to manoeuvre, this would have required more skill than we perhaps appreciate.[5] Finally, the masked mummy would have been placed in its innermost coffin. Seventy days after entering the undertaker's workshop, Tutankhamen would have been transformed into a latent Osiris, ready for his funeral.

Autopsy, like excavation, is a destructive process. Once performed, it is impossible to put the subject back into its original state and only extensive recording and full publication can preserve the body, albeit in a virtual form, for future generations. Carter understood the destructive nature of archaeology very well, and was prepared to take infinite pains to conserve Tutankhamen's fragile grave goods. Yet he saw absolutely no reason why Tutankhamen's mummy should not be unwrapped immediately, even though that unwrapping would inevitably cause its destruction. Lacau, who as Director General of the Antiquities Service was responsible for the preservation of all of Egypt's ancient artefacts, mummies included, did nothing to halt the process. Indeed, Lacau insisted that he be present to observe – and perhaps to enjoy – the unwrapping, which was to be the climax of several theatrical stages in the excavation (the opening of the Burial Chamber and the opening of the sarcophagus being the two main others). It was the anatomist Douglas Derry who felt the need to justify the autopsy, although his principal argument – that the autopsy would preserve Tutankhamen's mummy – is not one that stands up to detailed scrutiny:

> *A word may fittingly be said here in defence of the unwrapping and examination of Tut-ank-Amen. Many persons regard such an investigation as in the nature of sacrilege, and consider that the king should have been left undisturbed ... It will be understood that once*

such a discovery as that of the tomb of Tut-ankh-Amen has been made, and news of the wealth of objects contained in it has become known, to leave anything whatsoever of value in the tomb is to court trouble ... The same argument applies to the unwrapping of the king, whose person is thus spared the rude handling of thieves, greedy to obtain the jewels massed in profusion on his body. History is further enriched by the information which the anatomical examination may supply, which in this case ... was of considerable importance.[6]

Carter, Lacau and their colleagues were reflecting early twentieth-century opinion, which saw the mummy as both uninformative and undecorative. Not everyone agreed with them, and, for the first time, Egyptologists had to deal with a backlash conducted via the letters pages of the national newspapers. The Bishop of Chelmsford was inspired to put pen to paper:

TO THE EDITOR OF THE TIMES
Sir – I wonder how many of us, born and brought up in the Victorian era, would like to think that in the year, say, 5923, the tomb of Queen Victoria would be invaded by a party of foreigners who rifled it of its contents, took the body of the great queen from the mausoleum in which it has been placed amid the grief of the whole people, and exhibited it to all and sundry who might wish to see it?

The question arises whether such treatment as we should count unseemly in the case of the great English Queen is not equally unseemly in the case of King Tutankhamen. I am not unmindful of the great historical value which may accrue from the examination of the collection of jewelry [sic], furniture and, above all, of papyri discovered within the tomb, and I realise that wide interests may justify their thorough investigation and even, in special cases, their temporary removal. But, in any case, I protest strongly against the removal of the body of the king from the place where it has rested for thousands of years. Such a removal borders on indecency, and traverses

*all Christian sentiment concerning the sacredness of the burial places
of the dead.*

    J.E. Chelmsford
    Bishopscourt, Chelmsford, Feb 1.[7]

The popular author Rider Haggard was less concerned about the
autopsy than about what would eventually happen to Tutankhamen's
remains. He had developed a profound dislike of the mummy room
in Cairo Museum and worried that Tutankhamen might soon be
added to its ghoulish collection. Writing to *The Times* ten days after
the Bishop, he proposed an ingenious solution:

*I urge … that after these remains have been examined, photographed,
and modelled in wax, as their own sepulchres are believed no longer
to be safe for them, they should, every king of them, be removed, laid
in one of the chambers of the Great Pyramid, and sealed there with
concrete in such a fashion that only the destruction of the entire block
of acres of solid stone could again reveal them to the eyes of man.*[8]

Petrie, speaking on behalf of the Egyptological community, disagreed; why spoil a good pyramid? he asked. Sir John Maxwell also
disagreed:

*If public opinion in this matter is genuine, then, to be consistent, all
bodies of the rich and poor alike should be recommitted to the earth,
and all national museums should take steps to return their mummies
to Egypt for reinterment. But it might be as well to remind good
people at home that at all museums on a Bank Holiday the crowd
dearly loves its mummy!*[9]

Throughout the nineteenth century Westerners had worried about
what would happen to their own corpses after death. Some worried

that they might be accidentally buried alive, and went to what now appear to be ridiculous lengths to ensure that they escaped this horror, designing safety coffins equipped with flags and bells, and 'waiting hospitals' where the dead would lie, uncoffined and closely observed, until putrefaction was established beyond any reasonable doubt.[10] Others – the vast majority – worried that they might not go intact and whole to the grave, and so might not be able to respond to the trumpet call that would surely herald the resurrection.[11] The idea of autopsy, of dissecting and desecrating the corpse, was to most people abhorrent, all the more so because it was in Britain for many years the last and most awful punishment meted out to executed criminals. Still warm, occasionally with still-beating hearts, the dead would be taken directly from the gallows to the dissecting room where, in front of an assortment of medical students, artists and the morbidly curious, they would be subjected to unimaginable indignities. Ultimately, the desecration over, they would be denied a proper burial. A shortage of hanged bodies naturally led to black market body-snatching – fresh, or nearly fresh corpses 'resurrected' from their graves – and eventually culminated in the passing of the 1832 Anatomy Act. From this time on it was the poor and the destitute, those whose bodies went unclaimed, who were destined for the autopsy table.

This concern for the protection and proper burial of the body rarely extended to long-dead Egyptians. Perhaps Egypt's corpses were simply too old, and too dead, to inspire respect? To many, they were not human remains, but an infinite resource to be dug up, bought, sold, displayed, destroyed and occasionally consumed. From the fifteenth century onwards mummy was a valued comodity, widely ingested as a medicine;[12] during the nineteenth it was used as an ingredient in the self-explanatory mummy-brown paint. The suggestion that mummies were also used to fuel the early Egyptian railways was simply a rumour started by author Mark Twain, although, as many tomb robbers discovered, mummies do burn exceptionally well.

In 1898 Thomas Cook & Son could boast of escorting 50,000 travellers to Egypt, providing splendid three-storeyed boats for the long Nile voyage.[13] As the mild Cairo climate was considered health-giving, these numbers increased from year to year. The tourists were welcomed by the Egyptians: they had a beneficial effect on the economy and on the rather neglected monuments, which the Antiquities Service was now forced to tidy up. But, like all tourists, they wanted souvenirs to remind them of their visit. Some found that a mummy or mummy fragment made the perfect reminder of the perfect holiday, and many respectable people thought nothing of returning home with a human body, or a head or hand, to display in their private cabinet of curiosities. These relics impressed their nearest and dearest and frightened their servants and – in some cases – would-be burglars. The most celebrated example of the protective power of the mummy was the home of Dr James Douglas in Phoenixville, Pennsylvania, which had two unwrapped mummies and their coffins prominently exhibited on a glazed veranda, and which was never robbed even though neighbouring houses often were.[14]

So great was the demand that some enterprising Egyptians were happy to manufacture mummies, either by wrapping together fragments of genuine old mummies (plus sundry rubbish) or by bandaging the not so long dead, for sale to gullible Europeans. Tales of 'ancient' mummies being recognised as recently vanished tourists were rife, and almost certainly apocryphal. The fact that dealing in antiquities – and, of course, in dead bodies – was illegal simply added to the thrill of the purchase. Even Amelia B. Edwards, who was later to found the Egypt Exploration Fund, a society dedicated to preserving and recording Egypt's antiquities, could be temporarily seduced into the murky world of the mummy trade:

...From that moment every mummy-snatcher in the place regarded us as his lawful prey. Beguiled into one den after another, we were

shown all the stolen goods in Thebes. Some of the things were very curious and interesting ... Pieces of mummy case and wall-sculpture and sepulchral tablets abounded; and on one occasion we were introduced into the presence of – a mummy ... Meanwhile we tried in vain to get sight of the coveted papyrus. A grave Arab dropped in once or twice after nightfall, and talked it over vaguely with the dragoman; but never came to the point. He offered it first, with a mummy, for £100. Finding, however, that we would neither buy his papyrus unseen nor his mummy at any price, he haggled and hesitated for a day or two, evidently trying to play us off against some rival or rivals unknown, and then finally disappeared. These rivals, we afterwards found, were the M.B.s. They bought both mummy and papyrus at an enormous price; and then, unable to endure the perfume of their ancient Egyptian, drowned the dear departed at the end of the week.[15]

This phenomenon was not confined to Europeans. As New York's *Harper's Magazine* told its readers:

The modern traveller is not content to collect merely beads and funerary statuettes and such small game. He must bring home an ancient Egyptian in properia persona. The amount of business done of late years in this grim kind of bric-a-brac has been very considerable. A foreign agent and wine merchant of Cairo assured me that when I returned from the Second Cataract in 1874, he had that very season 'passed' and shipped no less than eighteen Theban mummies; and many other agents were most likely equally busy and equally successful.[16]

If it was easy to collect human remains, it was less easy to dispose of them. Over time, as they started to decay, or as their owners died or simply moved on to new hobbies, many of their unwanted Egyptians were buried – and immediately forgotten – in Western gardens, where they still lie today, a potential cause of confusion for the archae-ologists of the future. A select few were given more elaborate burials. The decaying mummy of Amenherkhepeshef – who, despite his sus-piciously Ramesside-sounding name, had been identified as the infant son of the 12th Dynasty king Senwosret III – was cremated by stalwart Episcopalian George Walcott Mead. Mead interred the remains in his family plot in West Cemetery, Middlebury, Vermont, beneath a grave-stone which bore an *akh*, a *ba* bird and a cross. He made his views on the matter quite clear: 'This was once a human being. It is fitting and proper that it should have a Christian burial.'[17]

More often the unwanted mummies were donated, often stripped of their bandages, and frequently infested with mites and mould, to the local museum. Here they served as interesting but essentially uninformative exhibits to entertain the general public. Few of the mummies could boast a name, provenance or history. They might preserve a few basic facts about the deceased – gender, age, height, hair colour, perhaps even cause of death – but beyond this they were useless, their value limited to the jewellery which had once lain beneath their bandages. These mummies were of little interest to pro-fessional Egyptologists, many of whom were linguists rather than archaeologists or scientists. Some felt an instinctive revulsion at being associated with dead bodies (from his lack of interest in Tutankha-men's remains, it seems that Carter may have been one of these). Others regarded the mummies with distaste, as they represented the unfortunate, 'popular', side of Egyptology. The public, in contrast, were fascinated, and paid to attend mummy unwrappings, or unroll-ings. These were public entertainments rather than proper scientific investigations, although there were some honourable exceptions. The surgeon Thomas Pettigrew, for example, made a good income from buying and publicly unwrapping mummies, but he also kept detailed notes of his work and his 1834 *History of Egyptian Mummies* was a popular success.

The discovery of the two royal caches, in the late nineteenth century, heralded a change in attitude. Egyptologists were suddenly faced with a group of well-known, well-provenanced individuals whose bodies might make a real contribution to the understanding of Egyptian history. The royal mummy had crossed the boundary between impersonal artefact and real person. Nevertheless, it was considered entirely appropriate that these mummies be autopsied by Gaston Maspero, a fine Egyptologist and linguist, but a man with no medical training. His autopsies were conducted at a breathtaking pace: Ramesses II, one of Egypt's greatest pharaohs, was stripped in just fifteen minutes, with Maspero cutting straight through the bandages, making no attempt to unwind them. If this unwrapping were to be performed today – which it would not be – it would involve a team of experts and many months of intensive work. The royal mummies were subsequently re-examined by Smith, whose 1912 publication, *The Royal Mummies,* remains the standard authority on this subject.

In the Manchester Museum, in 1908, Margaret Murray, a former pupil of Petrie, did have some medical training. Murray assembled a team of experts to perform a double autopsy on a pair of 12th Dynasty mummies known as the 'Two Brothers'.[18] She took a robust approach to those who queried, not her technique, but her right to unwrap the mummies at all:[19]

> *To most people there are few ideas more repugnant than that of disturbing the dead. To open graves, to remove all the objects placed there by loving hands, and to unroll and investigate the bodies seems to many minds not merely repulsive but bordering on sacrilege … To such people I have nothing to say. Their objections, their opinions even – are an offence to science.*[19]

Murray's multidisciplinary approach has prospered, and today the KNH Centre for Biomedical Egyptology at Manchester University, headed by Professor Rosalie David, is dedicated to mummy research. The Manchester experts are engaged in the study of tissue types, parasites and diseases, and they hope that their work will not only explore the health of the long-dead, but also play a part in the eradication of one of Egypt's most persistent modern parasitic diseases, schistosomiasis (bilharzia). Meanwhile, in a curious twist of fate, Manchester Museum, no longer directly involved in mummy studies, found itself at the centre of an Egyptological storm when in May 2008 it decided on ethical grounds to cover the unwrapped and partially wrapped mummies displayed in its galleries. The bandaged mummies were left uncovered. The overwhelming public response was that museum visitors wanted to see the mummies. They did not regard this as voyeurism, or as an abuse of the rights of the dead Egyptians, and a significant number felt that this was what the Egyptians themselves would have wanted. Furthermore, they found the shrouded mummies both sinister and distasteful. After a period of experimentation and consultation the Manchester Museum policy has been modified, with just one stripped mummy remaining partially covered.

Just as Egyptology has advanced over the past century, so have medical techniques. Mummies are no longer routinely unwrapped and only when a mummy is irretrievably damaged – it is rotting beneath its bandages, for example – will biomedical Egyptologists pick up their scalpels. Instead, the experts rely on non-invasive procedures such as 3D X-rays, and the taking of minute tissue samples for DNA and histological analysis.

On 31 October 1925 the exterior trappings of Tutankhamen's mummy, including a floral collar, gold mummy bands, a pair of golden hands holding a crook and flail and a black resin scarab, were removed. The engraved mummy bands – two longitudinal bands and four transverse bands – had clearly been made for someone else, and were not a good fit. Furthermore:

> *In some cases cartouches have been deliberately cut out, plain gold*
> *inserted in their place, but in one instance the original cartouche*
> *which is that of Smenk-ka-Ra remains. Thus, leading to the assump-*
> *tion that these particular plaques were the residue from the burial of*
> *that King utilized for Tutankhamen.*[20]

Carter then attempted to extract the mummy from its innermost coffin, but to no avail. Both the mummy and its golden mask remained obstinately stuck, and Carter could not apply the force necessary to separate them without running the risk of severe damage to the fragile mummy. Hoping that the heat of the sun might soften the resin, Carter enlisted ten strong men to carry the coffin outside the tomb. After two days of sunbathing, Tutankhamen was still glued fast and Carter resigned himself to conducting the autopsy with the king stuck within his mask and inner coffin, which was itself still stuck in the middle coffin.

On 11 November the autopsy took place in the outer corridor of the tomb of Seti II, in the presence of officials from the Antiquities Service and various Egyptian and European guests, who, as Carter's diary reveals, soon got bored with proceedings and became impatient with the need to take frequent photographs. It was conducted by Derry, Professor of Anatomy in the Medical Faculty of the Egyptian University, and by Dr Saleh Bey Hamdi of Alexandria, the former director of the Medical School. Derry had previously worked on the 11th Dynasty mummies recovered from the temple-tomb of Nebhep-etre Montuhotep II, but he was not the obvious choice to lead the autopsy and his selection came as a blow to his former teacher Smith, who had been recommended to Carnarvon by Lythgoe of the Metropolitan Museum as 'the *only* one who should have responsibility of the evidence on that side'. There was a sharp and unpleasant exchange of letters between Smith and Carter, but Carter would not be swayed from his decision. Certainty that he would be called upon to perform this vital operation had inspired Smith to write for *The Times* as early as 15 December 1922:

> *It would be a misfortune if the shrouded corpses [Smith was hoping that Tutankhamen had been buried with Ankhesenamen] are not fully studied to recover this valuable information which is so urgently wanted by students of the history of mummification and of the so-called 'ritual of embalmment', for if full records and photographs are made of the external appearance of the mummy it will be possible to replace the outer wrappings after the examination has been made. But whether the mummies are unwrapped or not, it is of the utmost importance to obtain a series of X-ray photographs of them before anything else is done. For, even if the process of unwrapping is undertaken, the radiographs will provide an important record and will also be a useful guide to the investigator during the development of the mummy. Due preparation should be made before the mortuary chamber is opened for this X-ray examination to be made.*

Carter had indeed intended to have Tutankhamen X-rayed before his autopsy but the radiographer had died and, with no replacement available, the plan had to be abandoned to allow the autopsy to proceed as scheduled. This was unfortunate.

Having coated the outermost wrappings with melted paraffin wax, Derry made an incision straight down the middle of the mummy, cutting from the lower edge of the mask to the feet, slicing through the outermost sheet, which was bound to the body by linen bandages passing around (what were assumed to be) the ankles, knees, hips and shoulders. He had hoped that he would then be able to lift Tutankhamen from his outer wrappings, so that the autopsy might be conducted in a conventional manner. However, as he peeled back the stiffened linen, he realised that this would not be possible:

We had hoped, by removing a thin outer layer of bandage from the mummy, to free it at the points of adhesion to the coffin so that it might be removed, but in this we were again disappointed. It was found that the linen beneath the mummy and the body itself had been so saturated by the unguents which formed a pitch-like mass at the bottom of the coffin and held it embedded so firmly, that it was impossible to raise it except at the risk of great damage. Even after the greater part of the bandages had been carefully removed, the consolidated material had to be chiselled away from beneath the limbs and trunk before it was possible to raise the king's remains.[21]

Tutankhamen was in a far worse state of preservation than any of the 18th Dynasty mummies recovered from the two royal caches. They had been separated from their original bandages a mere century or so after burial. In Tutankhamen's case, 3,000 years of contact with lavishly applied unguents had had an oxidising effect, charring his skin and reducing his wrappings to the consistency of soot:

… the threads that once held the [gold] hands and trappings in place upon the outer linen covering were decayed, and in consequence the various sections fell apart at the slightest touch … the farther we proceeded the more evident it became that the covering wrappings and mummy were both in a parlous state. They were completely carbonised by the action that had been set up by the fatty acids of the unguents with which they had been saturated.[22]

Lucas identified this charring as a slow, spontaneous combustion. Physical anthropologist Robert Connolly agrees, and has been quoted as suggesting that Tutankhamen may have been a fire-risk in his own tomb: 'Huge heat was generated by the resin. If it hadn't been an airtight coffin, the whole tomb would have likely gone up in flames.'[23] In contrast, several authorities have suggested that the charring to the body may have been caused by Carter and Derry's misguided use of heat to separate the body from its mask and coffin.[24]

Derry was forced to work on the body from the legs upwards. After five days the torso and limbs had been exposed and he had reached the head, which was still covered by the mask. The two were separated with 'hot knives', leaving the mask still stuck in the otherwise empty coffin. Derry had extracted the body by dismantling it. Tutankhamen had been decapitated, his arms separated at the shoulders, elbows and hands, his legs at the hips, knees and ankles, and his torso cut from the pelvis at the iliac crest. With the scientific investigation complete he was re-assembled on a sand tray for photographs, and some sections were stuck together with resin to give the appearance of an intact corpse. His head, swathed in cotton, was photographed in a way that suggested it was still attached to the body. Carter's account of the autopsy, written for a general audience, makes no mention of the dismemberment. Whether this should be construed as an act of deliberate falsification – the guilty hiding of a desecration – or simply as a respectful means of allowing some privacy to a damaged king, has become a matter of heated debate.[25]

An entry in Carter's notebook, dated 1 October 1925, reveals that he originally intended to re-wrap the mummy: 'this scientific examination should be carried out as quietly and reverently as possible, but … I should delay re-wrapping the mummy until I knew whether the Ministers would like [to] inspect the royal remains'. His diary for 23 October 1926 suggest that this was done: 'The first outermost coffin, containing the King's Mummy, finally re-wrapped, was lowered into the sarcophagus this morning.' Yet in 1968 a team led by Ronald Harrison, Professor of Anatomy at Liverpool University, opened the sealed sarcophagus to find Tutankhamen unreconstructed and still lying on his sand tray. The Liverpool team took a skin sample and, as they had been refused permission to remove Tutankhamen from his tomb, used a slightly outmoded portable X-ray scanner to examine his remains.

Their work was filmed, and broadcast on British television in 1969, but, although articles by Harrison were published in *Buried History* and *Antiquity*, the radiographs were never published in the medical literature.[26] Ten years later a third examination, conducted by James E. Harris, Chairman of the Department of Orthodontics at the University of Michigan, again X-rayed the king, concentrating on his head and teeth.[27] It was apparent at this examination that Tutankhamen was deteriorating; there was damage to the ears, his skin had darkened, and his eyes had collapsed inwards.

The most recent work on Tutankhamen's remains has been performed as part of an extensive, ongoing programme of New Kingdom mummy studies by a Cairo-based team of experts under the leadership of Dr Zahi Hawass, then Chairman of the Supreme Council of Antiquities. This team has had access to a full range of modern analytical techniques, including DNA tests and computerised tomography (CT) scans. In 2005 Tutankhamen was scanned, and over 1,700 images were used to create a 3D reconstruction of his body.[28] In 2007 he was transferred to a new glass coffin with controlled temperature and humidity. There he rests today; the only king (as far as we know) to lie in his own tomb in the Valley of the Kings.

The Derry Autopsy

The Times, 14 November 1923
Luxor: Nov 12 – The mummy of Pharaoh Tutankhamen was taken out of its wrappings today. The body was found covered with gold, with stars of gold on the heart and lungs. A large golden dagger was with the body. It is expected that an official communiqué will be published tomorrow – Reuter.

Tutankhamen's bandaged feet had sustained some damage from

rubbing against the sides of his innermost coffin. This damage was, however, insignificant when compared to the damage caused by the charring within the bandages, which made it impossible to make a full and proper record of the wrappings. Carter estimated that the embalmers had employed sixteen layers of bandages, and that different grades of linen had been used, with the best – used for the innermost and outermost layers – resembling finest cambric. The limbs had been wrapped individually, as had the fingers and toes; the abdomen had been packed with linen sheets impregnated with resin, and the head had been topped by a curious pad of wadded linen whose conical shape reminded Carter of a crown. As far as Carter could tell, 'the mode of binding was as usually practised upon mummies of the New Empire'. However, 'whenever it was possible to discern details of [the] method of wrapping, the evidence was suggestive of hastiness – that was the consensus of opinion among the scientific element present'.[29]

As Derry picked away the bandages piece by piece, jewellery, amulets and clothing started to appear between the various layers. There were over 150 amulets, each intended to help the king on his journey to the afterlife. Tutankhamen wore bracelets on each arm (seven on the right and six on the left), rings on his fingers and an assortment of collars and pectorals on his chest. There were gold finger and toe stalls and a pair of golden sandals on his feet. A golden apron, or kilt, extended from his waist to his knees and two daggers, one of gold and one of that most exciting of new metals, iron, were attached to girdles. A beautiful, yet simple, golden diadem encircled Tutankhamen's head; beneath this a gold band held a fragile linen *khet* (bag-shaped) headdress in place. Under the headdress came several layers of bandaging, and finally a close-fitting beaded skullcap secured by another gold band. The linen of the cap had decayed, leaving the blue and red glass and gold beads in place. As this was clearly too fragile to remove, it was consolidated with paraffin wax and left in place. Today it has disappeared. It seems unlikely that it could have been stolen (not as an intact piece, anyway), and it is possible that the beads have simply fallen from the head.

Tutankhamen's body measured 1.63m long. Allowing for slight shrinking during mummification, this suggested that he may have stood 1.67m tall: the same height as the two guardian statues who guarded the doorway to the Burial Chamber. His arms had been flexed at the elbow and folded over his stomach, the left arm above the right. A 'ragged' embalming wound, just 8.6cm long, was situated, as expected, on the left side of the body running from the navel to the hip bone. Curiously, there was no embalming plate to cover and magically repair this wound, but an oval gold plate was discovered in the bandages on the left side of the body. Examining Tutankhamen's genitals – the scrotum flattened by the embalming process, and the penis (50mm in length) bound in the erect position – Derry could not see any pubic hair and was unable to determine if the king had been circumcised.

The skin on the king's body was greyish in colour, brittle and cracked; skin and flesh together were just 2–3mm deep, and could be easily lifted away from the bone. The skin on his face, which had been protected by the funerary mask, was darker in tone and marked with white natron spots. There was a large lesion or scab on his left cheek, over the jawbone near the ear. Tutankhamen was beardless – he had been buried with a full shaving kit, which had been stolen by robbers, leaving only the label behind – and his shaven head was covered in a white substance which Derry identified as fatty acid. His left earlobe bore a wide (7.5mm) piercing but was empty; his right earlobe was missing and was presumed to have come away with the bandages. His eyes were part open, his eyelashes still in place and his lips slightly parted to reveal the prominent front teeth which are observable in other 18th Dynasty royal mummies. His nose, which had been flattened by the bandages, was plugged with linen impregnated with resin. To Carter, Tutankhamen appeared 'of a type exceedingly refined and cultured. The face has beautiful and well-formed features. The head shows strong structural resemblance to Akh-en-aten.'[30] By Akhenaten, Carter meant the KV 55 mummy whom we last encountered in Chapter 2. Derry agreed that Tutankhamen's skull had the same distinctive shape, 'broad and flat-topped (platycephalic)', as the KV 55 skull.[31]

Derry noted that Tutankhamen's right upper and lower wisdom teeth 'had just erupted into the gum and reached to about half the height of the 2nd molar. Those on the left side could not be seen easily, but they appeared to be in the same stage of eruption.'[32] This is a curious observation for him to have made. Tutankhamen's closed mouth could not have been forced open without causing serious damage and without the use of X-ray technology, Derry could not have seen Tutankhamen's back teeth. This, combined with his statement that the skull was empty apart from its coating of resin (something that would not have been apparent with the nose-plugs in place), led Leek, himself a dentist well experienced in the investigation of ancient remains, to deduce that Derry must have cut into the head. Using a standard autopsy technique he probably made an incision beneath the chin, passing around the inner border of the jaw and continuing upwards to the floor of the mouth. The damage must then have been repaired with resin.[33]

However it was obtained, this dental evidence, combined with bone analysis (the examination of the epiphyses, or growth plates at the end of the long bones), indicated that Tutankhamen had died at between seventeen and nineteen years of age.

The Harrison and Harris Examinations

Agreeing with Derry, the Liverpool team estimated that Tutankhamen had died aged eighteen to twenty-two. This has occasionally been disputed – Leek suggested that he may have been as young as sixteen;

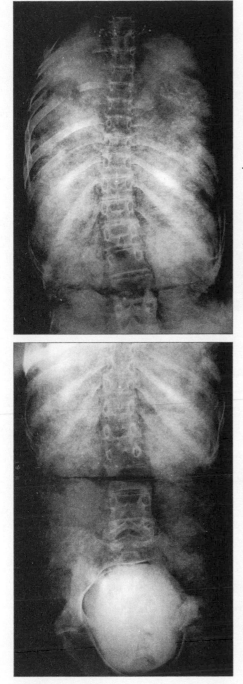

14. *Harrison X-ray of Tutankhamen's thorax, showing cut ribs on the right side and broken ribs on the left side. Most of the rib fragments are missing along with the entire front of the thorax and the sternum. At the top, several beads can be seen; these are presumably from the beaded vest which was originally on the body, and which was perhaps used to cover the accidental damage and the wholesale destruction of the thorax by the embalmers.*

15. *Harrison X-ray of the lower part of Tutankhamen's torso showing the dense packing in the pelvic cavity (presumably resin-soaked linen) and the destruction of the left side of the bony pelvis with many pieces missing. This is possibly the result of a 'fatal accident'. It is also possible to see packing in the lower part of the thorax and the zone of damage where Derry cut the body in two.*

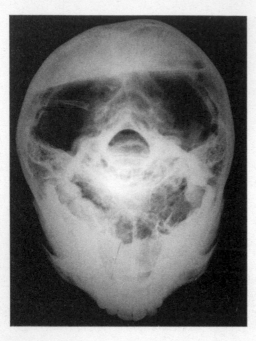

16. Harrison X-ray of the base of Tutankhamen's skull; the line of resin is visible.

Harris that he may have been as old as twenty-seven – but today it is widely accepted that Tutankhamen was approximately eighteen years old at death.

The skin sample showed that Tutankhamen and the KV 55 mummy shared the same, relatively rare, blood group (A2 with antigens MN present); in the same analysis, Akhenaten's grandmother Thuya was found to be A2N.[34] Harris's measurements later confirmed Derry's recognition of a close similarity in craniofacial morphology between Tutankhamen and KV 55 (and Tuthmosis IV, father of Amenhotep III). This similarity was strong enough to suggest that Tutankhamen and KV 55 were either brothers or father and son.

The Harrison X-rays confirmed that Tutankhamen's head had been part-filled with resin. Two distinct resin layers were observable and, as these were at right angles to each other, it seems that one must have been introduced when the body lay supine, the other when the head was tipped backwards or, more unlikely, the entire body hung upside down. A small piece of bone was identified in the skull cavity; it seemed likely that this was a fragment of the shattered ethmoid bone, and on the BBC film Harrison gave the opinion that it was a post-mortem artefact. However, closer examination of his X-rays has shown that the ethmoid bone was still intact in 1969 (although it had sustained some damage by 2005). This has led Connolly to suggest that Tutankhamen's brain was not extracted in the conventional manner, but had liquefied and trickled down his nose.[35]

The resin-hardened linen packing the chest cavity had prevented Derry from conducting a full examination of the upper torso. Harrison's X-rays therefore came as something of a shock: there was obvious and extensive damage in this region, and the sternum and part of the ribcage were missing. Clearly, Tutankhamen could not have been born without his breastbone. This damage must have occurred at or immediately prior to mummification, or, perhaps, during Derry's examination. Derry, however, makes no mention of removing the chest – it is difficult to understand why he would wish to do so – and it seems as if some at least of the ribs were broken in antiquity rather than cut during the autopsy. Harrison also noted that Tutankhamen's heart was absent: a curious omission given that the heart had important duties to perform in the afterlife. A black resin scarab, inscribed with *Book of the Dead* spell 29b, may have been intended as its replacement.

The heart was not the only body-part missing. Tutankhamen's penis was clearly visible in Burton's photographs, yet Harrison could not find it. For a long time the rumour circulated that it had been stolen as a ghoulish souvenir, probably during the Second World War when the tomb was not well guarded. This led to accusations of gross negligence – and a host of unfortunate puns regarding the lost 'crown jewels' – which only subsided when in 2006 the Hawass team discovered the penis hidden in the loose sand of the tray. Dr Eduard Egarter Vigl, an expert in mummified members, has since been able to confirm that although the penis had shrunk during the mummification process, and had been somewhat flattened by its bandages, the young king was 'normally built'.[36]

Recent Examination

Hawass's team confirmed that Tutankhamen's chest had suffered serious damage prior to mummification (or, less likely, during Derry's autopsy) and that his pelvic bones were almost entirely missing. They also noted that his left thigh had been broken at, or very close to, the time of death. Their work indicated that Tutankhamen may have suffered a whole host of health problems, including a left club-foot, diseased bones in his right foot, a cleft palate, scoliosis and malaria. Many of these conclusions have been challenged; in particular, the diagnosis of the congenital abnormality club-foot (*Talipes equinovarus*) is open to question, as it is not unknown for 'club-foot' to be the result of warping caused by over-tight bandages.[37] Was Tutankhamen a sickly king with mobility problems? His tomb included 130 walking sticks and canes, but the stick could also be a symbol of authority, a weapon and a piece of sporting equipment. Alongside the sticks there were armour, six chariots and an arsenal of bows and arrows, throwing sticks, slings, clubs, swords, shields and daggers. Images and artefacts from his tomb show Tutankhamen sitting to perform tasks – shooting, for example – where we might reasonably have expected him to stand, but they also show him standing to perform heroic deeds: the brave (or foolhardy?) Tutankhamen balances on a fragile papyrus boat to harpoon a hippopotamus in the marshes, or drives his chariot at speed as he chases ostriches across the desert. On his Painted Box he again stands triumphant in his chariot as he defeats his Syrian enemies. These images are conventional images of kingship. They conform to the centuries-old tradition which dictated that kings, whatever their actual appearance and character, should always appear physically

1. The Ramesside monarchs of the 19th Dynasty compiled lists of Egypt's kings, omitting any who did not conform to conventional notions of kingship. This extract from the king list taken from the Abydos cenotaph temple of Ramesses II is designed to be read from right to left. It shows the name of Amenhotep III, omits the Amarna pharaohs Akhenaten, Smenkhkare, Tutankhamen and Ay, and continues with the names of Horemheb and the first king of the 19th Dynasty, Ramesses I.

2. *Head of a colossal statue of Akhenaten, recovered from the Karnak temple. Akhenaten's earliest attempts to change the focus of state religion, and the monumental presentation of kingship, occurred at Thebes. He then abandoned the traditional New Kingdom religious capital to establish a new city dedicated to the solar god known as the Aten, at the new city of Amarna.*

3. *In this extreme example of the Amarna art style, Akhenaten exhibits a curious range of features which would have been emphasised by his tall crown: an elongated face, thick lips, almond shaped eyes and a long neck. Although some Egyptologists have interpreted Akhenaten's new, androgynous appearance as evidence of disease, most believe that it represents a new art-style which, in some way, reflects the theology of Aten worship.*

4. *Nefertiti, consort of Akhenaten, depicted as a mature woman. Egyptian queens are seldom shown as older women, but both Nefertiti and her mother-in-law, the politically powerful Queen Tiy, were depicted this way.*

5. *The Amarna royal family: Akhenaten, Nefertiti, Meritaten (with Akhenaten), Meketaten and Ankhesenpaaten (with Nefertiti). Although to modern eyes this appears to be a charming, informal scene, it is actually a carefully composed presentation of the quasi-divine royal family beneath the life-giving rays of the Aten.*

6. *Limestone relief head of Kiya, secondary wife of Akhenaten, recovered from Hermopolis Magna (modern Ashmunein). Kiya originally wore a 'Nubian-style' wig and characteristically large earrings. However her image has been re-carved, with alterations to the head and hairstyle, so that she becomes the eldest Amarna Princess, Meritaten.*

7. *A damaged votive stela of unknown provenance, dedicated by the soldier Pasi. The two unnamed Amarna kings have been variously identified as Akhenaten and his consort Nefertiti, Akhenaten and his son or lover Smenkhkare, and Akhenaten and his father Amenhotep III. The cartouches that would have named the couple are empty.*

8. *An Amarna king and an Amarna queen: again both are unnamed, but they are usually identified as Smenkhkare and Meritaten. Is the king carrying the staff which denotes his royal authority, or is he lame and using a walking stick?*

9. *The badly damaged head of the anthropoid coffin recovered from tomb KV 55. The face has been ripped away but the beard and the uraeus (rearing snake on the brow) are still in place. This evidence strongly suggests that the anonymous coffin was used for a royal burial.*

10. *This statue of the god Amen, in the Karnak temple, has the features of Tutankhamen. It is a visually striking example of the way in which Tutankhamen re-associated kingship with the traditional Amen-based religion at Thebes.*

11. *The god Amen and his consort Mut, in the Luxor temple. The pair have been given the distinctive facial features of Tutankhamen and his consort Ankhesenamen: the link between kingship and traditional theology is therefore obvious to all who see them. Although the Ramesside kings did not approve of Tutankhamen (see Plate 1), this image must have been considered acceptable, as it was re-inscribed by Ramesses II.*

12. *Reflections of the Amarna art style can be seen in the building work undertaken by late 18th Dynasty kings at Thebes. This image of Tutankhamen was later usurped by Horemheb. The king's blue war crown has obviously been re-carved and is not necessarily the crown that Tutankhamen originally wore: this crown would be very appropriate for Horemheb and his militaristic Ramesside successors.*

13. Unlabelled limestone head, recovered from Amarna, and believed by many to represent Tutankhamen.

14. *The goddesses Isis (left: west) and Serket (south) stand with outstretched arms to protect the gilded canopic chest containing Tutankhamen's preserved internal organs. The goddesses Nephthys (east) and Neith (north) protect the other two sides.*

15. *Tutankhamen, wearing the White Crown of southern Egypt, and carrying the staff and flail which denote his royal authority, stands on the back of a leopard (representing the south). This statue is one of two depicting the king's control over the natural world: two companion pieces show Tutankhamen wearing the red crown and harpooning in a boat (representing the Delta marshes).*

16. The golden face of Tutankhamen has become, for many, the defining image of ancient Egypt.

perfect and brave. We have no understanding of the king behind this propaganda: we cannot state whether Tutankhamen was either brave or physically whole. Nor can we be certain that he ever tested himself on the battlefield. New kings traditionally reinforced their claim to the throne by provoking a fight with Egypt's traditional enemies, the Nubians to the south, and the Asiatics to the north-east. Fragmented references from the Karnak, Luxor and Medamud temples suggest that Tutankhamen's troops did campaign against both enemies, while images from the Memphite tomb of General Horemheb show Asiatics and Libyans suing for peace. However, the simple fact that the early 19th Dynasty Ramesside kings would be forced to spend many years restoring Egypt's northern border suggests that whatever their propaganda would have us believe, and whatever campaigns they actually undertook, Tutankhamen and his successors, Ay and Horemheb, were not great generals who enjoyed multiple victories.

Much to Carter's disappointment, Derry was unable to determine how Tutankhamen had died. Some causes of death – those, such as smallpox, which left obvious signs on the body – could be excluded, but that hardly narrowed the field. For many years it was generally accepted – for no apparent reason – that Tutankhamen had died of tuberculosis. TB was finally ruled out as a cause of death when Harrison's X-ray of the king's back indicated that the epiphyseal plates were still in place.

As early as 1923, Mace had proposed a more dramatic scenario. Tutankhamen, too young to die a natural death, had perhaps been murdered by his successor, Ay:

> *The rest is pure conjecture ... We have reason to believe that he was little more than a boy when he died, and that it was his successor, Eye [Ay], who supported his candidature to the throne and acted as his*

advisor during his brief reign. It was Eye, moreover, who arranged his funeral ceremonies, and it may even be that he arranged his death, judging that the time was now ripe for him to assume the reins of government himself.[38]

In theory, this is a sustainable idea. Some kings were indeed assassinated by their subjects. Their deaths were not the work of political fanatics or random madmen, but the result of elaborate conspiracies hatched in the royal harem, where ambitious mothers and their equally ambitious sons schemed to divert the succession away from the intended heir. The best known of these plots resulted in the death of the 20th Dynasty Ramesses III, and was followed by a trial which saw the execution or forced suicide of all involved. An earlier, tolerably well-documented conspiracy involved the assassination of the founder of the 12th Dynasty, Amenemhat I. Regicide, therefore, cannot be automatically ruled out. But it is hard to see why anyone should have wished to murder Tutankhamen. His reign was slowly but surely correcting the chaos of the Amarna age, and there is no obvious sign that he was doing anything to upset anyone. More to the point, those closest to the king – the people most likely to kill him – had the opportunity to block his elevation to the throne when he inherited as a child. Why wait until the child became a man?

The murder theory would probably have died a natural death were it not for the 'evidence' provided by Harrison's 1968 skull X-ray and the publication of his *Buried History* article:

While examining X-ray pictures of Tutankhamen's skull, I discovered a small piece of bone in the left side of the skull cavity. This could be part of the ethmoid bone, which had become dislodged from the top of the nose when an instrument was passed up the nose into the cranial cavity during the embalming process. On the other hand, the X-rays also suggest that this piece of bone is fused with the overlying skull and this could be consistent with a depressed fracture, which had healed. This could mean that Tutankhamen died from a brain haemorrhage caused by a blow to his skull from a blunt instrument.[39]

The bone fragment – actually there are two, and both are on the right side of the skull rather than the left – is a red herring; a post-mortem artefact which may well have been created when Derry entered the cranial cavity.[40] Of greater interest was an area of darkness at the base of the skull, just where the head joins the neck. It has been suggested that it may represent a haemorrhage caused by a blow to the back of the head. Perhaps Tutankhamen had been attacked from behind while sleeping?[41] An area of clouding in the region of the thickening may, or may not, be evidence for a calcified membrane formed over a blood clot. If it is membrane, it complicates the issue by suggesting that he must have lived for at least two months after the blow to the back of his head.

Those who developed the blow-to-the-back-of-the-head murder theory had to rely on the one published radiograph. Recent re-examination of all the Harrison radiographs has shown that the 'calcified membrane' is merely one side of the posterior fossa floor projecting above the other:

> *All previously reported abnormal findings can be accounted for by post-mortem artefacts and an understanding of normal skull base anatomy … Currently proposed murder theories regarding Tutankhamen's death are not supported by critical appraisals of the radiographs of the young pharaoh.[42]*

This diagnosis is confirmed by the recent Egyptian examination of the mummy, which discovered no evidence of a blow to the head.

If he was not murdered by a blow to the head, how did

Tutankhamen die? Initially the Hawass team suggested that his shattered left leg may have triggered a fatal infection or a fat embolism, or
that Tutankhamen may simply have bled to death. Later, they suggested that he may have died from the effects of malaria on a consti-
tutionally weakened body. Several experts have since expressed the
view that this is unlikely, as, while malaria is life-threatening to young
children, adults will usually develop an immunity to the disease.
Others have proposed sickle cell disease or the hereditary metabolic
bone disease hypophosphatasia. There is, of course, no need to look
for exotic or unusual illnesses; in Tutankhamen's day simple diarrhoea
was a killer.

Statistical evidence drawn from our own, risk averse society confirms what common sense already tells us. Accidents are far more
common than murders, and accidents are the biggest cause of invol-
untary death among young males. The damage to Tutankhamen's
chest, and his shattered leg, lend support to the death-by-accident
hypothesis. Could he have been killed as has recently been suggested
by Benson Harer, by a hippopotamus?[43] Alternatively, the fact that he
was not mummified to the highest standard, and that his heart was
missing (maybe it was already putrefied?), suggests that there may
have been a delay in getting his body to the embalmers. Assuming that
this is not simply the result of post-mortem damage in the undertaker's workshop, it may well be evidence of death on a foreign
battlefield.

There is another possibility. Tutankhamen's golden ostrich-feather
fan is a beautifully constructed, self-referential object. The foil-cov-
ered handle tells us that the forty-two feathers, alternating brown and
white, which once adorned the top of the fan, were taken from
ostriches captured by the king himself while hunting in the desert to
the east of Heliopolis (near modern Cairo). The embossed scene on
the semi-circular top of the fan shows, on one face, Tutankhamen
setting off in his chariot to hunt ostrich, and on the reverse, the

*17. Tutankhamen's golden ostrich-feather fan (the feathers decayed long ago):
a self-referential object.*

triumphant king returning with his prey. Ostriches were important
birds, their feathers and eggs prized as luxury items. Hunting ostriches
– a New Kingdom royal sport that developed following the Second
Intermediate Period introduction of the horse and chariot – was an
ideal way for a king to demonstrate his control over the unruly forces
of nature. It was a substitute for battle and, as such, was a dangerous
occupation. This fan was recovered between the walls of the third and
fourth shrine in the Burial Chamber, close by the king's body. Could
it have a particular relevance to his death?

6

FAMILY

Very little is known about the origin of this king ... the early Egyptologists, Wilkinson, Leemans, Rougé, Mariette, believed him to be a younger son of this Pharaoh [Akhenaten], probably by a concubine ... As a side-light on this matter, we may add that Khuniatonu [Akhenaten] gave readily his daughters to husbands who were not or were only very slightly connected with his family: Touatânkhamanou may have had no more blood-ties with him than Aya. Whatever his origin, he came to the throne, under the name of Touatânkhatonou, through such a marriage. The daughter he married, Ankhousnepatonou was the third in the order of birth, but we have actually no means of deciding whether the event took place during the lifetime of her father or her brother-in-law Sâkerîya, or whether, having usurped the power after the death or deposition of Sâkerîya, he legitimised his usurpation by this alliance.

Gaston Maspero[1]

Maspero, writing in 1912, was confused as to Tutankhamen's exact place in the royal family. As I write, almost a century after Maspero, Egyptologists are, if anything, more confused, with every new piece of evidence seeming to contradict what has gone before. Nevertheless it is possible to use the evidence provided by his tomb, combined with information gleaned from Thebes and Amarna, to reconstruct a family – or, rather, a whole series of potential families – for Tutankhamen.

A key element in this work is genetic testing, or DNA analysis. In an ideal world this would allow any mummy to be slotted directly into its family tree. However, as always in Egyptology, things are not quite that simple. Ancient DNA does not preserve well in hot climates; it may simply prove impossible to obtain a valid sample for analysis. Contamination poses a real problem. Tutankhamen, for example, lay exposed in the embalmer's workshop for up to forty days before his bandages were applied; 3,000 years later he again lay exposed as Carter's team worked, sweated, shed skin and occasionally smoked around him. This leads directly to a third problem. While we undoubtedly have the mummies of many members of the 18th, 19th and 20th Dynasty royal families, we cannot be absolutely certain that we have identified these mummies correctly, and the fact that almost everyone buried in the Valley is likely to be related in some way to everyone else simply adds to our confusion. Without a precise understanding of who exactly is who, DNA results, no matter how accurate, become essentially meaningless.

We know that Tutankhamen is Tutankhamen – or, more accurately, we know that those who buried him believed him to be Tutankhamen – because he was discovered within his sealed shrines. Similarly, we are confident that Yuya and Thuya are who they say they are. But all the other royal mummies have been wrapped and re-wrapped in antiquity, and their identifications are based on the labels scribbled by necropolis officials centuries after their deaths. Some of these labels can be accepted without quibble. The mummy labelled Ramesses II, for example, is that of an extremely old man, and this seems reasonable, as history tells us that Ramesses ruled 19th Dynasty

Egypt for over sixty years. Other labels are less convincing. In particular, the mummy identified as the veteran 18th Dynasty warrior Tuthmosis I appears to be a young man in his early twenties, and this is clearly incompatible with his known history.[2] Of more relevance to our study of Tutankhamen, the badly damaged mummy labelled Amenhotep III, which should be that of the father of Akhenaten and the grandfather of Ankhesenamen, has come in for a great deal of scrutiny as it exhibits an anachronistic packing technique and may therefore not belong to the late 18th Dynasty.[3]

Conversely, our fascination with the Amarna royal family, and our familiarity with named individuals, has led us to focus on this period while ignoring others. The Younger Lady (KV 35YL), discovered in the side chamber of the cache tomb of Amenhotep II, is an excellent example of this. Although, superficially, there is little to suggest that this is an Amarna body, every investigation over the past decade has started with the assumption that it is. It is therefore curious that, while the Elder Lady (KV 35EL) and the Younger Lady have been subjected to intense scrutiny, the anonymous 'prince' who lay with them has been virtually ignored. If these three are, indeed, Amarna bodies, could he be Akhenaten's prematurely deceased brother, Tuthmosis? Or, could he be Akhenaten's unnamed son? Or even a husband to the second-born Amarna princess, Meketaten?

At first read this seems very negative and discouraging. It is not meant to be. It is merely an explanation as to why we cannot simply analyse Tutankhamen's DNA then slot him straight into his family. The evidence is not as cut and dried as the popular press would have us believe, and other factors have to be taken into account. These include the more traditionally obtained anatomical and dental data and, of course, the historical and archaeological evidence.[4]

One matter that can be immediately resolved is that of Tutankhamen's age at death and, from that, his age at accession. It was always understood that Tutankhamen had enjoyed a relatively brief reign.

Prior to 1922 there had been some speculation that he was an elderly courtier who, in the absence of an obvious male heir, became king through his marriage to the one surviving Amarna princess, Ankhesenamen, before dying of old age. This is now firmly disproved, as his body is undeniably that of a young man who died at somewhere between seventeen and twenty-two years old. As eighteen is the age most commonly cited, it is the age that we will use in our discussion. Tutankhamen's last undisputed regnal year, confirmed on a wine jar sealing discovered in his tomb, is Year 9. A 'Year 10' sealing was also found; this is likely to refer to Tutankhamen, but it crucially omits the royal name and so could just possibly refer to a different king. A 'Year 31' sealing belonging to another anonymous king probably refers to vintage wine sealed during the reign of Amenhotep III.

Combining this evidence, we may deduce that Tutankhamen came to the throne as a child of approximately eight years, and that he died in the tenth year of his rule, aged eighteen. This is supported by a consideration of his wardrobe, which includes at least one small-sized garment decorated with his cartouche: cartouches were only used by kings and queens. His age seems to prove that he became king by right – that he was born royal – rather than by force. It is difficult to imagine anyone supporting an eight-year-old candidate for the throne who was not directly in the line of succession.

Additional support for Tutankhamen's royal birth comes from the fact that, while still a child, he married the third-born daughter of Akhenaten and Nefertiti. Princesses, in the 18th Dynasty, did not marry outside the royal family; they married their brothers and half brothers and, very occasionally, their fathers, or they married no one. The argument that Tutankhamen must have married Ankhesenamen because she was a royal heiress who would transmit the right to rule to her husband is an entirely erroneous one: we can see, by considering the marriages of Amenhotep III and Tiy, and Akhenaten and Nefertiti, that kings had no need to marry an 'heiress'.

Tutankhamen's Father: Akhenaten?

Outside his tomb, Tutankhamen seems to confirm his own royal pedigree. Many of the stone blocks used to build the Amarna temples were recycled in the later buildings of the neighbouring city of Hermopolis Magna (modern Ashmunein). One such inscribed block, isolated from its fellows and badly damaged, mentions 'the bodily son of the king, his beloved, Tutankhaten', Tutankhaten being the name used by the young Tutankhamen while resident at Amarna. It seems likely that this was part of a larger scene, and that Tutankhamen originally faced a princess whose name is represented by the 'Aten' element.[5]

Who is this 'bodily father'? Given that Tutankhamen can have been no more than eight years old when the scene was carved, there are just three possibilities: Amenhotep III, Akhenaten and Smenkhkare. Under normal circumstances we would expect a king to be the son of the previous king. However, in this case we are not actually sure who the previous king was – did Smenkhkare enjoy a brief independent reign of up to two years, or did he die Akhenaten's co-regent, his own reign entirely lost within Akhenaten's own? Without Smenkhkare's body, we are unable to tell if he lived long enough to leave an eight-year-old son to succeed to the throne. However, if we assume that Smenkhkare was in the direct line of succession – a child of Akhenaten and Nefertiti, or Akhenaten and another wife, born two years before the oldest daughter, Meritaten – he would have been approximately fourteen years old when Tutankhamen was born. If Smenkhkare was a child born to Amenhotep III and Tiy (or Amenhotep III and a different queen), he could have been much older at Tutankhamen's birth.

Tutankhamen appears to settle the matter himself. The 'Prudhoe Lions' are a pair of 18th Dynasty red granite statues whose multiple inscriptions reflect their complicated history. Created to guard the temple of Amenhotep III at Soleb in Nubia, they were, in the third century BC, transferred to the Nubian city of Gebel Barkel by the Nubian king Amanislo. Finally they were transferred to the British Museum. A text carved on Tutankhamen's behalf (which was later usurped by Amanislo) announces, in no uncertain terms, that Amenhotep III is his father:

> *He who renewed the monument for his father, the King of Upper and Lower Egypt, Lord of the Two Lands, Nebmaatre, image of Re, Son of Re, Amenhotep Ruler of Thebes.* [6]

This is reinforced by his dedication, recorded on the handle of a wooden astronomical instrument, housed in the Oriental Institute Museum, Chicago, to the 'father of his father', Tuthmosis IV.

Unfortunately, we cannot accept these statements at face value. 'Father', in the Egyptian language, might also be used to describe a grandfather, great-grandfather or more generalised ancestor, while 'son' might also mean son-in-law, or grandson. The fact that Akhenaten reigned for seventeen years (his reign length confirmed by two jar labels) suggests that Amenhotep III died seventeen years before Akhenaten. He could only have left an eight-year-old son to rule after Akhenaten if he himself had first shared a nine-year co-regency with Akhenaten, with each king using his own year dates so that Akhenaten's Year 1 was Amenhotep's Year 29. If we are to insert a brief reign for Smenkhkare, or for the enigmatic Neferneferuaten, or for both, between the reigns of Akhenaten and Tutankhamen, the co-regency would have to have been even longer. While not entirely impossible, it seems highly unlikely that such a lengthy co-regency would pass unmentioned in the historical record.[7]

It seems most likely that Tutankhamen was the son either of Akhenaten or of Smenkhkare. There is no sign of a royal son at the Amarna court, but this does not mean that there was no son: in this case, absence of evidence can definitely not be taken as evidence of absence. The many images of the Amarna royal family cannot be read as the ancient equivalent of family portraits; even less can they be interpreted as casual snapshots of royal family life. While royal daughters would always remain a part of their birth family, and would be depicted offering their continuing feminine support to their father, sons were potential kings; heirs, and to a certain extent rivals, to their father. They were excluded from family groups which should best be interpreted as illustrating the king and his most devoted supporters; a combination of his mother, his consort and his daughters. This is well illustrated by Akhenaten's own birth family. We know that his mother, Tiy, bore at least six children: two sons (Tuthmosis and Amenhotep) and four daughters (Sitamen, Henut-Taneb, Isis and Nebetah). However, the two princes are completely overshadowed by their sisters, who appear regularly alongside their parents in formal art. This gives the curious effect of Akhenaten stepping forward from nowhere to take his father's throne, and has led to ingenious but misguided theories as to why he has a 'hidden' childhood.

A potential flaw in the Akhenaten-as-father theory is the often-stated assumption that Akhenaten was incapable of fathering children because he carried a genetic abnormality. This assumption flies in the face of evidence that Akhenaten considered himself the father of Nefertiti's six daughters plus other children in the royal harem, and it begs the question of Smenkhkare's parentage. Here, of course, we are having to assume that Nefertiti, and the other ladies of the harem, were not serially unfaithful to Akhenaten.

The infertility theory is based, not on medical evidence, but on Akhenaten's artwork. For over a thousand years the rules of artistic representation had decreed that elite Egyptians should appear physically perfect, with no flaws or blemishes. Men should be either eternal youths with firm bodies and tanned skins, or mature statesmen with pendulous breasts and soft rolls of fat. Women should be beautiful, slender, pale and young (and presumably fertile), although very occasionally an older woman might be presented as a wise elder. Initially Akhenaten adhered to this tradition, and his early portraits show a conventional if slightly plump 18th Dynasty monarch. By the end of Year 5, however, he appeared strikingly different to all previous pharaohs. His narrow head had become elongated, its length emphasised by his preference for tall headdresses and the traditional false beard. His face featured almond-shaped eyes, fleshy earlobes, a pendulous jaw, long nose, hollow cheeks, pronounced cheekbones and thick lips. His shoulders, chest, arms and lower legs were weedy and underdeveloped and his collar bone excessively prominent, yet he had wide hips, heavy thighs, rounded breasts, a narrow waist and a rounded stomach. Many early Egyptologists sought to interpret this highly feminised image as a true representation of the king himself. This led to the assumption that Akhenaten must have suffered from a serious medical condition: among the many suggestions that have been put forward are Marfan's disease, Fröhlich's syndrome, Wilson-Turner X-linked mental retardation syndrome and Klinefelter syndrome.[8] Some, but not all, of these diseases would have made Akhenaten infertile.

Diagnosing illness via art is a process fraught with danger: we have already seen how the young Ankhesenamen's misshapen head, once cited as evidence for the practice of infant head binding, was 'corrected' in her husband's artwork. Today, while the theory of the sick Akhenaten remains popular in alternative histories, most Egyptologists agree that Akhenaten's art cannot be read too literally; that his artists set out to depict the essence of their king, rather than his outward appearance. Furthermore, his 'new' art is not a sudden development. Akhenaten was merely speeding up and exaggerating an ongoing artistic evolution that had started during his father's reign. His new image may be loosely based on his own appearance – indeed, Tutankhamen's garments suggest a family tendency to carry weight on the hips – but this is likely to have been exaggerated to reflect his interest in a genderless, self-creating deity.

Tutankhamen's Father/Brother: KV 55 Revisited

The damp and decomposing mummy which Davis discovered in KV 55, and which he quickly reduced to a skeleton, is today housed in Cairo Museum. Despite Davis's conviction that these were the remains of Queen Tiy, it is universally agreed that the remains are male, and that they are the remains of someone closely related to Tutankhamen. That is, however, almost all that is agreed. The experts cannot even agree on the condition of the bones, with some classifying them as very bad, others as good; meanwhile the skull shape has been described as both wide and flat, and long. So striking are these discrepancies that it is tempting to speculate that the experts may not always have examined the same body.[9]

Tomb KV 55 yielded artefacts originating from the Amarna royal tomb. It was originally sealed with Tutankhamen's seal: this suggests that Tutankhamen was responsible for emptying the Amarna tomb and transferring its contents to Thebes. As Tutankhamen was responsible for the abandonment of Amarna, this makes sense. But Tutankhamen himself died at approximately eighteen years of age; he could not have buried an adult son. The KV 55 mummy is therefore likely to be his father (Akhenaten or Smenkhkare or some other royal individual) or his brother (Smenkhkare, an unknown royal individual or, as a very remote possibility, Akhenaten). Clearly, age at death is the crucial factor here. The older the remains, the more likely they are to be Akhenaten; the younger they are, the more likely they are to be Smenkhkare. Unfortunately, this is a matter of continuing expert debate. Smith initially estimated an age at death of twenty-five or twenty-six years. He was quite adamant about this:

> ... the estimated age of twenty-five or twenty-six years might, in any given individual, be lessened or increased by two or three years, if his growth was precocious or delayed, respectively. The question has been

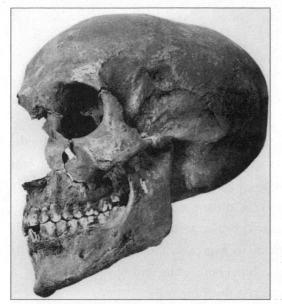

18. *The skull of the KV 55 mummy: Akhenaten to some, Smenkhkare to others.*

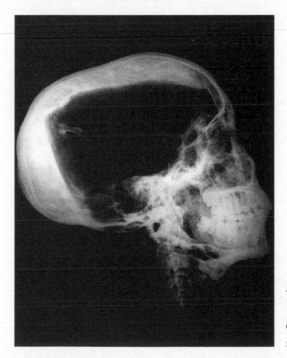

19. *The Harrison X-ray of Tutankhamen's skull: the two layers of resin within the skull are clearly visible.*

put to me by archaeologists: 'Is it possible that these bones can be those of a man of twenty-eight or thirty years of age?' ... No anatomist would be justified in denying that this individual may have been twenty-eight, but it is highly improbable that he could have attained thirty years if he had been normal. [10]

Smith was, however, influenced in his unswerving belief that the bones were the remains of Akhenaten. Admittedly Akhenaten was generally supposed to have lived for at least thirty years, and probably far longer, but, if he came to the throne as a child of nine or ten, and/ or if he had a long co-regency, it was not impossible that he was fairly young when he died. This does, however, raise questions about the birth of Meritaten, who was born before the end of his regnal Year 1. Smith then reconsidered his conclusion:

I do not suppose that any unprejudiced scholar who studies the archaeological evidence alone would harbour any doubt of the identity of this mummy, if it were not for the fact that it is difficult from the anatomical evidence to assign an age to this skeleton sufficiently great to satisfy the demands of most historians, who want at least 30 years into which to crowd the events of Khouniatonou's [Akhenaten's] eventful reign ... If, with such clear archaeological evidence to indicate that these are the remains of Khouniatonou, the historian can produce irrefutable facts showing that the heretic king must have been 27, or even 30, years of age, I would be prepared to admit that the weight of the anatomical evidence in opposition to the admission of that fact is too slight to be considered absolutely prohibitive. [11]

Derry restored the broken skull and made a full anatomical examination of the remains, deducing that the pattern of fused and unfused epiphyses, poorly developed interdigitated cranial sagittal sutures and an unerupted right upper third molar indicated that their owner could have been no more than twenty-five years old at death.[12] Harrison concurred: KV 55 had died at less than twenty-five years of age and, indeed, 'if certain variable anatomical criteria … are to be utilized, it is possible to be more definite that the age at death occurred in the 20th year'.[13] Anatomist Joyce Filer also agrees: '[the skeletal evidence] points to somebody perhaps no more than mid-twenties; certainly, by the teeth, I would go even younger than that.'[14]

In stark contrast, Wente and Harris, basing their analysis primarily on the head and teeth, agree with Smith, suggesting an age of between thirty and thirty-five.[15] The most recent analysis, by the Supreme Council of Antiquities team, goes even higher, with an estimated age at death ranging from between thirty-five and forty-five years to a more improbable sixty.[16] As many commentators have spotted, if Akhenaten died aged sixty, he would actually have been several years older than his own mother Tiy (as identified by the same team as KV 35EL), who died, apparently in her forties, no more than ten years before his own death. Citing DNA evidence, the Egyptian team have identified KV 55 as both the father of Tutankhamen and a son of Amenhotep III and Tiy: this would indicate that he is either Akhenaten, Akhenaten's elder brother Tuthmosis, or an otherwise unknown brother, who could, of course, be Smenkhkare. Their conclusion is that he is 'most probably Akhenaten'. This identification, which appears to contradict the evidence offered by the bones, has provoked widespread debate, and many would still identify KV 55 as the relatively young Smenkhkare. The link with the mummy known as Amenhotep III is a curious one, as it seems highly likely that this mummy has been mislabelled, as we have already seen.

In 2010, a toe from the KV 55 mummy was returned from Liverpool University to Egypt via Switzerland. The toe, borrowed with full permission by the Harrison team in 1968, had been used by Robert Connolly to determine the mummy's blood group (A2 with antigens M and N; the same as Tutankhamen).

Tutankhamen's Mother: Nefertiti?

If Tutankhamen's father is Akhenaten, the obvious choice for his mother has to be Nefertiti, mother of Ankhesenamen.[17] As she was Akhenaten's consort, or chief queen, Nefertiti's son would be first in line to inherit Akhenaten's throne. Only if she failed to produce an heir would Akhenaten be expected to look elsewhere for his successor.

Like Queen Tiy before her, Nefertiti was a woman of non-royal birth. She was not, however, a woman without connections. A younger sister, Mutnodjmet, appears in Amarna court scenes, where she is often accompanied by dwarves. More interesting is the Lady Tiye, whose titles include 'Favourite of the Good God, Nurse of the King's Great Wife Nefertiti, Nurse of the Goddess, Ornament of the King'.[18] In their shared Amarna tomb, Tiye and Ay stand together to receive a reward of golden necklaces from their king and queen. For a wife to be honoured in this way is unprecedented; clearly, Tiye was a lady of the highest importance. Could it be that she is not simply Nefertiti's nurse, but her stepmother? Meanwhile circumstantial evidence suggests that her husband Ay may have been a second son born to Yuya and Thuya; if this is correct, he was brother to Queen Tiy, and Nefertiti was Akhenaten's first cousin. Ay's constant use of Yuya's title 'God's Father' supports the idea that he, too, was father-in-law to the king.

Nefertiti gave birth to six surviving, well-documented daughters, the eldest three being born at Thebes, and the youngest three at Amarna. We are able to estimate their birth-years by referring to their appearances in their father's art. This is by no means an infallible system – daughters may be missing even when we suspect they are still alive, and there may be a time-lag if daughters are not featured until they have been weaned – but no daughter is likely to appear before she has been born. This evidence suggests the following family timetable:

- Meritaten (Beloved of the Aten): born no later than Year 1, most probably before her father came to the throne.
- Meketaten (Protected by the Aten): probably born in Year 4.
- Ankhesenpaaten (Living through the Aten): born before the end of Year 7, most probably before year 6.
- Neferneferuaten-the-Younger (Exquisite Beauty of the Sun-Disc): probably born by Year 8.
- Neferneferure (Exquisite Beauty of Re): born before Year 10.
- Setepenre (Chosen of Re): born before Year 10.

There is nothing to suggest that Nefertiti bore a son. This does not mean, however, that she did not; she may, indeed, have been the mother of many sons. Nefertiti did not produce a daughter each year, and she could have been married to Akhenaten for several years before Meritaten was born. Could the 'gaps' be the years that she gave birth to sons? Of course, these could simply be natural gaps (times, perhaps, when Akhenaten was distracted by his harem queens) or years when babies were born and died.

Nefertiti's death is never mentioned, but this is far from unusual: queens' deaths are rarely mentioned. Her mummy has never been discovered, and all we have is a single *shabti*, recovered in two pieces, inscribed for:

> *The Heiress, high and mighty in the palace, one trusted of the King of Upper and Lower Egypt Neferkheperure Waenre, the Son of Re, Great in his lifetime, The Chief Wife of the King, Neferneferuaten-Nefertiti, Living for ever and ever.* [19]

There is no means of telling whether this *shabti* was ever used in Nefertiti's burial, but if, as Cyril Aldred suggested, it was inscribed during her embalming period, its wording would indicate that she died and was buried at Amarna during her husband's reign, most probably in Year 14.[20] However, just as Tutankhamen's untimely death has attracted many and varied murder theories, so there has been huge and widespread reluctance to accept that Nefertiti either died a natural death during her husband's reign, or that she simply retired from public life. Indeed, in the alternative Egyptological worlds there has been a reluctance to accept that she died at all.[21] As she vanishes from the archaeological record not long after Akhenaten's Year 12, a denial of her death or retirement has to go hand-in-hand with the assumption that she changed her identity: that she is still present in the archaeological record, but that we cannot see her because she is in disguise. This is not as far-fetched as it might at first seem: the Amarna royal court were prone to changing their official names to reflect their beliefs.

The royal names Ankhkheperure Smenkhkare and Ankhkheperure Neferneferuaten (or its feminine counterpart, Ankhetkhepherure Neferneferuaten) have been discovered in sound archaeological contexts in association with Akhenaten's name; some of the Neferneferuaten names bear the epithet 'effective for her husband'.[22] These names could refer to one individual or two (or, less likely, three) individuals.[23] The Smenkhkare version has been discovered alongside Akhenaten's name on a calcite jar recovered from Tutankhamen's tomb; both names were erased in antiquity. The Neferneferuaten version is found alongside Akhenaten's name on a fragment of an Amarna stela, and on a box in Tutankhamen's tomb, which also gives Meritaten's name as a 'Great Queen'.

In the 1970s John Harris used this philological evidence to suggest that Nefertiti did not die during her husband's reign but remained at Amarna where, under an evolving succession of names, she ruled first as co-regent to, then as successor to, Akhenaten.[24] He demonstrates quite convincingly that during the earlier part of Akhenaten's reign, Nefertiti's name evolved from the simple Nefertiti, the name used at the time of her marriage, to Neferneferuaten Nefertiti (adopted at the end of Year 5). At the same time, she started to use the double cartouche (the prerogative of kings) and an enhanced form of the consort's title 'King's Great Wife', which emphasised her unique status. Far more speculative is the subsequent evolution, towards the end of Akhenaten's reign when Neferneferuaten Nefertiti has disappeared, to the use of a king's prenomen and nomen that allows Neferneferuaten Nefertiti to become Akhenaten's co-ruler Ankhkheperure Neferneferuaten (or the feminine Ankhetkhepherure Neferneferuaten). Following the death of Akhenaten, Ankhkheperure Neferneferuaten then rules alone as Ankhkheperure Smenkhkare, promoting her eldest daughter Meritaten (already married to Smenkhkare) to the necessary role of queen consort. When she dies, she is succeeded by Tutankhamen. In a variant of this theory, Neferneferuaten Nefertiti serves as Akhenaten's female co-regent Ankhkheperure Neferneferuaten; the couple are then succeeded by the male king Ankhkheperure Smenkhkare and his consort Meketaten.

A graffito scribbled in a Theban tomb (TT 139) by the draftsman Pawah is of interest here. Pawah is addressing a prayer, not to the Aten, but to the traditional god of Thebes, Amen. He dates his writings to Year 3 of the king 'Ankhkheperure beloved of the Aten, the son of [the sun god] Re: Neferneferuaten beloved of Waenre [Akhenaten]'.[25] Pawah mentions a Theban building known as the 'Mansion of Ankhkheperure': clearly, Ankhkheperure Neferneferuaten is financing construction outside Amarna. This may be contrasted with a wine jar label from the 'house of Smenkhkare' which bears the regnal date Year 1. Are these two independent solo reigns, or is either a co-regency running alongside Akhenaten's own year dates?

Neat though the theory of Nefertiti as Ankhkheperure Neferneferuaten is, there are a couple of obvious stumbling blocks. First, although she was undoubtedly a powerful consort – there are unique scenes of her smiting the enemies of Egypt, for example, an action normally reserved for the king – there is no direct evidence to indicate that Nefertiti ever ruled Egypt either as a co-regent or as a solo king, and a great deal of precedent to suggest that this would have been considered an impossible move. No king of Egypt had ever promoted a wife, let alone a wife of non-royal birth, to the role of co-ruler. Akhenaten was not famed for his mindless adherence to tradition, but all his innovations had the effect of reinforcing his own position rather than diminishing it.

Secondly – and this is an instinctive, gut reaction – it appears unduly complicated and unnecessary. Why, with Tutankhamen to succeed him (either as a son or grandson), would Akhenaten even consider going down the tortuously difficult route of appointing a female co-ruler? Would this have been accepted? Why, first as co-regent then as king, would Nefertiti need to keep changing her name?

Tutankhamen's Mother: Sitamen?

Princess Sitamen was the eldest and most prominent daughter of Amenhotep III and Tiy.[26] She has few monuments of her own, however, and is best known from the items of her furniture that were dedicated to the burial of her grandparents, Yuya and Thuya. Here, on the back of an ornate throne, two images of Sitamen are shown in mirror-image. Sitamen sits on a throne. She wears a tall lotus-blossom crown ornamented with two gazelle heads in place of a uraeus, and she holds *menyt* beads and a *sistrum*; feminine items which link her with the cult of the goddess Hathor.[27]

Towards the end of her father's reign Sitamen started to use the title King's Great Wife, although she never took precedence over her mother, Tiy. The obvious implication is that Sitamen must have married Amenhotep III. Father–daughter marriages are very rare, however, even in the incestuous royal family, and there remains the possibility that she married one of her brothers; a brother who, perhaps, served as co-regent alongside Amenhotep III. Could she be a mother for Tutankhamen? The flaw here is her apparent marriage to Amenhotep III; as we have already seen, he is an unlikely father for Tutankhamen. It is difficult to imagine her marrying Akhenaten after Amenhotep's death, as widowed queens, in the 18th Dynasty, did not re-marry. Sitamen could therefore only be Tutankhamen's mother if, rather than Amenhotep III, she had originally married her brother (Amenhotep's co-regent) Akhenaten. That such a marriage would go unnoticed is unlikely.

Sitamen's mummy has never been identified.

Tutankhamen's Mother: An Unknown Harem Queen?

Although Tutankhamen's father must have been a prominent royal, his mother may simply have been an anonymous harem queen. This was a far from unusual situation, as, while Akhenaten himself was the son of a queen consort (Tiy), his father Amenhotep III was the son of a non-royal harem queen (Mutemwia), as was his grandfather, Tuthmosis IV (Tia). If this is the case, we would not expect to learn much about Tutankhamen's mother during her husband's reign, when she would have been just one among many, but we might have expected Tutankhamen to have mentioned her on his own monuments: his unexpected death may well have prevented this.

A parallel may be drawn here with Mutemwia, a woman of non-royal birth, with no public profile prior to her son's accession.[28] It is tempting to speculate that Mutemwia was born into the powerful family of Yuya of Akhmim – that Yuya was, perhaps, her brother – and that she engineered her son's marriage to his cousin Tiy, although there is no proof of this. Amenhotep was happy to promote his mother during his own reign, when he featured her as an important (and necessary) element in his own birth legend. In so doing, he re-started the early 18th Dynasty tradition of respect for strong and supportive women – mothers, wives and daughters – that was to continue until the end of his family line. Amenhotep included his mother's statue in his memorial temple, and she figures at a small scale beside the left leg of the huge seated statues of Amenhotep, known today as the Colossi of Memnon, which still stand in their original position outside his now-vanished memorial temple gateway. Accompanying Mutemwia are Tiy and one of his four daughters; thus Amenhotep stresses his relationship with three generations of royal women – a king's mother, king's wife and king's daughter – only one of whom was actually born royal.

Tutankhamen's Mother: Tadukhepa of Mitanni?

Included among the harem queens were high-ranking foreign brides acquired through diplomatic marriages that cemented the political alliances of the Near East. Brides travelled in one direction only. As Amenhotep III was forced to explain to Kadashman-Enlil I of Babylonia, Egyptian kings did not allow their daughters to marry foreigners. Kadashman-Enlil argued, then pleaded – he even asked for an Egyptian woman whom he could pass off as a princess – but to no avail.[29] The all-powerful king of Egypt could impose whatever rules he liked. While we know little of Akhenaten's harem, we know that his father married two princesses from Babylonia (southern Iraq), two from Syria, one from Arzawa (south-western Anatolia) and two from Mitanni (northern Syria/northern Iraq).

Included in Akhenaten's harem was Tadukhepa, daughter of King Tushratta of Mitanni. Tadukhepa had been contracted to marry the elderly Amenhotep III, but her bridegroom had died while she was travelling to Egypt and the marriage remained unconsummated. Rather than return home with her splendid dowry, breaking the diplomatic link, Tadukhepa married the new king, Akhenaten. She may therefore, in theory, be Tutankhamen's mother. However, it is debatable that a half-Mitannian son, whose foreign relatives might have been tempted to claim his Egyptian inheritance, would ever have been considered a satisfactory candidate for the throne.

Tutankhamen's Mother: Kiya?

A stronger contender for the role of mother to Tutankhamen must be the prominent harem queen Kiya, whom we last encountered in KV 55.[30] We have no confirmed Kiya sculpture, but her two-dimensional image has survived on blocks from Amarna, enabling us to recognise her face, which appears both softer and rounder than Nefertiti's more angular face. Kiya favours a bobbed wig and large, round earrings, so that there is a temptation to classify any Amarna woman sporting large earrings as Kiya (Plate xx).

Kiya, like Nefertiti, is a woman of obscure origins. This is entirely understandable, if frustrating: if neither was of royal birth, both would have been entirely defined by their relationship to the king and nothing else would have been worth recording. If either was of royal birth, a king's daughter, we would expect them to tell us, as this important title would have never lapsed. Kiya is a slightly unusual name; it is perhaps a contraction of a longer Egyptian name, or it may be an Egyptianised version of an unpronounceable foreign name. That Tadukhepa might have become Kiya, Akhenaten's beloved, is an attractive and popular theory – it is the stuff of romantic fiction – but it is completely unproven.

Kiya never bore the consort's title of 'king's wife' (nor the family title 'king's daughter') and never wore the royal uraeus on her brow, yet she was allowed to play a unique role in the rituals of Aten worship, which had, until now, been confined to Akhenaten and Nefertiti. Not only did Kiya have her own sunshade temple – a female-based temple or chapel associated with the cult of the Aten – which would have come with its own endowment of land and therefore its own income, she was allowed to officiate both alongside Akhenaten and, most surprisingly, alone.[31] This should have been impossible: traditional theology taught that kings were the only mortals capable of communicating with the gods. Yet images recovered from Thebes show that Nefertiti, too, was able to make offerings to the Aten. In Nefertiti's case she was accompanied by her eldest daughter, Meritaten (or, more rarely, by Meketaten or Ankhesenpaaten), who played the vital role of her consort.

There is good circumstantial evidence to suggest that Kiya bore Akhenaten at least one daughter: two badly damaged blocks, recovered from Hermopolis Magna, name a king's daughter (whose name is now lost) in association with Kiya's name and title, while images of Kiya with a daughter are later altered to show Meritaten with a daughter.[32] The Amarna royal tomb offers more circumstantial evidence that she gave Akhenaten at least one child: either the same anonymous daughter, or someone else.

Akhenaten's tomb was carved in the Royal Wadi – a dried riverbed cutting through the cliffs that formed the eastern boundary of his capital city. This, like his father's Theban tomb, was a large structure designed for multiple occupancy. Archaeological evidence – fragments of funerary goods, and wall paintings – suggests that, although it was never finished, it was used for some burials. Unfortunately, by the time it was rediscovered in the 1880s the tomb had been robbed both in antiquity and in recent times, and there were no intact burials. Again, Rider Haggard was inspired to write to *The Times*:

> *About the year 1886 or 1887 the late Rev. W. J. Loftie told the late Mr. Andrew Lang and myself that when he was spending the previous winter at Alexandria, according to his custom, some Arabs who had*

discovered the tombs of Queen Thi and her daughter-in-law, Queen Nefertiti, the wife of Khuenaten (presumably at Tel el-Amarna) had brought to him the gold ornaments which they found with these bodies. He added that he believed the bodies to have been broken up and destroyed after they were plundered. Mr Loftie said that he purchased all these ornaments, except the gold winding-sheets and two private or personal gold rings, one taken from the mummy of each Queen. These he had left behind because he had no more money with which to pay for them. [33]

Haggard tells us that Loftie ultimately returned to purchase the rings, and that Lang bought the 'Thi' ring (which bore a representation of Bes) while Haggard purchased the Nefertiti ring (inscribed with the words 'the living Bes, Bes the living'). The remainder of the collection was sold by the Reverend Loftie, and eventually entered the collections of Edinburgh Museum.

The plastered and decorated tomb walls have suffered extensive damage, but most of the surviving scenes show the king and his family being blessed by the rays of the Aten. In Room Alpha, Wall F, however, we see images that would be extraordinary in any ancient Egyptian context.[34] Two registers, one above the other, may be presumed to tell a continuous story. In the first scene, which is set at the palace, we see Akhenaten and Nefertiti with their right arms raised to their heads in grief. They are standing before something or someone who has unfortunately vanished. Outside the room a woman is holding a baby in her arms, while an attendant holds a fan, the symbol of royalty, over the baby. In front of them female attendants grieve, and a group of male dignitaries raise their arms in sorrow. In the second scene we see the stiff body of a woman lying on a bier. Akhenaten and Nefertiti are again shown in an attitude of mourning, and Akhenaten reaches out to grasp his wife's arm in a poignant gesture that speaks to us over the centuries. There is no sign of any baby, but female attendants again weep and one, overcome by sorrow, is supported by two men.

It seems that a mother has died giving birth to a child; an all too common tragedy in ancient Egypt, but a scene rarely depicted in a Burial Chamber, which was a place of rebirth. It may actually be that the baby is the deceased herself, being re-born after death. Alternatively, if we separate the baby from the death scene, it may be that we are witnessing the death of one or two of the younger princesses.[35] However, if we read the scene at its most literal level we see a mother dying in childbirth in the presence of the king and queen. As Nefertiti can be identified by her unique flat-topped crown, we know that she is not the deceased. It is possible that the dead mother is one of the royal daughters but this seems unlikely, as Meketaten's death is depicted elsewhere in the same tomb while Meritaten and Ankhesenpaaten, the only other daughters old enough to bear children during their father's reign, apparently outlived their parents. It is far more likely that the lady on the bed is Kiya, dying as she gave birth to one of Akhenaten's children.

Kiya vanishes – and has presumably died – by the end of Akhenaten's Year 12, although a solitary wine label hints that she may have been alive as late as Year 16.[36] Her mummy has never been identified but, as we have seen, some of her funerary goods were included amongst the artefacts in KV 55, where they were mingled with those of Akhenaten and Tiy. This, surely, is confirmation that she was accorded a burial befitting a woman of highest status. And, in ancient Egypt, the highest status that a commoner-born woman could achieve was that of king's mother. Did she bear Akhenaten's male heir or heirs? Again, there is a stumbling block. No one could have known that Kiya was to become a king's mother until Akhenaten had died and her son(s) actually succeeded to the throne. Until that point she, like Mutemwia before her, should have been just one of (we assume, many) fertile harem queens. So, is Kiya a red herring?

After her death, the sculptors set to work chiselling out Kiya's name and titles and, in many cases, replacing them with the name of the eldest princess, Meritaten. Kiya's three-dimensional image was altered, somewhat clumsily, so that her usually sleek bob was converted into a side lock of youth worn on an unnaturally elongated bald child's head. This rewriting of history may simply have been a practical response to a crisis: for example, an immediate replacement may have been necessary for the continuation of Kiya's female orientated cult, whatever that might have been – we have no real understanding of Kiya's religious role at Amarna. Alternatively, but less likely, it may be a sign that Kiya died in disgrace. Whatever its rationale, it caused a great deal of confusion when Egyptologists, recognising that Meritaten's name was superimposed over that of another royal woman, assumed that she had replaced her mother, Nefertiti. From this mistake grew a plethora of unsupported theories that Nefertiti herself had been banished or somehow disgraced.[37]

Tutankhamen's Mother: Meketaten?

We have already considered the death scene in the Amarna Royal Tomb, Room Alpha. In a very similar scene in Room Gamma, Wall A, we again see Akhenaten and Nefertiti grieving at the foot of a bier, with two young women (Meritaten and Ankhesenamen perhaps, or servants?) mourning at its head.[38] Again, there is an anonymous baby present. This time, however, we can name the deceased. The inscription above the bier, which is now badly eroded, originally read 'King's Daughter of his body, his beloved Meketaten, born of the Great Royal Wife Nefertiti, may she live for ever and eternally.' A scene on the next wall (Wall C) shows Meketaten, or perhaps her statue, standing in a garden pavilion whose papyrus columns are entwined with convolvulus and lotus blossom. Meketaten wears a long robe, a short wig and a perfume cone. She faces her parents and three of her sisters who raise their arms in mourning. Neferneferure and Setepenre are absent from the group, and may already be dead. Beneath the mourners are tables laden with food, drink and flowers. Meketaten's bower is reminiscent of the birth bowers used by women in labour, and adds weight to the suggestion that she has died in childbirth. However, booths holding food and drink were a part of the Memphite funerary ritual, and so the connection with childbirth may be a more subtle one, with Meketaten's symbolic bower signifying her own rebirth.

Our interpretation of the scene depends very much upon its dating. We know that Meketaten was born at Thebes, probably during her father's fourth regnal year, and certainly before Year 7, when Ankhesenpaaten was born. If the scene dates as early as Year 13 she would have been no more than nine years of age and unlikely to conceive a child; if it dates to the end of her father's seventeen-year reign (but how, then, do we explain the presence of the otherwise vanished Nefertiti in the scene?) she would have been thirteen years old, and probably old enough to die in childbirth. We have no knowledge of the average age of menarche during the 18th Dynasty, but there is no reason to suppose that it was substantially different to the average age of menarche in the mid-twentieth century, which is estimated as twelve to fourteen years.[39] A parallel may perhaps be drawn with the English Lady Margaret Beaufort, who in AD 1457 gave birth to Henry VII as a thirteen-year-old widow. Complications, caused by the mother's small size and immature body, meant that both mother and baby nearly died at the birth, and Margaret was unable to have further children.

Tutankhamen's Mother: Meritaten?

The Lady Maia, or Mayet, 'wet nurse to the king, educator of the god's body and great one of the harem', was buried in an elaborately decorated rock-cut tomb in the Sakkara cemetery. Amid more conventional scenes, her tomb walls show Tutankhamen sitting on Maia's lap, and Maia standing before Tutankhamen. This apparent closeness, combined with the lady's unusual name, has led Egyptologist Alain Zivie to suggest that Maia might be the eldest Amarna princess, Meritaten, and that she might actually be Tutankhamen's mother rather than his wet nurse or foster mother.[40] This is an interesting theory, but it is not one that has gained wide acceptance. Its most obvious stumbling block is that Maia, if she was indeed a king's daughter, king's wife and king's mother, would surely have mentioned this on her tomb walls.

If the link between Maia and Meritaten is broken, could Meritaten still be Tutankhamen's mother? Meritaten is conspicuous throughout Akhenaten's reign as a precocious royal child, but in the Amarna tomb of Meryre II she appears as a mature woman.[41] On the south wall of the main chamber we see Akhenaten, Nefertiti and five of the six princesses standing on the palace balcony known as the 'Window of Appearance' to hand golden collars to the miniature Meryre. Setepenre is missing, presumably because she is too young to take part in the ceremony. On the east wall of the same chamber we see the royal couple, now with all six princesses, enjoying the international festival or 'durbar' that we know occurred at Amarna in the second month of Akhenaten's Year 12. This is the last time that we see these seven women together: it may be argued that this is the last securely dated event preceding the accession of Tutankhamen.[42]

The north wall of Meryre's tomb is very different. The image is unfinished and damaged, but it clearly shows a king and queen standing beneath the rays of the Aten. The royal couple are depicted in typical Amarna style, and could easily be Akhenaten and Nefertiti. The cartouches which accompanied them were, when the tomb was recorded during the late nineteenth century, those of the 'King of Upper and Lower Egypt, Ankhkeprure son of Re, Smenkhkare Djeserkheperure' and the 'King's Great Wife' Meritaten.

Meritaten, then, was both wife of Smenkhkare and queen of Egypt. She was at least sixteen years old when Akhenaten died, and could have borne one or more surviving children: two unexplained Amarna princesses, Meritaten-the-younger and Ankhesenpaaten-the-younger, may well be her daughters. We don't know when Smenkhkare died, but, if he died two years after Akhenaten, Meritaten could have had an eight-year-old son ready to succeed him. If that is the case we might have expected to see her guiding her infant son in the first years of his kingship. Could she, rather than Nefertiti, be the enigmatic, female Neferneferuaten?[43]

Tutankhamen's Mother: The Younger Lady?

The Younger Lady (KV 35YL), recovered in a side chamber in the cache tomb of Amenhotep II, has a confused recent history. Loret, perhaps misled by the mummy's bald head, initially identified it as a young man. Soon after, the 'young man' was recognised as female. Marianne Luban was the first to propose, on the grounds of skull shape, bone structure, the shaven head and evidence of ear piercing, that this mummy may be Nefertiti.[44] But when a team from York University carried out a non-invasive examination of the mummy, and came to the same conclusion, the situation was almost immediately complicated by the publication of a report from the Egyptian Supreme Council of Antiquities, which stated, on the basis of DNA testing, that the 'Younger Lady' was male.[45] It now seems that this analysis may have been performed on a detached arm, found in the same chamber, as the most recent testing has confirmed that the mummy is indeed female.

The most recent DNA analysis performed by the Supreme Council of Antiquities research team has suggested that the Younger Lady was both Tutankhamen's mother and a previously unknown sister of KV

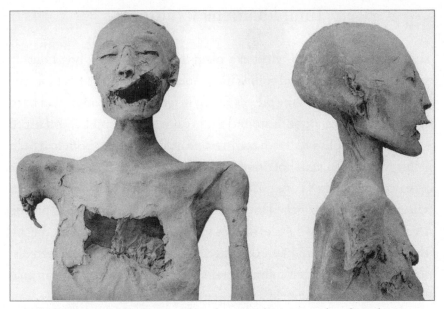

20. The 'Younger Lady' discovered in the Amenhotep II cache of royal mummies.

55/Akhenaten, although a member of the team has since been quoted in the German press as stating that she may equally well be the grand-daughter of Tiy (here identified as the Elder Lady: KV 35EL) rather than her daughter.[46] Finally they suggest that the Younger Lady was killed by a sharp blow to the face, although others believe that the undeniable damage to the face occurred post-mortem. This identification has provoked intense debate; it is certainly hard to imagine the circumstances where such a prominent woman would go unmentioned in the Amarna record. If she is a sister of Akhenaten, could she be Sitamen? Or, if KV 55 is not in fact Akhenaten, could the Younger Lady be either Meritaten or Ankhesenamen?

Tutankhamen's Children?

Tutankhamen's Treasury yielded a plain and unassuming box housing two miniature anthropoid coffins lying side by side and head to foot, one measuring 49.5cm and the other 57.7cm in length. The coffins had been tied shut with linen ribbons around the neck, waist and ankles, and sealed with the necropolis seal. Both coffins were made of wood, both had been painted with resin, and both bore conventional inscriptions naming the deceased simply as 'Osiris'. They barely fitted into their box and, in a reflection of what happened to Tutankhamen's own coffin, it had proved necessary to cut away the toes of the larger coffin in order to shut the lid. This lid, which had originally been tied and sealed in place, had been displaced in antiquity. Each coffin contained an inner coffin covered in gold foil, and each of these held a tiny, perfectly bandaged mummy.

The first mummy wore a golden cartonnage funerary mask that was too large for its head. It was unwrapped by Carter, then autopsied by Derry, who identified it as the body of a premature girl, measuring 25.75cm from the vertex of the head to the heels.[47] Although there was no sign of an abdominal incision, and therefore no sign of how preservation had been achieved, she was in good condition even though her grey skin was somewhat brittle. She had been wrapped with her arms fully extended and her hands resting on the front of her thighs. She had neither eyelashes nor eyebrows, but she did have fine hair on her head, which Derry thought was probably the remains of lanugo (fine baby hair). A portion of the umbilical cord was still attached. Derry estimated that this child had died at five months' gestation.

The second mummy was also well bandaged, but lacked a golden mummy mask. It seems likely that the miniature mask, recovered by Davis in his 1907 excavation of Tutankhamen's embalming refuse (KV 54), and now housed in Cairo Museum (JE 39711), originally came from this mummy, even though it is slightly too small to have fitted neatly on the wrapped head.[48] Derry unwrapped this mummy himself.

He discovered a second baby girl, measuring 36.1cm from the vertex of the head to the heels. Although there was an obvious embalming incision, and the body and skull cavity had been packed with resin-impregnated linen, she was less well preserved than the other mummy. Her extended arms lay beside the thighs. She had eyebrows and eyelashes and her eyes were wide open. Although there was little head hair, Derry felt that this may have come away with the bandages. There was no umbilical cord but Derry felt, from the condition of the navel, that this had been cut away rather than withered naturally, suggesting that she was stillborn at approximately seven months' gestation. Harrison, who radiographically re-examined the body, believed the child to have been a stillbirth of eight or nine months' gestation. He suggested that she had suffered Sprengal's deformity of the clavicle in conjunction with spina bifida and lumbar scoliosis.[49] More controversially, it has since been suggested that the two girls may have been stillborn twins, their difference in size being attributed to intrauterine growth discrepancy resulting from Twin–Twin Transfusion syndrome.[50]

We have no explanation for these bodies and, with no other intact royal tomb, no parallel to consider. But, although it is entirely possible that they are Tutankhamen's baby sisters, or even that they are included in the tomb as ritual objects rather than family members, it is difficult to escape the gut-reaction that these are two stillborn daughters born to Tutankhamen and Ankhesenamen. We don't have Ankhesenamen's body, but the recent genetic analysis conducted by the Supreme Council of Antiquities has indicated that they may be the children of Tutankhamen and an otherwise unidentified 18th Dynasty mummy (KV 21A) recovered from a private tomb in the Valley of the Kings.[51] This is a strange development, unless we are to identify KV 21A, who has previously been assumed to belong to the earlier 18th Dynasty, with Tutankhamen's only known wife, Ankhesenamen. But this cannot be the case, as further examination of the genetic data published by the Egyptian team indicates that the foetuses could not be the children of Tutankhamen plus any daughter fathered by KV 55 whom they identify as Akhenaten.[52] Either Tutankhamen had one or more unknown wives who were the mothers of the foetuses, or KV 55 is not Akhenaten, father of Ankhesenamen, who is herself the mother of the foetuses, or the foetuses are not immediate family members.

Did Tutankhamen have any other children? Just two independent, circumstantial and rather weak pieces of evidence have been used to argue that he may have had.[53] The first is a letter written by the Babylonian king Burnaburiash, in which he uses a standard, formal greeting to address '… your house, your wives, your children…'; it is impossible to assess the importance of what might be a simple slip of the cuneiform stylus. The second is an illustration on an ivory chest, recovered from his tomb, which shows the king and queen in a garden, with two anonymous children nearby. These two children may indeed belong to Tutankhamen and Ankhesenamen; however, they might equally be the king and queen themselves.

Tutankhamen was succeeded by Ay. This unlikely choice of heir – at an estimated sixty years of age Ay was already elderly, and can surely have been no more than a caretaker king – is a strong indication that Tutankhamen had no living child to follow him. We might have expected Horemheb, Ay's own far younger successor, to step forward at this point; his title of regent suggests that this may well have been Tutankhamen's intention. But it seems – without being absolutely proven – that in Year 9/10 Tutankhamen's troops were engaged in failing to re-take the Syrian city of Kadesh, which had fallen under the influence of the Hittite king Suppiluliumas.[54] We have few specific details of this campaign, but random carved scenes recovered from Luxor (the probable remains of Tutankhamen's memorial temple), plus tribute scenes carved in the Karnak temple and scenes on the walls of Horemheb's Memphite tomb, suggest that the Egyptians faced a coalition of Syrian-Palestinian forces rather than Hittites. Horemheb played no part in Tutankhamen's funeral arrangements;

presumably, if he was fighting in Syria, he could not return to Thebes in time. But he would subsequently decorate the walls of his memorial temple with scenes of Asiatic campaigns that – if they really happened – were probably conducted entirely during Tutankhamen's reign.

Confirmation of the lack of royal sons comes from a letter recovered from the royal archives of the Hittite capital, Boghaskoy (Anatolia). The letter is written in cuneiform 'wedge' text, the standard text used in 18th Dynasty diplomatic correspondence:

> *...But when the people of Egypt had heard of the attack on Amka, they were afraid. And since, in addition, their lord Nibkhururriya had died, therefore the queen of Egypt, who was Dahamunzu, sent a messenger to my father and wrote to him thus: 'My husband has died. A son I have not. But to thee, they say, the sons are many. If thou woulds give me one son of thine, he would become my husband. Never shall I pick out a servant of mine and make him my husband ... I am afraid.' When my father heard this, he called forth the Great Ones for council, saying 'Such a thing has never happened to me in my whole life!' So it happened that my father sent forth to Egypt Hattusaziti, the chamberlain (with this order): 'Go and bring thou the true word back to me. Maybe they deceive me. Maybe (in fact) they do have a son of their lord. Bring thou the true word back to me.'*[55]

At first sight, this is a simple, poignant tale. A widowed queen of Egypt has written to Suppiluliumas, asking him to send one of his sons as her bridegroom. The king's name, Nibkhururriya, seems to be a Hittite version of Tutankhamen's prenomen, Nebkheperure. The name of the letter writer, 'Dahamunzu', is a phonetic version of the standard Egyptian queen's title *ta hemet nesu* (king's wife).[56] As Ankhesenamen is Tutankhamen's only prominent wife, it seems that she must be the lonely letter writer. But, here doubts set in. As Suppiluliumas knew, Egyptian princesses did not marry foreigners, and widowed queens did not re-marry. Ankhesenamen, as the last surviving Amarna princess, would have been next in line for the throne in her own right and, as the earlier 18th Dynasty female pharaoh Hatshepsut had proved, queens could rule unmarried. Furthermore, the Hittites and the Egyptians were not exactly good friends. Ankhesenamen did, however, need a husband if she was to produce the next heir to the throne, and she may have wished to draw the lingering and expensive hostilities with the Hittites to an end. Rather than the simple plea of a helpless woman, is this an intelligent attempt to find a diplomatic solution to two of Egypt's problems?

The canny Suppiluliumas sent his chamberlain to make further enquiries in Egypt. The timing must have been tight – it would have taken many days to make the long journey from Boghaskoy to Memphis and back again, and all the while Egypt would have been waiting for a king to bury Tutankhamen. Many weeks later Hattusaziti returned. He had questioned the queen, and she in turn had sent a terse message via her own envoy Hani:

> *Why didst thou say 'they deceive me' in this way? Had I a son, would I have written about my own and my country's shame to a foreign land? Thou didst not believe me and hast even spoken thus to me. He who was my husband had died. A son I have not. Never shall I take a servant of mine and make him my husband. I have written to no other country. Only to thee have I written. They say thy sons are many: so give me one of thine. To me he will be husband, but in Egypt he will be king.*[57]

Optimism overcame experience, and Suppiluliumas dispatched a son, Zannanza, who died on route to his wedding. Whether or not this was a natural death is unclear; but it certainly caused a rift in the already lukewarm relationship between Egypt and the Hittites. By the time the artists painted the scenes on the wall of his Burial Chamber,

Tutankhamen's successor was decided and Ay was king of Egypt.

It has been suggested that Ankhesenamen would have been desperate to acquire a royal, if foreign, husband because she was appalled at the idea that she would be compelled to marry the elderly Ay, her probable grandfather, to reinforce his right to the throne. This theory, a persistent one in popular literature, is based upon the entirely erroneous 'royal heiress' theory, and is supported by just one dubious piece of evidence: a blue glass ring engraved with the names of Ay and Ankhesenamen.[58] In the event, Ay came to the throne with his long-standing wife Tiye as his consort. We do not see Ankhesenamen again, and her body has never been identified.

7

RESTORATION

*There are, we are tempted to believe, certain characteristics
which become innate in man in those dim ages as yet but
slightly touched by archaeological research. There are glimmer-
ing atavisms of which we are barely conscious, and it may be
that these awaken in us sympathy for the youthful Tut.ank.
Amen, for his queen, and all the life suggested by his funerary
furniture. It may be that these instincts which make us yearn to
unravel the mystery of those dim political intrigues by which we
suspect he was beset, even when following his slughi hounds
across marsh and desert, or shooting duck among the reeds with
his smiling queen. The mystery of his life still eludes us – the
shadows move but the dark is never quite uplifted.*

Howard Carter[1]

It is not possible to tell the full and accurate story of Tutankhamen's
life and death. There are still too many unanswered questions; too
many blank areas. It may be that some spectacular future discovery – a
lost diary, perhaps – eventually allows us to understand everything,

21. Tutankhamen: a modern reconstruction by artist J. Fox-Davies.

but this seems highly unlikely: the ancient Egyptians did not, as far as we are aware, keep personal diaries. What is far more likely to happen is that regular, small amounts of new information – derived from the re-analysis of already known artefacts, further scientific examination of Tutankhamen's body, the discovery of a new text or statue fragment – will continue to expand our knowledge. For me, like many other Egyptologists, this does not really matter; it is the journey towards the complete story, the intricate teasing out of detail and the linking together of disparate facts, that fascinates. It is probably no coincidence that many Egyptologists, both professional and amateur, have a longstanding and occasionally productive interest in detective fiction.[2]

In the meantime, anyone who claims to be able to write a 'warts and all' biography of Tutankhamen is being either economical with the truth, or naive, or, perhaps, works in television: the reluctance of television producers to accept that Egyptology is a developing subject with few black-and-white answers is one that causes professional Egyptologists to grind their teeth in annoyance as they endure yet another 'documentary' that simplifies a highly complex subject down to its most basic level.

Everyone who attempts a biography of Tutankhamen will write a different story. What follows here is not the definitive account of his life, merely the one which, in my opinion, fits best with the evidence – biological, historical and archaeological – to date. At some points these different types of evidence contradict and so, although I have tried to make this account evidence-based, I have had to make some assumptions. The most important of these are:

- That there was no lengthy co-regency between Amenhotep III and his son Akhenaten.
- That the Amarna court continued the tradition of including royal females in official art while excluding the royal males.

- That the traditional anatomists are correct, and the KV 55 bones are those of a young man of between twenty and twenty-five years of age.

Where there is doubt, I have followed the principle of Occam's Razor: entities must not be multiplied beyond necessity (often paraphrased as 'other things being equal, the simplest explanation is usually the correct one'). Because this is my own interpretation of the evidence already presented in this book, I have avoided the use of footnotes.

ఈ ఈ ఈ

Nebmaatre Amenhotep III, son of Tuthmosis IV, was born to the harem queen Mutemwia. As Tuthmosis had other, more important, wives, it was unlikely that the young prince would ever succeed to his father's throne. But the gods smiled on Amenhotep and his mother and, at maybe ten years of age, he inherited the richest and most powerful kingdom in the Mediterranean world.

Egypt's kings could not rule without a queen by their side. Amenhotep's consort, Tiy, was to become one of Egypt's most influential and conspicuous queens. Her name and image were included alongside her husband's on official monuments and more personal items, she appeared alongside him in statuary, she was even mentioned in the diplomatic correspondence that linked the great Near Eastern states of the Late Bronze Age. Tiy was a fertile queen, and she bore her husband many children, including four daughters and two sons.

After thirty prosperous years on the throne Amenhotep celebrated a *heb sed* jubilee; a festival of renewal and rejuvenation which was marked by an impressive building programme and nationwide revelry. From this time onwards he indulged a developing interest in his own divine nature; a divinity which he expressed through art and architecture. Traditional theology decreed that only at death could Egypt's semi-mortal kings become fully divine. Yet already, preserved for eternity on the walls of the Luxor temple, Amenhotep's birth legend hinted at an earlier, more earthly divinity. In far away Nubia he took things a step further, by dedicating a temple to himself as the divine being 'Amenhotep Lord of Nubia', while a subsidiary temple at nearby Sedeinga celebrated his equally divine consort, Tiy. This interest in personal divinity went hand-in-hand with an increasing interest in solar religion. While the traditional state cults were never neglected, Amenhotep paid particular attention to an ancient and hitherto obscure sun god known as the Aten. The genderless Aten is difficult to classify, but appears to represent the light of the sun, rather than the sun itself.

A further two jubilees followed and then, after thirty-eight years of rule, Amenhotep died and was buried in a large and beautifully finished tomb in the Western Valley. He did not intend to lie alone; his architects had provided additional suites of rooms for his closest female relatives, and for Queen Tiy. His highly conspicuous memorial temple, the largest royal temple ever to be built, was situated on the desert edge. Filled with colossal statues of the king as a god, its avenues lined with images of jackals and sphinxes and an astonishing 770+ statues of the goddess Sekhmet, it was an awe-inspiring sight. Today all that remain of this magnificence are the Colossi of Memnon; two figures sitting in splendid isolation beside the dusty modern road.

As her eldest son, Tuthmosis, had predeceased his father, Tiy's second-born son succeeded to the throne as Neferkheperure Waenre (the transformations of Re are perfect, the unique one of Re) Amenhotep IV. The new king was already married to his cousin Nefertiti, daughter of Tiy's brother Ay. She, like her aunt, proved to be a fertile queen, supplying her husband with six living daughters and an unrecorded number of sons.

Amenhotep IV started his reign as an entirely typical – albeit extraordinarily wealthy – 18th Dynasty king, crowned by the god

Amen and ruling from Thebes and Memphis. As the workmen started to cut his tomb in the Western Valley, a new town was founded in Nubia, its temple dedicated to Amen. Meanwhile, building work continued in and around the Karnak temple where Amenhotep preserved *maat* – the ideal state of affairs – by completing his father's unfinished projects. Year 2, however, brought an unexpected change. There was to be a *heb sed* celebrated, not after the traditional thirty years of rule, but on the third anniversary of Amenhotep's accession. A festival required new buildings. Heliopolis, Memphis and Nubia benefited from new solar temples while Thebes – the heart of the cult of the great state god Amen – received a series of chapels and temples all dedicated to the worship of the Aten. This architecture would be dismantled and recycled soon after Amenhotep's death, so that, instead of a collection of impressive solar temples, we are today faced with a gigantic jigsaw made up of thousands of inscribed and painted sandstone blocks. The scenes preserved on these blocks make it clear that the traditional pantheon, Amen included, were very obviously excluded from Amenhotep's festivities. The Aten, in contrast, played a highly conspicuous role in the celebrations.

By the end of Year 5 the Aten had become Egypt's dominant state god. The copious offerings that had once been presented to the temples of Amen were now diverted to the Aten temples so that the cult of Aten grew rich as the cult of Amen grew poor. Soon the old temples were closed, and the decision was taken to relocate the court to the purpose-built city of Akhetaten in Middle Egypt (Horizon of the Aten; a city known today by the Arabic name Amarna). Rejecting the personal name which linked him with the despised Amen, Amenhotep (Amen is satisfied) adopted a new identity. From this time forward he would be Akhenaten (Living spirit of the Aten).

Akhenaten felt free to distance himself from his inherited obligations by turning his back on the state gods. This was a blatant rejection of the most important aspect of his kingship: his duty to maintain *maat*. By challenging the status quo he was embarking on a path fraught with danger for both himself and for Egypt. The ordinary people may not have been unduly troubled by this; they had always been excluded from state religion, and what little evidence there is suggests that they simply continued to revere the eclectic mix of demi-gods, ancestors and local deities that had been worshipped for many generations. But the elite – the courtiers who surrounded Akhenaten and who were forced to follow him to Amarna – must have found it very difficult, as they were required to show public acceptance of the new regime. The new god, a faceless, bodiless disc, shone down on the royal family alone. While Akhenaten, Nefertiti and their children worshipped the Aten, the elite worshipped through Akhenaten and his family, helped in their private devotions by stelae bearing images of the king and queen. As the royal family effectively replaced the old gods, they assumed the roles formerly played by the solar creator god Atum (now the Aten), and his twin children Shu (the atmosphere: Akhenaten) and Tefnut (moisture: Nefertiti). Their growing band of daughters was featured alongside the royal couple; they offered their feminine support to their king and his god while serving as living reminders of their parents' fertility.

This was unusual, but it would perhaps not have been too bad. What would really have hurt is the fact that, along with many of the old gods, Osiris and his kingdom of the dead had been swept away. Denied access to an afterlife in the Field of Reeds, Akhenaten's courtiers were condemned to dwell in their tombs until the end of time. This new theology is reflected in the tombs that they cut high into the cliffs to the east of the city. Traditionally, 18th Dynasty tombs would be decorated with images of the tomb owner going about his daily business. At Amarna, however, the tomb owners are mere specta-tors, or, at best, bit part players, in the lives of the royal family. Even Ay and Tiye, the most important of Akhenaten's courtiers, are rela-tively insignificant in their own tomb.

Egypt's new capital lay on the east bank of the Nile, almost equidistant from the southern capital, Thebes, and the northern capital, Memphis. Construction started during Year 5 and progressed swiftly; by the end of that year the king was staying in temporary quarters while he inspected progress on his palace. By Year 9 Amarna was fully functional, and a ready-made population had been imported. The city offered a full range of amenities: stone sun-temples, mud-brick palaces, spacious villas, workshops and offices. Outside the innermost city a workmen's village housed the craftsmen who laboured in the elite tombs and the multi-chambered royal tomb, hidden in the Royal Wadi. In defiance of the long-established tradition that the king should be peripatetic, constantly displaying himself to the people of his long, thin country, Akhenaten rarely if ever left his new city – he showed no interest in participating in the occasional military campaigns, for example – and all his younger children were born here. It was therefore at Amarna, in Year 12, that the most important event of his reign occurred. A great and unique festival, the 'durbar', saw a host of ambassadors and vassals summoned from Nubia, Libya, the Mediterranean islands and the Near East. There was feasting, self-congratulation, many hours spent standing in the hot sunlight, and the reception of a huge amount of tribute including horses, chariots, women and gold. This was a time of plague in the Near East; it may therefore not be a coincidence that Tiy and the three younger princesses died soon after the celebration.

Within a couple of years Nefertiti, too, was dead and buried in the Amarna royal tomb. So, too, was Kiya, most prominent of Akhenaten's harem queens and mother of several of his children including Tutankhaten. With the sudden loss of almost all his female relations, Akhenaten needed a consort – a theoretical or actual wife – who could perform the female rites that would support his kingship. He solved the problem by elevating his eldest surviving son by Nefertiti, Smenkhkare, to the position of co-regent, with Meritaten by his side as Great Queen. Now Meritaten could assume the religious and political roles played by Tiy, Nefertiti and Kiya. This she did with consummate ease; like Tiy, but unlike Nefertiti, her name was mentioned in diplomatic correspondence and her fame spread throughout the Near East.

Akhenaten died in the autumn of his regnal Year 17 and was succeeded, as he had planned, by his co-regent Smenkhkare, with Meritaten by his side. But barely had Smenkhkare interred his father in the Amarna tomb than he himself died. Smenkhkare was succeeded by his young half-brother, Tutankhaten, whose elevation to the throne was supported by his half-sister, the dowager queen Meritaten, and his great-grandfather, Ay. Meritaten interred her husband in his own tomb in the Royal Wadi – Amarna's own Valley of the Kings – then ruled Egypt as regent on behalf of the young king. When Meritaten died approximately two years after her husband, she too was given an appropriate Amarna burial. Tutankhaten, at just eight years old, married his slightly older half-sister Ankhesenpaaten, the only surviving princess, and started to rule – theoretically – alone.

Of course, an eight-year-old could not rule unaided. Tutankhamen inherited a group of advisers who were all too well aware of the problems which beset both the monarchy and the country. Prominent among these advisers were Ay and Maya and the two viziers, Pentu and Usermont. Amenhotep-Huy was viceroy of Kush (Nubia), his wife, Taemwadjsi, was chief of the harem, and Generalissimo Horemheb was commander-in-chief of the army. Horemheb is a curiously opaque character who managed to achieve the near impossible feat of maintaining a relatively low profile throughout the Amarna Period while retaining a position of authority. He was not only a high-ranking soldier, he was 'king's deputy in the entire land' and 'Noble of Upper and Lower Egypt'; titles which suggest that he was Tutankhamen's designated heir. If this literal interpretation of his titles is correct, it must surely have been a formality, as no one could reasonably have expected the young Tutankhamen to predecease Horemheb nor, indeed, to die without fathering a son.

Tutankhaten had been born during Akhenaten's reign. He had spent his entire, short life entirely within the boundaries of Amarna, where he had been raised to worship the Aten via his own family. He had known no other way of existence, no other god, but his advisers had, and they could see the damage wrought by Akhenaten's policies. Seventeen years of royal navel-gazing had left Egypt weak and vulnerable, her foreign policy in tatters and her internal economy corrupted. With Smenkhkare and Meritaten dead and buried, it was time to make a decisive break with the past. Tutankhaten was young enough to convert to the old, tried and tested ways. He could become a traditional New Kingdom monarch; an ideal combination of brave warrior, wise administrator and conscientious priest. By stressing his own personal orthodoxy, by restoring *maat* to chaos, without actually identifying his grandfather Akhenaten as the source of that chaos, the new king would prove his worth and Egypt would be renewed.

The new king did indeed inaugurate a new age. Superficially, he was able to accomplish much of what he intended. But the twenty years of Akhenaten's rule could not simply be forgotten. The lingering Amarna influence is most obviously detected in official art, which retains many of the Amarna features, but there is also a subtle alteration in the relationship between the king, the gods and the people, which is reflected in elite tomb art, where the enthroned god Osiris now displaces the king in the scenes that decorate the walls.

Akhenaten's dissolution of the state temples had struck at the heart of Egypt's prosperity. The traditional temples managed a wide portfolio of assets including land, ships, quarries and peasant labour. Effectively, and with little fuss, they had served as production, storage and distribution mechanisms, with their priests acting as highly skilled accountants and their grain-filled warehouses serving as a form of state bank which could be drawn on in a crisis. Tutankhaten was to be credited with re-establishing the traditional state gods, re-opening their temples, re-dedicating their statues and re-establishing their priesthoods. As a first step along the road to polytheism he was re-named Tutankh-Amen (Living image of Amen), Ruler of southern Heliopolis [Thebes], while his consort Ankhesenpa-Aten became Ankhesen-Amen (She lives for Amen).

Maya, now chief of the treasury, embarked on a tax-raising campaign. Visiting the major temples from the Delta to Aswan, he ensured that the dues that had once been diverted to the cult of the Aten were now being received by the state. He commenced the demolition of Akhenaten's stone buildings both at Thebes and at Amarna (the blocks being thriftily re-used in Tutankhamen's own building works), while assuming responsibility for the restoration of Amen's vandalised monuments. The Theban stone masons picked up their chisels and Tutankhamen's image was added to the third pylon (gateway) at the Karnak temple; by completing this pylon, originally started by Amenhotep III, Tutankhamen was able to make a public affirmation of his relationship with one of Egypt's most glorious kings. For similar reasons, Tutankhamen completed and decorated Amenhotep's entrance colonnade at the Luxor temple. Back at Karnak, an avenue of ram-headed sphinxes was created to run between the tenth pylon and the Mut temple, the sphinxes being craftily recycled from the sphinxes originally made for Akhenaten's Karnak temples. Tutankhamen was represented in colossal form – either as himself, or as a god bearing his face – at the Karnak and Luxor temples and at his own memorial temple, which was now under construction on the west bank. Scenes of Tutankhamen driving his chariot into battle against his Asiatic enemies, and campaigning against the Nubians, decorated his memorial temple walls; it is a moot point whether these scenes are to be interpreted literally or not. Meanwhile, hidden away in the Western Valley, his tomb was being excavated. As 'Overseer of Works in the Place of Eternity' and

'Overseer of Works in the West', the multi-titled Maya probably assumed responsibility for this as well.

Similar restorations and enhancements occurred throughout Egypt, although the evidence for this is now sadly lacking. Memphis, whose status as Egypt's administrative capital is testified by a marked increase in the number of tombs belonging to bureaucrats, has a couple of lintels inscribed with Tutankhamen's name. An Apis bull died and, for only the third time, was given a full, formal burial at Sakkara. Other information is more nebulous: there are references to a 'Resthouse' built by Tutankhamen near the Great Sphinx, and the northern official Maya mentions a mysterious 'House of Nebkheperure [Tutankhamen]'. Nubia benefited from major temple reconstructions at Kawa and at the Soleb temple of Amenhotep III, and Amenhotep-Huy raised a new temple at Faras, in Lower Nubia.

A series of artefacts recovered from Amarna – faience finger rings and a block that shows Tutankhamen, while still Tutankhaten, offering to Amen and Mut – testify to his early reign at Amarna. Abandoned workings in the Royal Wadi may even be the beginnings of his original tomb. Amarna, however, was not a good site for a capital city; it was remote, and too firmly associated with the cult of the Aten. Within four years of his accession Tutankhamen's advisers had made an important decision. Thebes would once again serve as Egypt's religious capital, while the civil service would be based at Memphis. Initially a significant population remained at Amarna, but, when it became clear that the court would never return, numbers dwindled and the mud-brick city crumbled. Only the workmen's village survived to be re-occupied and even expanded before its abandonment during the reign of Horemheb.

Abandoning Amarna meant abandoning the Amarna cemeteries. Most of the Amarna elite tombs were unfinished and it seems that only one, the tomb of Huya, Steward of Tiy, had actually been used. However, the Royal Wadi definitely had been used, and the royal tomb, plus, perhaps, neighbouring tombs used for Smenkhkare and Meritaten and the lesser princesses, housed a significant number of Tutankhamen's extended family and their valuable grave goods. Everyone knew what this meant. The Wadi would have to be guarded night and day and, even then, there was no guarantee that it would not be robbed. Who would guard the guards? Things came to a head when tomb security was breached, goods were stolen, sarcophagi were smashed, tomb walls were defaced and some of the mummies were damaged. The decision was taken to move the royal burials to the security of the Valley of the Kings as quickly as possible. Maya, in his role as overseer of works in the Valley of the Kings, would probably have assumed responsibility for this.

The Amarna royal tombs were re-opened and their contents – including the remains of Tiy, Akhenaten, Nefertiti, Kiya, Smenkhkare, Meritaten, Meketaten, Meketaten's husband (a younger brother to Smenkhkare?) and the three younger princesses – transferred to workshops in the Theban necropolis, one of these being the unfinished private tomb KV 55. The two New Kingdom caches, created during the Third Intermediate Period, suggest that the Amarna burials would have been immediately stripped of their valuables. These would have made a valuable contribution to Tutankhamen's coffers and, in some cases, to his own funerary provision. The mummies were then moved to more suitable resting places, with some of them eventually finding their way into the two New Kingdom caches. Tiy's burial was reassembled, as was the burial of Smenkhkare (albeit in Kiya's 'restored' coffin), and for a time the two lay side by side in KV 55. Then, early in Ay's reign, the tomb was re-opened, the burials were again plundered and Tiy – Ay's sister – was given a more appropriate burial alongside her husband in the Western Valley. Her shrine, cumbersome and unwieldy even when dismantled, was simply abandoned in KV 55. Smenkhkare – who may well have been thought to be Akhenaten – was given a travesty of a royal burial with the unwanted odds and ends that no one wanted. The tomb was then re-sealed and, fairly soon after, concealed beneath a layer of flood debris. With Ay dead and no one else left to mourn the Amarna court, it was simply forgotten.

Tutankhamen and Ankhesenamen had no living children. This was not a major problem; the king was still young, and he had a harem full of beautiful women to tempt him. However, it did become a problem when Tutankhamen died unexpectedly in a hunting accident in his regnal year 10. Funerary tradition dictated that Tutankhamen should be buried by his successor, as 'he who buries, inherits'. Not only would this ensure Tutankhamen the best possible afterlife, it would demonstrate to the gods and the people that his successor was indeed entitled to claim the throne. But his designated heir, Horemheb, was absent, campaigning, unsuccessfully, in the Near East. Under these highly unusual circumstances we might have expected Ankhesenamen, the most prominent surviving descendant of Akhenaten, a king's daughter and king's wife, to step forward. This would not have been without precedent: the 12th Dynasty Sobeknofru ruled as a female pharaoh under similar circumstances, and her reign was accepted by all. Instead, we find Ankhesenamen writing to the king of the Hittites, asking for a son who will become her husband. At the very least this suggests an atypical delay between Tutankhamen's death and his burial: a delay which allowed Ankhesenamen to wait for a response, receive the Hittite envoy, send him back home, and wait for her groom. It is a delay which would, presumably, have allowed Horemheb ample time to return home. We do not see Ankhesenamen again.

Tutankhamen's ministers settled the succession to their own satisfaction. The elderly Ay – a compromise candidate – interred his great-grandson in his own tomb; a pious gesture which ensured that Tutankhamen was adequately provided for, while allowing Ay himself to take over Tutankhamen's far larger tomb. The two stillborn daughters born to Ankhesenamen were interred alongside their father; here they could support and protect their father for all eternity. Four years after his accession Ay, too, died and was interred in Tutankhamen's original tomb. As his intended heir, his son or grandson Nakhtmin, had predeceased him, he was succeeded by Generalissimo Horemheb. Horemheb erased Tutankhamen's name from the Restoration Stela – Tutankhamen's manifesto – and inserted his own in its place. The Amarna Age had well and truly ended.

PART II

TUTANKHAMEN: LIFE AFTER DEATH

As human beings, we have an innate ability to make something out of nothing. We see shapes in the clouds, and a man in the moon; gamblers are convinced they have 'runs of luck'; we take a perfectly cheerful heavy-metal record, play it backwards, and hear hidden messages about Satan. Our ability to spot patterns is what allows us to make sense of the world; but sometimes, in our eagerness, we are oversensitive, trigger-happy, and mistakenly spot patterns where none exist.

Ben Goldacre[1]

Conspiracy Theory
The attribution of deliberate agency to something that is more likely to be accidental or unintended.

Aaronovitch[2]

Tyldesley's Law
Any theory about the behaviour, beliefs and abilities of the ancient Egyptians, no matter how unlikely, will be accepted as truth by someone.

– Tyldesley[3]

8

TUTANKHAMEN'S CURSE

In 1923 Carter wrote an article for *Pearson's Magazine*. 'The Tomb of the Bird' tells of strange, almost supernatural events immediately prior to the opening of Tutankhamen's tomb.[1]

It is the start of the 1922–3 season. Carter has bought a caged bird, which sings most beautifully every day. To the amusement of his sophisticated city friends, he takes the bird to Luxor where it is to be the companion of his loneliness in the desert. The workmen are charmed by the new arrival, and believe it to be a bird of good omen. It is not long before the first steps of the staircase leading to Tutankhamen's tomb are revealed:

'Ah!' exclaimed the leader of the working gang, 'that bird is truly Bakh heit – a luck bringer – and the notes he sings are magic!' But although we worked on feverishly, with the load above as yet to be removed, the real significance of our discovery was not made clear until after several days of toil ...

But you will wonder what this has to do with the bird. Well, one day when enough of the detritus, sand and silt had been removed, and a messenger came to my investigation of the staircase, I suddenly observed that it had become strangely silent and depressed – a depression still more observable when I gave orders for the work to cease until I could be present in the morning …

[With the sealed door uncovered] I decided to take no further steps until Lord Carnarvon arrived. A cable to London was therefore sent announcing the news, and the entrance to the tomb was again covered up. But on returning home in the evening – it was nearly dark, with only a faint glimmer of fading light in the sky – I was astonished to hear the bird singing belatedly, but with wonderful energy and charm.

Well, in due course, Lord Carnarvon arrived. Operations recommenced. Step by step the stairs were laid bare, until seventeen were revealed, and here we left work for the night. The excitement of all of us was intense, and except by the servants, the renewed depression of the bird, although pointed out to me, was scarcely noted.

The tomb door was opened, and the fill in the passageway removed to reveal the second, sealed doorway.

But it was at this point, when the nerves of all of us were at extreme tension, that the messenger brought news of the tragedy. The man, who was almost breathless, told me that a cobra had entered the house, passed down the passage, made its way to the room where we are now sitting, coiled up the leg of that table on which the bird cage was resting, and killed my pet!

And so, as I realised what had happened, the significance which accompanies a moving and odd coincidence made itself felt even through the overwhelming excitement of the moment, for the ray of light from our candle revealed the contents of the ante-chamber to the tomb, and shone on the head of the King bearing on his forehead the Uraeus – the symbol of royalty and protection – the cobra!

The Reises were awed; before them was the image of the serpent that had killed the lucky bird!

First they questioned themselves. What wretch, they asked, had cast an evil eye on the sweet bird that had grown dear to them – the bird that was the luck bringer – the beloved of Allah?

Then in their own way they realised the meaning of the Keys of Protection, and, becoming downcast, saw in the death of the bird a portent of evil omen in spite of the treasures spread out before them. What did it threaten? Had the Jinn which had protected the tomb for 3,000 years become enraged and hostile? 'May the evil omen be afar!' they muttered.

It became necessary to reassure them. The bird, we told them, would return – the lucky bird whose song had cheered us and guided us to these hidden treasures.

Well, a telegram was sent to Lady Evelyn Herbert, who brought from Cairo the canary which you can hear singing now in the next room. With the coming of the bird, cheerfulness returned to the staff, who made it the true possessor of the tomb – Bab-el-Asfour *– the Tomb of the Bird.*

A more down-to-earth account, recorded in a private letter written by Herbert Winlock of the Metropolitan Museum, confirms the essence of this much-repeated story. Carter did indeed have a much-admired songbird, which he kept in a cage in his house in the Valley. While Carter was away from home, meeting Carnarvon in Cairo prior to the tomb opening, Callender found a cobra in the cage 'just in the act of gulping the canary down'.[2]

As the son of Samuel John Carter, a celebrated Victorian animal portrait painter who was himself the son of a gamekeeper, Carter had been raised with a small menagerie of pets which the Carter children, all talented artists in their own right, used to practise their drawing. Carter continued this tradition in Egypt, where tame animals were allowed to roam free in his garden. Birds, in particular, gave him great pleasure; his notebooks mention tranquil hours spent floating in a small boat on the Nile floodwaters, watching the pelicans. However, life in the Valley, for Carter's pets, could be both brutal and short. A pair of young gazelles died, 'the story being too sad to repeat'; a young donkey was bitten in the mouth by a cobra and expired three painful hours later.[3] The story of a canary being eaten by a snake is startling – how did the cobra get into the house? – but not an unusual one, and Carter quickly replaced his lost pet.

What does make the story unusual is the hint of the supernatural which the down-to-earth Carter was prepared to allow in an article intended for a popular audience. It may simply be that, as a self-employed Egyptologist facing an uncertain future, he wanted to sell a good story that would encourage the readers of *Pearson's Magazine* to buy his book. He may have felt the need to compete with the other, equally lurid tales of the supernatural that were already in circulation. It may even be – as was later suggested – that he allowed the story to spread in order to frighten potential robbers away from a tomb that was under some form of spiritual protection. Whatever his motivation, the story had the entirely foreseeable effect of linking the tomb with the occult via the unimpeachable evidence of its excavator.

The belief that the dynastic Egyptians were possessed of a long-lost, esoteric knowledge can be traced as far back as ancient Greece and Rome. The mysterious, unreadable and surely magical hieroglyphic writings made this a very easy, and in many ways very attractive, assumption to make. By 1822, when Jean-François Champollion published his key to decoding the hieroglyphic script, the idea of Egypt as a powerful source of alternative understanding of all aspects of life and religion was deeply ingrained in popular culture. Now the hieroglyphic texts were no longer secret: anyone could buy a translation and read the words inscribed on the temple and tomb walls. There can, however, be a wide gulf between reading and understanding, and misconceptions over the true nature of Egyptian theology abounded. Meanwhile, Western Europe was rapidly losing the rock-solid comfort of unquestioning Christian faith. The Bible was no longer the revealed word of God; people were descended from monkeys; light and voices travelled through metal wires; men sailed through the air in giant metal birds. The world had become a more scientific place, yet life seemed more uncertain as things that would once have been fantastic suddenly became real.

Up to 16 million people died in the Great War (1914–18). This included almost an entire generation of young men whose bodies were buried in foreign fields. A further 50–100 million worldwide – an estimated 250,000 in Britain – died in the devastating flu pandemic that followed (1918–20). These tragedies naturally led to an increased interest in the occult as the living struggled to maintain contact with their dead. Seances, automatic writing and ouija boards (originally promoted as a parlour game, and not as a means of communicating with the 'other side') grew in popularity, and Egyptian religion, with its sinister mortuary rituals, held a great fascination for those who felt that they might be able to connect themselves to a lost knowledge simply by touching, or gazing at, ancient artefacts. The Theosophists – a sect who attempted to reach spiritual enlightenment through intuition and direct communication – were not the only ones to believe that the Egyptians had enjoyed strong magical powers which students of the occult might one day re-awake. Meanwhile, Tutankhamen's links with the 'heretic' Akhenaten made him a particularly suitable study for those interested in the development of religion and magic.

A large library of mummy-based horror stories ensured that Carter's public was pre-programmed to accept the mummy as a malevolent entity.[4] A corpse, so recognisably human many thousands of years after death that it carries the promise of resurrection, is indeed a frightening figure. While many of the published mummy tales had little to distinguish them from other run-of-the-mill horror stories, some were tightly crafted and sprinkled with semi-accurate Egyptological facts, names and locations, which allowed the reader to suspend disbelief. Inevitably, some readers accepted this heavily disguised fiction as fact.

The first mummy tale written in English – appropriately titled *The Mummy!* – was published anonymously by Jane Webb (later the garden expert Jane Loudon) in 1827. Webb was apparently influenced both by the work of Napoleon's Commission and, more directly, by the 1818 publication and popular success of Mary Shelley's (then Mary Godwin) *Frankenstein*. Her mummy, Cheops, is a likeable and relatively harmless creature and her book, set in 2126 England, more akin to science fiction than gothic horror: among the exotica, it features ladies who wear flame headdresses and, quite shockingly, trousers! Here her hero, Edric, confesses his dream of resuscitating a corpse using a 'galvanic battery'. Although he lives three centuries after his author, Edric has a nineteenth-century understanding of death, and he knows that the only way of being absolutely certain that a body is indeed dead is to observe the signs of putrefaction. This he is too squeamish to do. It seems that his experiment is doomed to fail before it starts, unless ...:

> *'If you could overcome your childish reluctance to trying an experiment upon a corpse,' said Father Morris, 'your doubts would be set at rest. For you could succeed in re-animating a dead body that had been long-entombed, so that it might enjoy its reasoning facilities in full perfection ...'*
>
> *'But where shall I find a body, which has been dead a sufficient time to prevent the possibility of its being only in a trance, and which yet has not begun to decompose? – For even if I could conquer the repugnance I feel at the thought of touching such a mass of cold*

mortality, as that presented in my dream, according to your own theory, the organs must be perfect or the experiment will not be complete.'

Edgar Allan Poe's satirical short story 'Some Words with a Mummy' (1845) echoes Shelley's and Webb's fascination with electricity, which, many suspected, could be used to bring the dead back to life:

Stripping off the papyrus, we found the flesh in excellent preservation, with no perceptible odour. The color was reddish. The skin was hard, smooth, and glossy. The teeth and hair were in good condition. The eyes (it seemed) had been removed, and glass ones substituted, which were very beautiful and wonderfully life-like, with the exception of somewhat too determined a stare. The finger and toe nails were brilliantly gilded.

Mr. Gliddon was of opinion, from the redness of the epidermis, that the embalmment had been effected altogether by asphaltum; but, upon scraping the surface with a steel instrument, and throwing into the fire some of the powder thus obtained, the flavor of camphor and other sweet-scented gums became apparent.

We searched the corpse very carefully for the usual openings through which the entrails are extracted, but, to our surprise, we could discover none. No member of the party was at that period aware that entire or unopened mummies are not unfrequently met. The brain it was customary to withdraw through the nose; the intestines through an incision in the side; the body was then shaved, washed, and salted, then laid aside for several weeks, when the operation of embalming, properly so called, began.

As no trace of an opening could be found, Doctor Ponnonner was preparing his instruments for dissection, when I observed that it was then past two o'clock. Hereupon it was agreed to postpone the internal examination until the next evening, and we were about to separate for the present, when someone suggested an experiment or two with the Voltaic pile.

The application of electricity to a mummy some three or four thousand years old at the least, was an idea, if not very sage, still sufficiently original, and we all caught at it at once. About one tenth in earnest and nine tenths in jest, we arranged a battery in the Doctor's study, and conveyed thither the Egyptian.

Théophile Gautier's *The Romance of a Mummy* (1858) is superficially more realistic. It tells the tale of the discovery of an intact tomb in the Valley of the Kings by the English Lord Evandale and his hired archaeologist Dr Rumphius, and introduces the idea that a mummy might remain beautiful – might even be an object of desire – beneath its bandages:

As a general rule mummies which have been filled with bitumen and natron resemble black simulacra carved in ebony; corruption cannot attack them, but the appearance of life is wholly lacking; the bodies have not returned to the dust whence they came, but they have been petrified in a hideous shape, which one cannot contemplate without disgust and terror. In this case, the body, carefully prepared by surer, longer, and more costly processes, had preserved the elasticity of the flesh, the grain of the skin, and almost its natural colour. The skin, of a light brown, had the golden tint of a new Florentine bronze, and the amber, warm tone which is admired in the paintings of Giorgione and Titian covered with a smoky varnish, was not very different from what must have been the complexion of the young Egyptian during her lifetime. She seemed to be asleep rather than dead. The eyelids, still fringed with their long lashes, allowed eyes lustrous with the humid gleam of life to shine between their lines of antimony. One could have sworn they were about to shake off, as a light dream, their sleep of thirty centuries. The nose, delicate and fine, preserved its pure outline; no depression deformed the cheeks, which were as round as the side of a vase; the mouth, coloured with a faint blush, had preserved its imperceptible lines, and on the lips, voluptuously moulded, fluttered a melancholy and mysterious smile, full of gentleness, sadness, and charm, – that tender and resigned smile which pouts so prettily the lips of the adorable heads which surmount the Canopean vases in the Louvre.

In 1869 Louisa May Alcott, more famous as the author of *Little Women*, published 'Lost in a Pyramid, or The Mummy's Curse'. In this sinister tale a female mummy – a sorceress – causes the living death of an innocent but curious bride who must suffer for her husband's actions:

Evelyn, my dearest! Wake up and answer me. Did you wear that strange flower today?' whispered Forsyth, putting the misty screen away.

There was no need for her to answer, for there, gleaming spectrally on her bosom, was the evil blossom, its white petals spotted now with flecks of scarlet, vivid as drops of newly spilt blood.

But the unhappy bridegroom scarcely saw it, for the face above it appalled him by its utter vacancy. Drawn and pallid, as if with some wasting malady, the young face, so lovely an hour ago, lay before him aged and blighted by the baleful influence of the plant which had drunk up her life. No recognition in the eyes, no word upon the lips, no motion of the hand – only the faint breath, the fluttering pulse, and wide-opened eyes, betrayed that she was alive.

Alas for the young wife! The superstitious fear at which she had smiled had proved true: the curse that had bided its time for ages was fulfilled at last, and her own hand wrecked her happiness for ever. Death in life was her doom, and for years Forsyth secluded himself to tend with pathetic devotion the pale ghost, who never, by word or look, could thank him for the love that outlived even such a fate as this.

Bram Stoker honed the mummy story into a more compelling, more realistic horror. *The Jewel of Seven Stars,* a mummy story similar in style and plot to the already successful *Dracula*, was published in 1903. It tells the tale of Queen Tera, whose unwrapping and resurrection in a lonely house in Cornwall led to a nasty ending for everyone involved. In fact his ending was considered so horrific that his publisher forced him to rewrite the final chapter for the 1912 revised edition. Unknown to everyone, Tera was a skilled magician:

> *Queen Tera was of the Eleventh, or Theban Dynasty of Egyptian Kings which held sway between the twenty-ninth and twenty-fifth centuries before Christ. She succeeded as the only child of her father, Antef. She must have been a girl of extraordinary character as well as ability, for she was but a young girl when her father died. Her youth and sex encouraged the ambitious priesthood, which had then achieved immense power. By their wealth and numbers and learning they dominated all Egypt, more especially the Upper portion. They were then secretly ready to make an effort for the achievement of their bold and long-considered design, that of transferring the governing power from a Kingship to a Hierarchy. But King Antef had suspected some such movement, and had taken the precaution of securing to his daughter the allegiance of the army. He had also had her taught statecraft, and had even made her learned in the lore of the very priests themselves. He had used those of one cult against the other; each being hopeful of some present gain on its own part by the influence of the King, or of some ultimate gain from its own influence over his daughter. Thus, the Princess had been brought up amongst scribes, and was herself no mean artist. Many of these things were told on the walls in pictures or in hieroglyphic writing of great beauty; and we came to the conclusion that not a few of them had been done by the Princess herself. It was not without cause that she was inscribed on the Stele as 'Protector of the Arts'.*
>
> *But the King had gone to further lengths, and had had his daughter taught magic, by which she had power over Sleep and Will. This was real magic — 'black' magic; not the magic of the temples,*

which, I may explain, was of the harmless or 'white' order, and was intended to impress rather than to effect. She had been an apt pupil; and had gone further than her teachers. Her power and her resources had given her great opportunities, of which she had availed herself to the full. She had won secrets from nature in strange ways; and had even gone to the length of going down into the tomb herself, having been swathed and coffined and left as dead for a whole month. The priests had tried to make out that the real Princess Tera had died in the experiment, and that another girl had been substituted; but she had conclusively proved their error ...

It was unfortunate, but perhaps predictable, that, with access to Tutankhamen's tomb restricted and few Egyptologists prepared to give the sort of speculative interviews that the press craved, popular authors specialising in this type of occult tale would become accepted as experts on all aspects of Egyptian religion and ritual. Included among the group of popular 'experts' were Sir Arthur Conan Doyle, the creator of Sherlock Holmes and author of two popular tales of ancient Egypt – 'The Ring of Thoth' (1890) and 'Lot No. 249' (1892), and Sir Henry Rider Haggard, author of *She* (1887) and *Cleopatra* (1889), whose 'Smith and the Pharaohs' had been serialised in the *Strand Magazine* in 1910. Most prominent of all was Marie Corelli, an immensely popular novelist and larger-than-life figure whose gothic works were regarded by some as complete tosh, but by many more as a true and exciting glimpse into lost worlds. At the peak of her success, Corelli was Britain's most widely read author and her opinions carried a great deal of weight with her supporters, if not with her critics. As her biography, published during her lifetime, delicately explains:

Marie Corelli is bold; perhaps she is the boldest writer that has ever lived. What she believes she says, with a brilliant fearlessness that sweeps aside petty argument in its giant's stride towards the goal for which she aims. She will have no half measures. Her works, gathered together under one vast cover, might fitly be printed and published as an amplified edition of the Decalogue [the Ten Commandments].

It is small wonder, then, that she has not earned the approbation of those critics who are unable to grasp the stupendous nature of her programme; they, having always held by certain canons, and finding those canons brutally discarded, retort with wholesale condemnation of matters that they deem literary heterodoxy, but whose sterling simplicity is in reality altogether beyond their ken. [5]

The idea that Tutankhamen's tomb might be under some form of remote protection surfaced as soon as Carnarvon's illness was first reported in the London press. On 24 March 1923 – the day that *The Times* recorded an improvement in the invalid's condition – the *Daily Express* reported Corelli's concerns over his safety:

I cannot but think that some risks are run by breaking into the last rest of a king of Egypt whose tomb is specially and solemnly guarded, and robbing him of possessions.

According to a rare book I possess, which is not in the British Museum, entitled 'The Egyptian History of the Pyramids' (translated out of the original Arabic by Vortier, Arabic professor to Louis XVI of France) the most dire punishment follows any rash intruder into a sealed tomb.

This book gives long and elaborate lists of the 'treasures' buried with several of the kings, and among these are named 'divers secret poisons enclosed in boxes in such wise that those who touch them shall not know how they come to suffer'.

That is why I ask: 'Was it a mosquito bite that has so seriously infected Lord Carnarvon?'

When, just few days later, Carnarvon succumbed to his illness, Corelli was hailed as a clairvoyant. Other mediums, less impressively, published their predictions of tomb-based death immediately after the event. 'Velma' had apparently warned Carnarvon of the perils of resuming his work in the Valley; 'Cheiro' had received a warning transmitted by one of Akhenaten's daughters, and had forwarded it to the Earl.

Carnarvon died aged fifty-seven at a time when average male life expectancy at birth in the UK was just under fifty-seven years; in 1866, the year of his own birth, a male industrial worker would have been lucky to reach forty-five years of age.[6] As a member of the well-fed, leisured elite Carnarvon might reasonably have expected to live a longer than average life, but his health had been severely weakened by a near-fatal car crash in 1901. An account of this accident is given by his sister, Lady Winifred Burghclere, who provides an idiosyncratic but eminently readable and affectionate tribute to her brother as an introduction to Carter and Mace's 1923 Tutankhamen publication. From this we learn how Carnarvon had been driving at speed along a straight and apparently empty road in Germany when he surmounted a hill only to find, in a hidden dip, the road completely blocked by two bullock carts. Unable to stop, he wrenched the car off the road, straight into a heap of stones. As the tyres burst, the light car over-turned and landed on its driver. The chauffeur, Edward Trotman, was thrown clear and protected by his thick coat, but Carnarvon was trapped. Trotman was able to drag the vehicle off his master, then, seizing a bucket of water from a workman in a nearby field, threw it over his unconscious form. According to Lady Burghclere, the shock of the water re-started her brother's heart. Carnarvon recovered from this ordeal, but he would never be the same again: 'Nothing that skill or care could effect then or later was spared, but throughout the remainder of his life he suffered from perpetually recurrent operations and dangerous illnesses.'[7]

His accident left Carnarvon weak, underweight and vulnerable to chest infections. His doctors, worried about the effects of a damp British winter, recommended a visit to Egypt, and so a new passion was born. That his immediate family accepted his death as entirely natural is made clear by Lady Burghclere:

> In his will he expressed the wish to be buried on Beacon Hill. It was therefore on the summit of the great down overlooking the home that he had so passionately loved, that he was laid to rest … Organ, music, choristers, there were none at this burying. The beautiful office, commanding 'the body of our dear brother to the ground in sure and certain hope,' had something of the stark grandeur of a funeral at sea. But the whole air was alive with the springtide song of the larks. They sang deliriously, in a passion of ecstasy which can never be forgotten by those who heard that song. And so we left him, feeling that the ending was in harmony with the life. [8]

Finally, the world's press had a story that they could publish without deferring to *The Times*: a human tragedy far more compelling than the disappointingly slow-moving events at the tomb. As with all celebrity deaths, the story rapidly gathered its own momentum. Soon there were reports of sinister goings on. At the very moment of Carnarvon's death all the lights in Cairo had been mysteriously extinguished and, back at Highclere, Carnarvon's dog, Susie, had let out a great howl and died. That all the lights in Cairo should fail – or, in some accounts, that all the lights in the hotel (or, wrongly, hospital) where Carnarvon died should fail – is so far from remarkable as to be unworthy of mention. Even today, the Cairo electricity supply is notoriously fickle and no one can ever explain just why the lights go on and off. The reports of the dog's death stem from Carnarvon's son, the 6th Earl, a man with an intense fear of Tutankhamen's curse: interviewed by NBC in New York, in July 1977, he apparently told his interviewer that he would 'not accept a million pounds to enter the tomb of Tutankhamen in the Valley of the Kings'.[9] In this case, as he was in Egypt at the time his father died, he cannot have been an eyewitness to events at Highclere. Indeed, it is unlikely that there were any witnesses, as Susie died early in the morning:

> *Father died shortly before two o'clock Cairo time. As I learned later, something very strange happened here in Highclere about the same time, shortly before 4 am London time. Our fox terrier bitch, who had lost her front paw in an accident in 1919 and whom Father loved very much, suddenly began to howl, sat up on her hind legs, and fell over dead.* [10]

Carnarvon's death certificate confirms that he died in Cairo shortly before 2 a.m. In 1923 there was a two-hour time gap between the two countries but England, being the more westerly country, was two hours behind Egypt. Rather than enjoying simultaneous deaths, Susie actually died four hours after her master.

Marie Corelli was the first to mention the ancient curse 'death comes on wings to he who enters the tomb of a pharaoh'. Soon it was an accepted fact that this, or a slight variant, 'death comes on swift wings to him that toucheth the tomb of the pharaoh', was carved over the entrance to Tutankhamen's tomb, or carved above the entrance to the Burial Chamber, or inscribed on a mud-brick tablet found in either the Antechamber or the Burial Chamber. Naturally, so potent a curse could not be allowed to taint the excavation:

> *Neither Carter nor Gardiner [the presumed translator of the curse] nor any of the other scholars present feared the curse then or took it seriously. But they worried that the Egyptian labourers would, and since they were dependent on native helpers, mention of the clay tablet was wiped from the written record of the tomb's discovery. Even the*

tablet itself disappeared from the artefact collection – but not from the memory of those who read it. (The tablet and the curse on it are cited everywhere, but it was never photographed and is considered lost). [11]

A second, slightly less explicit curse was apparently written on the back of 'a statue … this magic figure was discovered in the main chamber of the tomb':

It is I who drive back the robbers of the tomb with the flames of the desert. I am the protector of Tutankhamen's grave. [12]

This is a mangled version of the genuine inscription on a small reed torch discovered immediately in front of the Anubis shrine in the Treasury. The torch was covered in gold and mounted on a brick-like pottery pedestal bearing the simple yet explicit spell, 'to repel the enemy of Osiris [the deceased] in whatever form he may come':

It is I who hinder the sand from choking the secret chamber, and who repel the one who would repel him with the desert-flame. I have set aflame the desert (?), I have caused the path to be mistaken. I am for the protection of Osiris [the deceased]. [13]

Soon it was rumoured that the last line of this inscription, '… I will call all those who cross this threshold into the sacred precincts of the King who lives for ever', had been erased by Carter to prevent panic spreading among his workforce. Meanwhile, a 'necromancer' and self-proclaimed archaeologist announced yet another curse discovered in the tomb:

Let the hand raised against my form be withered! Let them be destroyed who attack my name, my foundation, my effigies, the images like unto me. [14]

While 'scientific' and Christian Westerners were only too eager to believe in the supernatural curse, Egyptians ancient and modern were not unduly troubled by it, and were certainly not averse to violating the tomb and stealing from the dead. They may have believed in ghosts, but they did not accept the Western phenomenon of the vindictive, re-awakened mummy. Scrutiny of the original excavation photographs, available to everyone via the website of the Griffith Institute, Oxford, confirms that they were correct in their disbelief. There is in fact nothing written above either the tomb entrance or the doorway to the Burial Chamber, and there never was. Nor, as this is a royal tomb, would we expect there to be. To understand why Tutankhamen would not have felt the need to protect his tomb with curses, we need to consider the role of the ancient Egyptian tomb in more detail.

The tomb served several purposes. It was a magical place, furnished with ritual artefacts, where the latent mummy could be transformed into a living being.[15] At the same time it was the home of the deceased, furnished with grave goods appropriate to his or her social status. At its most basic level, however, it was simply an elaborate storage box designed to protect the mummified tomb owner until the end of time.

Life beyond death meant different things to different classes of people at different times, but fundamental to all beliefs was the idea that the *ka* spirit needed to live close to the corpse. If the mummy was destroyed and the *ka* could not find an alternative home – a statue perhaps, or an image or even a memory – the deceased would die the terrible Second Death, from which there could be no return. It was therefore vital that no one should interfere with the tomb and its mummy. This could have been achieved with remarkable ease had the Egyptians been prepared to revert to the Predynastic tradition of burial in simple pits cut into the desert sands. There would then have been no need of artificial mummification, as the hot and sterile sand would have created a naturally dried mummy and, with no grave goods, no one would have had any desire to disinter the newly impoverished dead. But that was never an option. The elite could not face eternity without a vast array of material goods, and their insistence on burial in what were essentially ill-guarded warehouses full of desirable objects made the vulnerable dead far richer than many of the living. Naturally, thieves were attracted to the cemeteries.

Many of the dead were robbed before they even reached the tomb. We have no means of knowing how many families paid for amulets and jewellery which unscrupulous undertakers simply neglected to place within the wrappings, but with the benefits of modern science we are able to peek beneath the neat bandages and see that some superficially perfect mummies, particularly those dating to the Late and Graeco-Roman Periods, are nothing more than a jumbled mass of bones and rubbish. The undertakers were not the only ones to rob the dead. The workmen who built the elite tombs, the grave diggers who worked in the public graveyards, and even the cemetery guards and priests; all might have been tempted to profit from their specialised knowledge. Once the thieves had accessed the burial chamber, the jewellery and amulets within the bandages made the wrapped corpse particularly vulnerable to attack. Mummies were hacked to pieces, or burned, in the frantic search for metals, glass and semi-precious stones.

It was therefore important that wrongdoers be discouraged from entering the tomb. The easiest way to do this was to seal the tomb, then hide it away. But the pyramid-building kings of the Old and Middle Kingdoms had no wish to hide their tombs; they wanted them to stand proud and tall, as a permanent memorial to their own greatness. The royal architects experimented with a range of physical barriers, incorporating hidden entrances, false chambers, stone portcullises and backfilled corridors in their designs, but all these systems failed. With the move to the Valley of the Kings, and the separation of the memorial temple from the burial, the 18th Dynasty pharaohs reduced the likelihood of robbery by random thieves but remained vulnerable to those who built and guarded their tombs.

Non-royal tomb owners were equally conflicted. Their tombs included both an accessible chapel (the sacred place where families and well-wishers would leave the offerings that would nourish the *ka*) and a hidden burial chamber (the sacred place where the mummy rested). Tomb owners wished to attract family members, friends and decent passers-by who might be persuaded to leave offerings, and so their tombs had to be conspicuous. At the same time, they wished to discourage those who might rob or vandalise the tomb. And so, from the 5th Dynasty onwards, we find written messages from the non-royal dead to the living, designed to warn against any improper behaviour. For example, a loose stone block from a private tomb, found near the pyramid of Teti at Sakkara, bears an obviously unheeded warning to 'any man who shall take stone from this tomb or who shall not enter in a pure state'.[16] Usurpation was a constant worry, as it was far easier and quicker to eject a long dead owner from either part of, or all of, an old and unvisited tomb, or to dismantle it and re-use its pre-cut blocks, than it was to build a new tomb from scratch. The façade of the tomb of Ankhi at Sakkara provides a dire warning to anyone who might be tempted to do this:

Every workman, every stonemason, or every man who shall [do] evil things to the tomb of mine of eternity by tearing out bricks or stones from it, no voice shall be given to him in the sight of any god or any man. [17]

In a land where maybe just 5 per cent of the population was literate, it seems unlikely that those tempted to rob could have actually read and understood this warning, but that, of course, would not have prevented the warning from becoming effective. It was accepted that the dead had the power to interfere with the living. They could help those in need, and might even punish those who had done wrong. And so, in the Giza tomb of Peteti, we read how:

> Any person … who shall enter this (tomb) and do something therein which is evil … it is the crocodile, the hippopotamus or the lion which shall consume them.
>
> Any person who shall do anything evil to this (tomb) … the crocodile shall be against them in the water and the snake shall be against them on land, the hippopotamus shall be against them in the water and the scorpion shall be against them on land. [18]

Royal tombs were, however, a different matter. They did not have integral offering chapels – they had memorial temples where the deceased could receive offerings without any need for the living to approach the resting place of the dead. During the Old and Middle Kingdoms these temples had been included within the pyramid complex; during the New Kingdom they were situated on the desert edge, a considerable distance away from the rock-cut tombs of the Valley. A similar system existed for the few non-royals buried in the Valley; Yuya and Thuya, for example, lay in the Valley but would have received their mortuary offerings in a dedicated place – a small chapel, stela or statue within a larger temple, perhaps – somewhere else. No one was expected to visit the tomb itself and, without visitors, and random passers-by, there was no need to include warning messages on the tomb walls.

The absence of a written curse (which some, naturally, believe has been suppressed by 'the authorities') has done nothing to stem the idea that Tutankhamen first killed Carnarvon, and then went on to kill others. For example:

> *Tutankhamen is the key figure in the curse which has, to date [1975], cost the lives of at least three dozen scientists, archaeologists and scholars ... Tutankhamen was only the front man for a cabal of priests. His real importance stems from the relatively late discovery of his tomb, which, unlike those of other pharaohs, had not been plundered, and from the fact that a series of mysterious deaths followed the grave's excavation. The curse of the pharaohs then began to excite scientists for the first time.* [19]

The number of curse victims varies from account to account, but the list generally includes the following:

- **George Edward Stanhope Molyneux Herbert, 5th Earl of Carnarvon:** his story has already been told. Died in 1923, aged fifty-seven.
- **Prince Ali Kemal Fahmy Bey:** a visitor to the tomb. Shot by his wife, 'The Tragic Princess', in a corridor of the Savoy Hotel, London. Died in 1923, aged twenty-three.
- **Aubrey Herbert:** half-brother to Lord Carnarvon. Had his teeth extracted in a misguided attempt to cure his blindness, and blood poisoning soon followed. Died in 1923 aged forty-three.
- **Hugh Evelyn-White:** an archaeologist and classicist at Leeds University, who committed suicide leaving a note blaming his death on an unspecified curse. Died in 1924, aged forty.
- **Georges Bénédite:** Head of the Department of Antiquities at the Louvre Museum, Paris. Fell after seeing the tomb (a stroke?). Died in 1926, aged sixty-nine.
- **Arthur Mace:** Assistant Keeper in the Department of Egyptian

Antiquities, Metropolitan Museum of Art, New York, and Carter's colleague and co-author. Retired on the grounds of ill-health before the tomb could be fully emptied. Died in 1928, aged fifty-three.

- **Richard Bethell**: a member of the committee of the Egypt Exploration Society who acted as Carter's assistant secretary during the 1923–4 excavation season. Died of natural causes in the Bath Club in 1929, aged forty-six.
- **Mervyn Herbert**: half-brother to Lord Carnarvon. Contracted 'malarial pneumonia'. Died in 1929 aged forty-six.
- **Richard Bethell, Lord Westbury:** father of Richard Bethell. Committed suicide by throwing himself out of a window following his son's death. On the way to the cemetery his hearse ran over an eight-year-old child, killing him. Neither Lord Westbury nor the unfortunate child is known to have entered Tutankhamen's tomb. Died in 1930, aged seventy-eight.
- **Albert Lythgoe**: Egyptologist at the Metropolitan Museum of Art, New York . Died in 1934, aged sixty-six:

> *In Boston last week wintry winds whined around the Massachu-setts General Hospital but their mournful sound went unheard by a tall thin patient who lay at death's door. The critical illness of Albert Morton Lythgoe, 66, made headlines in newspapers the length & breadth of the land, not because he was once Curator of Egyptology in Manhattan's Metropolitan Museum of Art, but because ten years ago he saw opened the sarcophagus of a footling little man named TutankhAmen who ruled Egypt 13 centuries before Christ. Was it not written: 'Here lies the great King and whoso disturbs this tomb, on him may the curse of the Pharaoh rest'?*
>
> *Dr. Lythgoe's wife ordered the hospital not to disclose the nature of his illness. But when the Press, eager to build up a*

'curse' story labelled his malady 'mysterious,' friends promptly revealed that Dr. Lythgoe had cerebral arteriosclerosis, the by no means rare condition of hardening of the brain arteries.

Initially the curse was confined to those who had actually entered the tomb at, or shortly after, the time of the discovery, but very soon pretty much any Tutankhamen-related incident could be attributed to his curse. The flight crew that brought Tutankhamen's 1972 exhibition to London appear to have been particularly vulnerable: two were killed (one dying in 1976, one in 1978); one broke the leg that had accidentally kicked the crate holding the death mask; one had his house burn down; one got divorced. Meanwhile, eminent pre-Tutankhamen Egyptologists were added to the list of curse victims: these include Champollion (1790–1832), who was apparently killed because he decoded the hieroglyphic script, Heinrich Brugsch (1827–94), who was not killed but given schizophrenic tendencies, and Flinders Petrie (1853–1942), who died because of his lifelong interest in the Great Pyramid.

Carter found it necessary to repeat, time and time again, that Tutankhamen's tomb contained no biological booby traps, no poisons and no curse. His position was quite clear:

It is not my intention to repeat the ridiculous stories which have been invented about the dangers lurking in ambush, as it were, in the Tomb, to destroy the intruder. Similar tales have been a common feature of fiction for many years, they are mostly variants of the ordinary ghost story, and may be accepted as a legitimate form of literary amusement. But there is another and a serious side to this question which calls for protest. It has been stated in various quarters that there are actual physical dangers hidden in Tut-ankh-Amen's tomb – mysterious forces, called into being by some malefic power, to take vengeance on whomsoever should dare pass its portals. There was probably no place in the world freer from risks than the Tomb. Sci-entific research had proved it to be sterile. Whatever foreign germs there may be within it today have been introduced from without, yet mischievous people have attributed many deaths, illnesses and disas-ters to alleged mysterious and noxious influences in the Tomb. Unpar-donable and mendacious statements of this nature have been published and repeated in various quarters with a sort of malicious satisfaction. It is indeed difficult to speak of this form of 'ghostly' calumny with calm. If it be not actually libellous it points in that spiteful direction, and all sane people should dismiss such inventions with contempt. So far as the living are concerned curses of this nature have no part in the Egyptian Ritual.[20]

He was, of course, wasting his time. Speculation simply grew, with many choosing to believe that Carter himself was collaborating with 'the authorities' to hide the evidence. In 1934 Herbert Winlock, frus-trated by the public's willingness to accept superstition as fact, started to collate information about those he deemed most vulnerable to the curse.[21] His work may be summarised as follows:

- Of the twenty-six people present at the opening of the tomb, six died within a decade.
- Of the twenty-two people present at the sarcophagus opening, two died within a decade.
- Of the ten people present at Tutankhamen's autopsy, none died within a decade.

Of those who had first crept into the Burial Chamber, only Lord Carnarvon – a man already in ill health – had died prematurely. Lady Evelyn, who accompanied her father into the burial chamber, would not die until 1980. She was not the only one to enjoy a long life. Alan Gardiner, a member of the original team, died in 1963 at the age of eighty-four; Douglas Derry, the man who did most physical damage to Tutankhamen, died aged eighty-seven in 1969. Carter died in 1939, aged sixty-four; he outlived Carnarvon by sixteen years. Others have conducted similar research and, unsurprisingly, reached similar conclusions. For example, in 2002 Australian scientist Mark R. Nelson concluded that 'There was no significant association between exposure to the mummy's curse and survival and thus no evidence to support the existence of a mummy's curse.'[22] These statistics have made – and continue to make – not a jot of difference.

Initially the curse was regarded as an entirely magical or mystical phenomenon. The deaths were caused by undetectable elementals or forces invoked 3,000 years ago by the necropolis priests. This idea was enthusiastically promoted by Conan Doyle, who was, in spite of his medical training, a firm believer in paranormal phenomena including ghosts, fairies and elementals.[23] In April 1923 he was engaged on a mission to promote Christian spiritualism in the United States, and this gave him regular access to the American press:

> *An evil elemental may have caused Lord Carnarvon's fatal illness. One does not know what elementals existed in those days, nor what their form might be. The Egyptians knew a great deal more about these things than we do.*

Asked why no one else been slain by the curse, he famously replied:

> *It is nonsense to say that because 'elementals' do not harm everybody, therefore they do not exist. One might as well say that because bull- dogs do not bite everybody, therefore bulldogs do not exist.*[24]

Today there are many who continue to accept that the Egyptians were capable of harnessing ancient energies: for example, in their employment of pyramid-power, which, some believe, can be used to sharpen razor blades, desiccate fish and restore calm to those suffering from the stresses of modern life. Rider Haggard, however, begged to differ, and his views were published in the *Daily Mail* on 7 April 1923:

> *All this nonsense about Lord Carnarvon having been brought to his end by magic is dangerous nonsense. Dangerous because it goes to swell the rising tide of superstition which at present seems to be overflowing the world.*

More recently, remote death by 'elementals' has been abandoned in favour of more 'scientific' curse explanations. The tomb obviously contained something that killed. This may have been a deliberate trap, set by the ancient priests, but it may equally well have been an unfortunate combination of circumstances that made Tutankhamen into the accidental murderer of Carnarvon and, maybe, Mace. The best known, and best argued, of the theories are as follows:

Infected Bite: The suggestion that Carnarvon might have been infected by a bite from a mosquito which had itself been contaminated by drinking Tutankhamen's embalming fluids was first put forward by the *Daily Mail*. It gained in popularity when the mummy autopsy revealed the scar on Tutankhamen's face; this was widely accepted as a mosquito bite linking Tutankhamen to Carnarvon. The theory of death by poison via a mosquito can be quickly squashed as, before the Aswan High Dam raised Egypt's water table in the 1960s, there were no mosquitoes in the dry Valley of the Kings.

Poison or Infection: Conan Doyle was the first to suggest that poisonous spores may have been included in the tomb to punish those who might threaten the king's mummy. Leaving aside the practicalities of the necropolis priests being able to perform this complex operation without killing themselves, this is an extremely unlikely scenario. Ancient Egyptian medicine, although advanced for its time, did not understand the causes of illnesses and, with bacteria and germs unknown, sicknesses were attributed to malevolent spirits. In any case, the tomb had to remain accessible to the officials who might need to restore it following a robbery or a damaging flood.

There was no obvious sign of any poison within Tutankhamen's tomb. Could Carnarvon have met an invisible, accidental killer: a virus, bacterium or fungus? Anthrax perhaps, as anthrax is known to linger for many years, or fungi related to aspergillosis, a lethal disease linked with modern climatic conditions in ancient tombs and caves. Lucas, as a down-to-earth chemist, was vehemently opposed to this idea:

So far as can be ascertained, no life of any kind, even of the lowest form, existed in the tomb when it was first found. Thus the morning after the sealed doorway of the Burial Chamber was opened, sterile swabs were taken into the extreme corner of the chamber near the back of the shrines, some six yards beyond where anyone had trod for more than 3,000 years, and were wiped on the walls, on the bottom of the outer shrine and under some reeds on the floor. These swabs, which were kindly supplied by Dr A. C. Thaysen of the Bacteriological Laboratory of the Royal Naval Cordite Factory, near Wareham, were examined at that laboratory by Mr H. J. Bunker, and out of five swabs from which cultures were taken, four were sterile and the fifth contained a few organisms that were undoubtedly air-infections unavoidably introduced during the opening of the doorway and the subsequent inspection of the chamber, and not belonging to the tomb, and it may be accepted that no bacterial life whatever was present. The danger, therefore, to those working in the tomb from disease germs, against which they have been so frequently warned, is non-existent. [25]

He emphasises that, while there was some evidence for fungus growing on the walls, and a small selection of beetles and spiders, all had clearly been dead for many hundreds of years. Even the wood-worm that had started to eat through the furniture were, after 3,000 years, dead.

Bat Droppings: Could Carnarvon have been poisoned by inhaling the ancient and toxic bat dung that was heaped on the tomb floor? No, because no bats had been able to penetrate the sealed tomb. The suggestion made by Geoffrey Dean, Director Emeritus of the Medico-Social Research Board of Ireland, that bats might have colonised the tomb after its opening, during the period before a proper door was fitted when the tomb was protected by a metal grille, is more credible. There are accounts of bats flying into the tomb at night, and Carter ordering their removal each morning.[26] Histoplasma flourishes in bat dung, and can be inhaled to cause histoplasmosis: fever, enlarged glands and pneumonia.[27] Carter, who had worked in tombs for all his adult life, may well have developed an immunity to the disease; Mace and Carnarvon may not.

Radiation: The idea that Carnarvon might have been killed by radiation within the tombs has become increasingly popular as our own fears about radiation and nuclear activity have grown: 'It is definitely possible that the ancient Egyptians used atomic radiation to protect their holy places. The floors of the tombs could have been covered with uranium. Or the graves could have been finished with radioactive rock. Rock containing both gold and uranium was mined in Egypt. Such radiation could kill a man today.' [28] There is no evidence to support this theory.

If it is impossible to study Tutankhamen without referring to Howard Carter, it is equally impossible to study the development of Tutankhamen's curse without referring to his sometime colleague Arthur Weigall.[29] Carter and Weigall had much in common: both fell into Egyptology almost by accident (Carter as an artist; Weigall as a student of family history); both served as Antiquities Inspector in the Valley of the Kings; neither was rich; both had strong principles which could make them unpopular with their contemporaries. It perhaps goes without saying that they were not the best of friends. Unlike Carter, however, Weigall was a fluent and highly successful author. His popular writings, at a time when he had been excluded from all official information about the excavation of the tomb, did much to encourage the worldwide belief that Carnarvon had been killed by an ancient curse. It was therefore inevitable that when Weigall himself died, on 2 January 1934 at just fifty-three years of age, the *Daily Mail* had no hesitation in pointing the finger of blame: 'Death of Mr A. Weigall, Tut-ankh-Amen Curse Recalled'.

Weigall had never been a member of the Tutankhamen excavation team and so it seems somewhat unfair that Tutankhamen might have considered him a suitable candidate for death by curse. But Weigall had been Antiquities Inspector for southern Egypt in the early 1900s, he had been the *Mail's* own Tutankhamen correspondent, and he had lectured and written about Tutankhamen in Britain, Europe and America. Indeed, in America he had occasionally (much to Carter's irritation) been advertised as the discoverer of the tomb: perhaps Tutankhamen, too, had become confused? He was also widely credited with predicting Carnarvon's death: seeing him enter the tomb in good humour at the opening of the Burial Chamber, Weigall apparently observed, 'if he goes down in that spirit, I give him six weeks to live'.[30]

His own writings, in contrast, deny the existence of any curse within the tomb:

> *Millions of people throughout the world have asked themselves whether the death of the excavator of this tomb was due to some malevolent influence which came from it, and the story has spread that there was a specific curse written upon the wall of the royal sepulchre. This, however, is not the case.* [31]

Weigall had left Egypt in 1914, returning to England to become both a stage-set designer and a popular author, journalist and novelist. His hugely successful *Life and Times of Akhenaten, Pharaoh of Egypt* (1910) had introduced the general public to the Amarna Age, and underpinned much popular thought about Tutankhamen's family. With the discovery of the tomb, he travelled to Luxor as special correspondent for the *Daily Mail*, full of hope that his insider knowledge and personal contacts would allow him to file informative reports that would delight his readers and earn him a large fee. In this he was, however, disappointed, as the excavation team was not prepared to grant him any privileges. Not unnaturally, Weigall took this rejection badly and his *Daily Mail* reports included stinging denunciations of Carnarvon's high-handed approach to the tomb and his assumption of a monopoly over one of the world's greatest assets.

Weigall included the already well-known tale of Carter's unfortunate canary in 'The Malevolence of Ancient Egyptian Spirits', a self-explanatory chapter in *Tutankhamen and Other Essays* (1923), a book which he wrote to take advantage of the public's insatiable demand for information. Under normal circumstances it would be unthinkable for a reputable Egyptologist to usurp a colleague's research and publish it. But these were not normal circumstances. *The Times'* exclusivity deal still rankled, and there were important financial considerations. A valuable Tutankhamen industry was developing in Europe and

America and, as a self-employed author, Weigall wanted to be a part of it. He was not the only one. Carter and Mace had to hurry the first volume of *The Tomb of Tut.ankh.Amen* into print in order to beat the 1923 Tutankhamen-themed publications being offered by several eminent Egyptologists, including Wallis Budge of the British Museum (*Tutankhamen: Amenism, Atenism and Egyptian Monotheism*: a book which, despite its title, focuses on Akhenaten), and Grafton Elliot Smith, whose slim *Tutankhamen and the Discovery of His Tomb by the Late Earl of Carnarvon and Mr Howard Carter* was based on a series of articles written for the *Daily Telegraph*. As Smith cheerfully admits:

> *As they were merely comments on the descriptions of the actual tomb and its contents the separate issue of these topical and ephemeral notes seemed at first to lack any justification, but I have received so many requests for information and guidance that I thought it might serve some useful purpose to redraft my articles and give such bibliographical references as would help the general reader to understand the results that have so far been attained and to appreciate the value of the more important discoveries that next season's work will certainly reveal.*[32]

Meanwhile, Tutankhamen was entering the world of fiction. In 1923 the American Archie Bell published the lengthily titled and curiously punctuated *King Tut-Ankh-Amun: His Romantic History. Relating how, as Prince of Hermonthis, he won the love of Senpa, priestess of the temple of Karnak, and through her interest achieved THE THRONE OF THE PHARAOHS*. This, a thrilling tale of seduction and murder on the banks of the Nile, was just the first in a series of imaginative lives of Tutankhamen which has continued unbroken until the present day. It was just one step from page to screen: the short film *Tutankhamen* and the longer *Dancer on the Nile*, which featured 'Prince Tut', were both released in 1923.

Weigall could not write a complete Tutankhamen book; he had no idea what, if anything, lay behind the Burial Chamber wall. He needed something to pad out his text, and dead songbirds and guardian snakes fitted the bill exactly. He understood the fascination of the Egyptian paranormal and had been one of the first to point out what is obvious to anyone who has spent any time in Egypt: that the modern Egyptians themselves believed strongly in the supernatural:

The ancient magic of Egypt is still widely practised, and many of the formulæ used in modern times are familiar to the Egyptologist. The Egyptian, indeed, lives in a world much influenced by magic and thickly populated by spirits, demons, and djins. Educated men holding Government appointments, and dressing in the smartest European manner, will describe their miraculous adventures and their meetings with djins. An Egyptian gentleman holding an important administrative post, told me how his cousin was wont to change himself into a cat at night time, and to prowl about the town. When a boy his father noticed this peculiarity, and on one occasion chased and beat the cat, with the result that the boy's body next morning was found to be covered with stripes and bruises. The uncle of my informant once spoke such strong language (magically) over a certain wicked book that it began to tremble violently, and finally made a dash for it out of the window. [33]

That these 'primitive' beliefs were routinely picked up and elaborated by supposedly well-educated tourists was, to Weigall, as inexplicable as it was unsuitable. As Antiquities Inspector he had made a stand against superstition, and banned desperate infertile women from offering before statues of the ancient goddess of healing, Sekhmet. His ban had absolutely no effect: even today, local guides lead women – locals and tourists alike – around the Sekhmet statues to enhance their fertility. In *Tutankhamen and Other Essays* Weigall expands on this theme:

The large number of visitors to Egypt and persons interested in Egyptian antiquities who believe in the malevolence of the spirits of the Pharaohs and their dead subjects, is always a matter of astonishment to me, in view of the fact that of all ancient people the Egyptians were the most kindly and, to me, the most loveable ... I will therefore leave it to the reader's taste to find an explanation for the incidents which I will here relate. [34]

He then, consummate popular author that he is, proceeds to tell the story of Carnarvon and the mummified cat. The year is 1909, and Carnarvon is excavating the elite Theban tombs when he discovers a cat-shaped wooden coffin, coated in black pitch. He takes the coffin to Weigall's house and, as Weigall is away from home, the coffin is placed in his bedroom. Returning home in the dead of night, Weigall stumbles over the coffin. He rings the bell, but no one comes. So he goes to the kitchen, where he finds the servants grouped around the butler, who has been stung by a scorpion. The butler passes into a state of delirium, and imagines that a large grey cat is pursuing him. Weigall returns to bed and lies watching the cat coffin, now illuminated by a shaft of moonlight. A branch of a tree swaying in the wind casts a flickering shadow which causes the cat's eyes to appear to open and shut. On the verge of sleep, Weigall starts to imagine that the cat has turned to look at him. Eventually he falls asleep, only to be rudely roused by a noise like a pistol shot. He leaps out of bed, and as he does, a large grey cat springs on to the bed, scratches his hand, and flees through the window. Weigall sees that the cat coffin has cracked in two. The cat mummy is now exposed, its bandages ripped open at the neck as if something has burst out of them.

Weigall then, making a quick change from storyteller to scientist, explains that a change in humidity must have caused the coffin to crack open with a loud noise. The mysterious grey cat is, in fact, his own pet tabby.

His next story is more sinister. He tells how one day he received a little earthenware lamp through the post. This is not an unusual situation: many tourists, having purchased Egyptian souvenirs, became unaccountably scared by them, and many museums have benefited from fear-inspired donations. Weigall learned that the lamp had been sent by a lady who had suffered bad luck ever since it came into her possession – the only example of bad luck that he was able to recall, however, is that she spilt ink on her dress. Weigall forgot about the lamp until one day a titled lady visitor asked for a souvenir. He gave her the lamp, and again forgot about it. Later, at a dinner party in London, he met a lady who had experienced such bad luck since acquiring an Egyptian earthenware lamp that she eventually threw it into the Thames. Weigall made enquiries, and discovered that his earthenware lamp had been given to the London lady by the titled lady.

These two personal stories are followed by an account of the malevolent British Museum mummy. This harmless artefact – a painted 'mummy board' rather than an actual mummy[35] – is generally supposed to have caused endless misery to all who owned it. And so he goes on, teasing his readers with stories of possibly supernatural happenings that might also be explained away in a rational manner. This tendency for professed non-believers to suggest evidence of curse activity before denying its existence continues today. Christopher Frayling, for example, outlines a worrying series of near-disasters while filming a BBC television series in Egypt: these included failures in light and sound when standing near Tutankhamen or his mask, a terrifying elevator plunge caused by a snapped cable, a severe respiratory attack following a day spent filming in a tomb filled with dry bat droppings, an attack of gallstones and, in a reflection of a similar story told by Weigall, almost the entire crew contracting conjunctivitis after a night spent filming in the Valley of the Queens. As I have no curse story of my own to offer, it seems appropriate to allow Frayling the last word on the subject:

For believers in 'the curse' this would all doubtless count as hard evidence; for myself, I prefer to believe that the causes had more to do with the Egyptian climate in April, the micro-climate inside the tombs, the power supply (we were sometimes plugged into a wiring system originally installed by Howard Carter, just after the turn of the century), eccentric ideas about machine maintenance, sheer coincidence and – where more mundane manifestations of 'the curse' were concerned – the caterers, than with the wrath of Tutankhamen. But there's no persuading some people. [36]

9

SECRETS AND LIES

I ... think it is right for me to solemnly affirm — not arrogantly or defiantly — that profanation is the very last idea of a true archaeologist. In his research work his one and sole idea is to rescue remains of the past from destruction, and that when in the course of his work he passes inviolate thresholds, he feels not only an awe and wonder distilled from their tremendous past, but the sense of a sacred obligation. I would add, everything goes to prove that if scientific research of this kind ended tomorrow, greater would be the number of unauthorised persons sacking graves that would yield gold and precious objects who sold and 's[c]attered far and wide'; and, for all practical purposes, that would be the end of them.

Howard Carter[1]

As we have already seen, Tutankhamen's tomb yielded no significant writings. So curious does this seem to our own, highly literate eyes that it has prompted Egyptologist Nick Reeves to make the intriguing suggestion that Carter may simply have looked in the wrong place;

that some of the royal and divine wooden figures recovered from the tomb might actually incorporate funerary papyri, sealed beneath their layers of gilding and paint.[2] This would not be without precedent; wooden statuettes were commonly included in New Kingdom royal burials and one, recovered from the cache tomb of Amenhotep II, included a cavity apparently designed to hold a papyrus. However, it is at present unproven. The most likely repositories for any such documents in Tutankhamen's tomb would be the two guardian statues that stood either side of the entrance to the Burial Chamber. These life-sized wooden images show Tutankhamen with a gleaming black, resin-painted, skin. They wear golden headdresses (one a *khat* head-dress, the other a *nemes* headcloth[3]) and golden jewellery, and each carries a stick that reinforces his authority. Their golden kilts, which stand proud of their bodies, providing a possible hiding place for documents, are inscribed with Tutankhamen's name and titles, and one (the figure with the *khat* headdress) claims to be the *ka*, or spirit, of the king and, perhaps of his brother statue: 'the good god, of whom one be proud, the sovereign of whom one boasts, the royal *ka* of Hora-khte, Osiris, the King Lord of the Lands, Nebkheperure'.[4] Sadly, X-ray examination has confirmed that their kilts do not conceal anything.

The idea that Carter, for some reason of his own, suppressed Tut-ankhamen's papyri has become a perennial favourite in alternative histories and popular fiction. Almost invariably, these 'lost writings' relate to the Biblical Exodus and seek to link Tutankhamen to Moses, or Akhenaten to Moses, or, in some more extreme cases, Tutankha-men to Jesus. To non-believers this is a curious idea – surely, if there was anyone in the Amarna royal family who was not a monotheist, it was Tutankhamen – and it probably reflects the preoccupation of the 1920s West with the establishment of a national home for the Jewish people. The idea is pushed to its limits in Gerald O'Farrell's *The Tut-ankhamen Deception*, in which the author suggests that Carter and Carnarvon actually discovered Tutankhamen long before 1922. They then looted the tomb of four-fifths of its contents before re-sealing it and 'discovering' it. The mummy's curse was actually a string of murders necessary to conceal the truth; papyrus scrolls, which were indeed hidden in the guardian statues, proved a link between the Amarna court, Moses and Jesus. The consequences of this deception were dire indeed:

> They [Carter and Carnarvon] manipulated the media and the politicians of the world with an adroitness that would be the envy of any modern press baron or spin doctor, but, in the course of their robbery, which took them nearly ten years to pull off, they uncovered a secret so potentially explosive that even they didn't know how to exploit it. By suppressing the truth they changed the course of history, perhaps costing millions of people their lives, and in the end they were almost certainly murdered for what they knew, along with a number of others. [5]

Without involving the unnecessary complications of lost religious writings and multiple murders, the Egyptian workmen always assumed that Carnarvon and Carter were looking for treasure – most probably gold – that they would sell at a great profit. Why else would they keep everything hidden from view in the tomb? The locals almost certainly knew about the first, 'secret', nocturnal visit to the Burial Chamber and, as Weigall wrote to Carter in January 1923: 'the natives all say that you may therefore have had the opportunity of stealing some of the millions of pounds' worth of gold …' [6] Some of their colleagues wondered about this, too. It is highly likely that Carter supported himself by dealing in antiquities during his precarious period of self-employment, before he teamed up with Carnarvon. He certainly dealt during the Great War – a time when tourism and prices slumped, and there were many bargains to be had – when he helped his patron to acquire many valuable pieces. In the early twentieth century collecting and dealing were not the absolute taboo for archaeologists that they are today, and Carter was far from the only Egyptologist to dabble. However, there was already a growing feeling that ethical excavation, and selling artefacts to the highest bidder, did not sit comfortably together. As Inspector for southern Egypt, Carter had acquired specialist knowledge of the tombs and their contents. Now, suddenly, he had changed from gamekeeper to poacher and was helping to sell items that, many believed, should not have been sold at all.

It was not illegal to buy legally acquired antiquities from a licensed dealer. However, despite a system of inspections and compulsory registers, it was not always possible to determine what had been, and what had not been, legally acquired. Too many dealers were supplied by unofficial excavators, or by workmen who happily stole artefacts from under the noses of their archaeologist employers: we have already seen this happening with the KV 55 artefacts. These objects, stripped of their archaeological context, were beautiful but valueless from an archaeological viewpoint. As for the official excavators, Antiquities Service rules generally allowed legally excavated finds to be split 50:50 between the excavator and the Egyptian authorities, with the authorities deciding which objects should be retained by Cairo Museum. Only in the case of exceptional or unusual items could the Museum claim everything. Following the 'division' of the finds, the excavator was free to do as he wished with his share: usually it was distributed between his backers as a reward for their financial contribution to the excavation, but occasionally it entered a private collection and effectively vanished (maybe to re-appear years later, as a gift to a local museum), or was sold as a means of recouping the cost of the excavation.

Reputable Western museums, intent on building up their Egyptian collections, did not always shy away from dubious deals and their eagerness pushed prices ever upwards, making illicit excavation even more rewarding. Wallis Budge, Keeper of Egyptian and Assyrian Antiquities at the British Museum (1893–1924), frequently bought antiquities – both legitimately and on the black market – thus saving his museum the trouble and expense of conducting its own excavations. He is certainly not the only museum professional to have done this, but he is the only one to have published a highly embroidered account of his adventures. The sense of shock that comes from reading his autobiography, *By Nile and Tigris* (1920), is caused not by the events themselves, but by the fact that Budge was prepared to boast quite openly about them. Here, for example, he tells how he outwitted both the Egyptian Antiquities Service and the police. We join him the day after he has purchased Papyrus Ani, a beautifully illustrated 19th Dynasty copy of the *Book of the Dead*:

> *… The officer in charge of the police told us that the Chief of the Police of Luxor had received orders during the night from M. Grébaut, the Director of the Service of Antiquities, to take possession of every house containing antiquities in Luxor, and to arrest their owners and myself …*
>
> *Now, among the houses that were sealed and guarded was a small one that abutted on the wall of the garden of the old Luxor Hotel. This house was a source of considerable anxiety to me, for in it I had stored the tins containing the papyri, several cases of anticas, some boxes of skulls for Professor Macalister, and a fine coffin and mummy from Akhmim … This house had good thick mud walls and a sort of sardâb, or basement, where many anticas were stored. As its end wall was built up against the garden wall of the Luxor Hotel, which was at least two feet thick, the house was regarded as one of the safest 'magazines' in Luxor. When the Luxor dealers, and other men who had possessions in the house saw it sealed up, and guards posted about it, and heard that it would be one of the first houses to be opened and its contents confiscated as soon as Grébaut arrived, they first invited*

the guards to drink cognac with them, and then tried to bribe them to go away for an hour; but the guards stoutly refused to drink and to leave their posts. The dealers commended the fidelity of the guards, and paid them high compliments, and then, making a virtue of necessity, went away and left them. But they did not forget that the house abutted on the garden wall, and they went and had an interview with the resident manager of the hotel, and told him of their difficulty, and of their imminent loss. The result of their conversation was that about sunset a number of sturdy gardeners and workmen appeared with their digging tools and baskets, and they dug under that part of the garden wall which was next to the house and right through into the sardâb of the house ... As I watched the work with the manager it seemed to me that the gardeners were particularly skilled house-breakers, and that they must have had much practice.

...It seemed unwise to rely overmuch on the silence of our operations, and we therefore arranged to give the police and the soldiers a meal, for they were both hungry and thirsty. M. Pagnon, the proprietor of the hotel, had a substantial supper prepared for them i.e. half a sheep boiled, with several pounds of rice, and served up in pieces with sliced lemons and raisins on a huge brass tray. When all were squatting round the tray on the ground, a large bowl of boiling mutton fat was poured over the rice, and the hungry men fell to and scooped up the savoury mess with their hands. While they were eating happily, man after man went into the sardâb of the house and brought out, piece by piece and box by box, everything which was of the slightest value commercially ... In this way we saved the Papyrus of Ani, and all the rest of my acquisitions, from the officials of the Service of Antiquities, and all Luxor rejoiced.[7]

While Budge was busy 'saving' artefacts for his museum, at the opposite end of the scale curator Émile Brugsch was strongly suspected of selling artefacts from the Cairo Museum collection for personal gain. Again, this needs to be set in context. Curious as it now seems, this was a time when museum curators regarded their collections as their own personal property, to use and dispose of as they wished, and it was far from unknown for museum visitors to return home with a 'worthless' pot or string of beads, the gift of a friendly curator. Cairo Museum even sold unwanted artefacts – strings of mummy beads – in its own Museum shop.

In his own defence, Carter would probably have argued that the antiquities trade was a far from black-and-white issue and that, as an Egyptologist turned dealer, he was performing a function that was all too necessary. If he did not identify the more valuable pieces, and direct them towards suitable collectors, either private or institutional, no one would, and the artefacts would simply disappear, undocumented, along with the wealthy tourists who bought souvenirs – genuine artefacts recovered from the Theban tombs, genuine artefacts 'imported' from other parts of Egypt, genuine artefacts embellished with modern writings, or outright fakes – on a whim. The discovery, in August 1916, of the tomb of three harem queens of Tuthmosis III in the remote Wadi Gabbanat el-Qurud (Valley of the Ape) on the Theban west bank makes this point for him.

This substantially intact tomb was revealed to Theban tomb-robbers following an intensive storm that resulted in severe flooding.[8] The tomb was plundered immediately and there is no record of its *in situ* contents, although contemporary accounts written by Egyptologists living in Egypt at the time of the discovery agree that there were three intact burials and a large number of grave goods, including many alabaster storage jars. The organic parts of the burial – the wood and the mummies themselves – had rotted away but the stone and gold remained. Inscriptions on their canopic jars tell us that the three queens were Manuwai, Manhata and Maruta; these non-Egyptian names suggest that all three came from the Syria/Palestine region. By the time of the official excavation in September 1916, the only objects left were those rejected by the robbers. Many of the grave goods fell into the hands of the dealer Mohammed Mohassib, who reportedly paid a spectacular £1,100 for the haul. While the Antiquities Service showed no interest in retrieving the stolen goods, Carter was able to reconstruct the story of the robbery and to buy most of the surviving artefacts from Mohassib and other dealers, using money supplied by Carnarvon. These were subsequently purchased, in seven lots over five years, by the Metropolitan Museum of Art for a price of £53,397; they are still displayed in New York today. As Carter routinely charged 15 per cent commission, his personal profit on this deal would have been substantial. No one would argue that this is an ideal chain of events, yet without Carnarvon's and Carter's intervention, the unique collection would have been split up and effectively lost.

ﯼ ﯼ ﯼ

The spring of 1924 saw Carter and his team locked out of Tutankhamen's tomb. Carter eventually left Egypt to embark on the American lecture tour that would secure his financial future. Herbert Winlock, the universally liked and exceedingly diplomatic representative of the Metropolitan Museum, was left behind to negotiate a settlement on his behalf; a role which, when Carter decided to publish his own devastatingly frank version of events, including private correspondence with Winlock himself, drove the normally placid Winlock almost to the end of his tether.

With Carter absent and unlikely to return, the Egyptian Antiquities Service took the opportunity to appoint a committee to conduct a thorough survey of Tutankhamen's tomb, and of the associated tombs used for storage, conservation, photography and recreation. As the committee set to work, Winlock, in turn, insisted that Carter's foreman, Reis Hussein, provide him with a daily report of events in the Valley. Thus Winlock was informed almost immediately when the committee, searching the luncheon tomb (KV 4), discovered a near life-sized wooden head of Tutankhamen neatly packed inside a Fortnum & Mason wine box. The head, which had been plastered and painted, showed Tutankhamen as the young sun god Re, emerging from the lotus blossom at the beginning of the world.

As the head lacked the notes and object number that normally accompanied Carter's methodical work, the Egyptian members of the committee took the view that Carter had stolen, or was intending to steal, the head from the tomb. A telegram was sent to Prime Minister Zaghlul, and the head was dispatched immediately to the Cairo Museum, where it was held as evidence. Lacau and Chief Inspector Rex Engelbach, who knew Carter, were inclined to believe that there might be another explanation: the head may not be from Tutankhamen's tomb, and may even have been purchased from a dealer; one of the workmen may simply have placed the head incorrectly in the luncheon tomb; the head may have been recovered from the stairwell and passageway before Carter's formal recording system was developed. It certainly made no sense for Carter to have abandoned a stolen item where anyone might find it. Winlock sent a coded telegram to Carter:

> *Send all the information you can relating to origin STOP Advise us by letter if any inquiry is made we shall be prepared STOP Made a bad impression on Egyptian members it was announced by telegram to Zaghlool immediately and sent by express to Cairo STOP Lacau and Engelbach have suggested to them you have bought for account of Earl last year from Amarna do not know whether they believed that actually.*

Carter's reply was immediate and precise.

> *The piece mentioned belongs like all other pieces belonging tomb in number four to material found in filling of passage STOP They are*

noted on plan in group numbers but not yet fully registered on index STOP[9]

He followed up with an explanatory letter. The head had been recovered amid the debris blocking the passageway, in a very fragile condition. It had been conserved, then put to one side at a time when KV 4 was the only tomb available for storage. It had then, presumably, been forgotten, as Carter's description of the contents of the passage-way in the 1923 publication omits any mention of it. It is included, and illustrated as Plate I, in the 1933 publication. Carter ended his letter asserting his annoyance that such a valuable item should have been sent off to Cairo without proper preparation for the journey.

This explanation – an eminently reasonable one, given the vast amount of material that Carter had to deal with – was accepted without further question, and the matter was officially dropped, leaving Lacau and Carter closer allies than they had ever been. It seems likely that Lacau was now starting to feel some resentment over the degree of control that Morcos Bey Hanna was imposing on what he regarded as his own domain. However it left a lingering doubt over the accuracy of Carter's record keeping and, in some minds, over his honesty.[10]

🐆 🐆 🐆

It was almost certainly Carter who came up with the bright idea that excavation expenses – including his own salary – might be defrayed by buying good antiquities cheaply and selling them on at a handsome profit. This appealed to the gambler in Carnarvon. However, despite dealings with the British Museum and the Metropolitan Museum, among others, relatively little money was raised from the scheme, as Carnarvon, who was a collector as well as a dealer, was unable to resist keeping many of the purchases for his own collection. By the time of his death the Carnarvon collection, housed at Highclere, was one of

22. *Tutankhamen as Re emerging from a lotus, initially discovered 'in filling of passage' and later re-discovered in KV 4.*

the finest private collections of Egyptian antiquities in the world.

Carnarvon's will left his antiquities to his wife, Almina. As Lady Carnarvon's family money had financed the collection this does not seem entirely unreasonable, although Carnarvon's heir, Lord Porchester, may have viewed things differently. Lady Carnarvon had an expensive lifestyle and very little interest in ancient Egyptian art. Carnarvon realised that she would almost certainly sell his collection and so, in a codicil to his will, he advised:

> *Should she find it necessary to sell the collection, I suggest that the nation – i.e. the British Museum – be given the first refusal at £20,000, far below its value, such sum however, to be absolutely hers, free of all duties. Otherwise I would suggest that the collection be offered to the Metropolitan, New York, Mr Carter to have charge of the negotiations and to fix the price.*

> *Should my wife decide to keep the collection I leave it absolutely*
> *to her whether she leaves it to my son or to the nation or to Evelyn*
> *Herbert. I suggest, however, that she consult Dr Gardiner and Mr*
> *Carter on the subject.*[11]

The specified price of £20,000 was far below the market value of the collection, estimated by Carter to be in the region of £35,000, and Lady Carnarvon was reluctant to take her husband's advice. Initially she planned to dispose of the collection by putting it up for auction, but Carter persuaded her that this was not a good idea. It is not clear whether or not the collection was ever offered to the British Museum: there are persistent rumours that they were given first refusal for £20,000 if they would accept by 4 p.m. that same day (which they evidently were unable to do), but there is nothing to back up this story. The collection was eventually sold to the Metropolitan Museum for $145,000; then little more than the £20,000 suggested by Carnarvon.

In 1924 Carter was charged with packing the collection for deposit in the Bank of England. He listed 1,218 objects, or groups of objects, then added the comment 'A few unimportant antiquities not belonging to the above series I left at Highclere'.[12] The 6th Earl, a man with a strong aversion to Egyptology in general and Tutankhamen in particular, was not interested in these pieces. A few were dotted around the house as ornaments, but most – over 300 objects – were stored in two cupboards set into the thick wall between the drawing room and smoking room.[13] Gradually these pieces were forgotten until only Robert Taylor, butler to the 6th Earl, knew that they were there. Taylor had rediscovered the collection in 1972, while making plans for a party, but had thought nothing of it. In 1987 the death of the 6th Earl made it necessary to create an inventory of Highclere. Taylor came out of retirement to help the 7th Earl, and was able to show him the cupboards. Astonished, the 7th Earl ordered a search of the castle, and more objects came to light; the housekeeper's room, for example, yielded a fragment of stone carved with hieroglyphs. This forgotten collection includes objects dating from the Middle Kingdom to the Ptolemaic Period, and the legally obtained share of Carnarvon's earliest work in Thebes and the Delta, including pieces recovered from the tomb of Amenhotep III. None of the pieces has any connection with Tutankhamen. The circumstances of their re-discovery, however, led to entirely incorrect speculation that these might be hidden Tutankhamen finds.

Howard Carter, too, left a collection of antiquities. His will was a simple one. Harry Burton and Bruce Ingram, editor of the *Illustrated London News* (the one British publication which had retained its interest in Tutankhamen) were named as his executors. His house on the West Bank and all its contents were to go to the Metropolitan Museum and, after sundry minor bequests including one to his loyal servant Abdel-Asl Ahmad Said, the remainder of his estate was to go to his niece, Phyllis Walker, the daughter of his sister Amy. Here Carter, like Carnarvon before him, had a word of advice to offer:

> *...and I strongly recommend to her that she consult my Executors as to the advisability of selling any Egyptian or other antiquities included in this bequest.* [14]

Miss Walker sensibly took this advice and consulted Burton, Newberry and Gardiner. All reached the same conclusion – that Carter's private collection included objects from Tutankhamen's tomb. The items, as listed by Burton for Engelbach, the new Head of the Egyptian Antiquities Service, were as follows:

1 green-blue glass headrest
1 large shawabti [*shabti*: servant figure], green faience
1 pair lapis shawabti
1 small libation glass
1 sepulchral dummy cup, faience
1 ankle amulet
9 gold-headed nails
3 gold ornaments for harness
1 metal 'tennon'

While some of these items were of negligible commercial or historical importance, the inscribed glass headrest was a unique and correspondingly valuable item. It is not clear how or when these objects had been acquired, or who took them from the tomb, and it is entirely possible that some, if not all, had been removed by Carter from Carnarvon's private collection immediately prior to its sale to the Metropolitan Museum. Margaret Orr, daughter of Carter's fellow excavator and co-author Arthur Mace, is on record as stating that her mother, Winifred, did not approve of Carter because he openly displayed antiquities (presumably taken from the tomb; though this cannot be proven) in his London home.[15]

Burton and Ingram now found themselves in a difficult, and potentially highly embarrassing situation. How could the objects be returned to Egypt with a minimum of fuss? Initially it was hoped that they could be returned in the 'diplomatic bag'. With Britain on the brink of war, however, the Foreign Office was reluctant to co-operate. Indeed, Under-Secretary Laskey was prompted to observe: 'I suppose the objects must be returned ... My own inclination is to have them dropped in the Thames.'[16] Eventually the objects were handed to the Egyptian Consulate in London – where they would remain throughout the war – then in 1946 returned by air to King Farouk, who personally presented them to Cairo Museum.

The objects in Carter's collection – minus the Tutankhamen objects – were valued for probate at just £1,093. They were sold through the London dealers Spink, or via Ingram and Burton, and eventually made their way into museum collections including the Ashmolean Museum, Oxford, and, inevitably, the Metropolitan Museum, New York.[17]

In 1978 Thomas Hoving published *Tutankhamun: The Untold Story*. Hoving was no alternative historian or fiction writer; he was the larger-than-life Director of the Metropolitan Museum (1967–77). His obituaries would refer to him as a 'charismatic showman and treasure hunter … one of the breed of brash, self-mythologising leaders', while in his autobiography, which is in some ways reminiscent of Budge's far earlier autobiography, he described his role as 'part gunslinger, ward heeler, legal fixer, accomplice smuggler, anarchist and toady'.[18] Despite its title, his book promised to reveal not the untold truth about Tutankhamen, but the untold truth behind his discovery. It is, by anyone's standards, a curious book for a museum director to have written:

> … *the full story is not altogether the noble, waxen, proper and triumphant tale so familiar to us. The truth is also full of intrigue, secret deals and private arrangements, covert political activities, skulduggery, self-interest, arrogance, lies, dashed hopes, poignance and sorrow – a series of events disfigured by human frailties that led to a fundamental and enduring change in the conduct of archaeology in Egypt.*[19]

Hoving wrote from the American rather than the British or Egyptian perspective, making full use of the Metropolitan's previously unpublished Tutankhamen archives. Today we regard Tutankhamen as an Egyptian king and a British discovery, but in the 1920s many Americans, labouring under the misapprehension that Carter was not only American but also a member of the Metropolitan Museum staff, thought otherwise. Only when they heard Carter speak, on his hugely successful 1924 lecture tour, did they realise their mistake:

> *Mr Carter spoke to his first public audience yesterday in Carnegie Hall of the 'Sahawra' desert, he 'ashuahed' them on 'behawf' of his colleagues of various reassuring things about Tutankhamen. Thirty-four years of grubbing about for ancient tombs have intensified his British vocal mannerisms, so that the person who started the report that Carter was an American should be captured, stuffed and placed in a glass case and labelled the most inaccurate of human observers.*[20]

One is tempted to wonder what this journalist would have made of Carter's natural Norfolk accent. While Carter was undeniably British, his team was Anglo-American. Yet the contribution of the Metropolitan Museum was rarely acknowledged outside America. Theirs was far from a disinterested assistance – the Museum had realistic hopes of receiving a substantial share of the tomb contents as a reward for their investment, and Lythgoe had already discussed this privately, with Carnarvon – but this treatment still rankled. Here, for example, Lythgoe writes in private to the Museum director, informing him of Carnarvon's deal with the (British) *Times*:[21]

> *Although we are doing the lion's share of the work in the tomb, the tomb is Carnarvon's and Carter's and the right to speak publicly of it in any definite way is solely theirs – at least for the present.*[21]

As the American press started to ask questions, Mace, a good friend to Carter, was forced to publish his views. *The Times* of 14 March 1923 carried the following:

> *Mr A. C. Mace, Associate Curator of the New York Metropolitan Museum of Art, now at Luxor, requests publication in The Times of*

the following letter addressed to the Editor of the Morning Post, who has decided not to publish it:

Sir – In the Morning Post *of February 10 your Luxor correspondent states that the members of staff of the New York Metropolitan Museum are feeling a good deal of annoyance at not being allowed to send information to the American newspapers. As the senior member of the Metropolitan Museum staff now working at the tomb of Tutankhamen, I should like to point out that there is not one word of truth in the assertion. Our relations with Lord Carnarvon and Mr Carter are extremely cordial in every way, and we have never expressed the slightest desire, or felt the slightest wish, to communicate details of the work to the Press of any country. Our interest in the tomb is purely scientific, and we deeply resent being exploited in this way by irresponsible mischiefmakers.*

 Yours Truly,

 A. C. Mace.

Hoving's major revelation is the unauthorised first visit to the Burial Chamber; a tale already published by Lucas. The remainder of his book focuses on the political events surrounding the excavation in general, and on Carter's interactions with the Metropolitan Museum in particular. It concludes with the startling suggestion that some small-scale items in the Metropolitan collection may have come, illegally, from Tutankhamen's tomb.[22] This allegation prompted a lengthy internal study of the collection which ended, in November 2010, with the Metropolitan Museum and the Egyptian government jointly anouncing that nineteen objects would be returned to Egypt. The nineteen objects included fifteen 'bits' or study samples sent to the Museum for analysis, a sphinx bracelet inlay and a small bronze dog acquired from Phyllis Walker from Carter's own collection, and a faience collar and part of a handle discovered in Carter's Egyptian house and sent to New York when the house was closed in 1948.

EPILOGUE:
TUTANKHAMEN ABROAD

The discovery of the tomb of King Tutankhamen was a defining moment in the cultural history of the early 20th century. It surpassed the boundaries of archaeology and fired the imagination of people all over the world, profoundly influencing high, as well as popular, culture and made millions of people aware of ancient Egyptian civilization.

Jaromir Malek[1]

The bout of Egyptomania which had greeted the 1922 discovery of Tutankhamen was exacerbated, in 1923, by the unveiling of a beautiful, and now world-famous, head of Nefertiti in Berlin. The plastered and painted stone head had been discovered at Amarna by Ludwig Borchardt in December 1912, but had never before been on public display. It would perhaps be unduly cynical to speculate that this timing was deliberate: that Nefertiti was a German 'spoiler', intended to direct attention away from the British Tutankhamen. If that was indeed the intention, it failed spectacularly. Nefertiti, who up to now had been regarded as a minor and relatively insignificant Amarna figure, immediately took her place alongside Akhenaten and Tutankhamen as an ancient world celebrity; Tiy, who until this point had been the senior queen, was somewhat unfairly relegated to a background role. The Amarna Period, a period whose art, fashions and even hairstyles sat so neatly alongside contemporary art deco styles, became familiar as it had never been before. This was not a new phenomenon; a comparable wave of Egyptomania had followed Napoleon's Egyptian campaign and the publication of the *Description*. Nor was it purely a Western phenomenon, although it is in the West that it is most obvious.[2] However, it was perhaps the first time that ancient Egypt had entered the lives of ordinary people via the media, mass production and the high street, where new shops, such as Woolworth's, were bringing an affordable, standardised style to almost every home. So intense was the fascination with the dynastic age that it was even suggested – fairly seriously – that an extension to the London Underground, which passed through Tooting and Camden Town, should be named Tootancamden.[3]

Those who could not travel to Egypt were able to visit Tutankhamen without leaving home. On 23 April 1924 – St George's day – King George and Queen Mary opened the British Empire Exhibition at Wembley. Included within the Amusement Park, alongside such bone-shaking attractions as the great dipper, the safety racer and the cake-walk, was a convincing (to those who had not seen the original) 'Tomb of Tut-Ankh-Amen'. Entry cost 1s 3d, or 8d for children, and for this the visitor was able to experience the most famous archaeological site in the world, which had been created: 'by the ingenious method of forming a walk in what in the actual tomb would be solid rock, the confined space is dealt with conveniently and the visitor views the objects as though framed in a picture'.[4] The glittering array of replica grave goods included the sarcophagus but not, of course, the coffins or mummy, as no one had yet seen them.

The artefacts were deemed extremely good replicas; the hiero-glyphs such faithful copies that they could be read and understood by linguists. They had been created for the exhibition by a dedicated team of twelve craftsmen employed by the firm of Messrs William Aumonier and Sons, and Weigall had been employed as a consultant to provide the required air of Egyptological authenticity and approval. The public were entranced: Carter, never a man to pander to popular taste, less so. Assuming that the replicas were based on the excavation's copyright plans and photographs, he made a determined attempt to stop the exhibition. On 22 April 1924, the day before the official opening, the front page of the *Daily Express* reported: 'Mr Carter's Wembley Bombshell – attempt to close the pharaoh's tomb – writ issued – replica said to be an infringement.' The same page announced the death of Marie Corelli, who, individual to the end, expressed a wish to have her time of death recorded as 7 a.m., even though she died at 8 a.m., because she did not approve of British Summer Time. Carter only dropped his case when he was assured that Aumonier had taken their information from the many, non-copyrighted photographs taken by Weigall, the *Daily Mail*, and others.

In 1992 cultural historian Christopher Frayling wrote *The Face of Tutankhamen*, a five-part television series for the BBC and accompanying book, exploring the way in which the discovery of Tutankhamen was received and interpreted by the non-specialist Western public. As a throw-away line, he mentioned that it was impossible to assess the accuracy of the Wembley replicas as, along with the other attractions from the Amusement Park, they were eventually sold off to other funfairs: 'occasionally, there are reported sightings, but so far they have proved to come from other strange and exotic "Egyptian" entertainments'.[5] In fact, they had made their way to Hull, home city of William Aumonier, where they were purchased by Mr Albert Reckitt. After some years in his private collection they were donated to the City of Hull Museums, and were displayed in the Mortimer

Museum in 1936. They were re-displayed in 1972 to coincide with the authentic, London *Treasures of Tutankhamun* Exhibition, and displayed again in 1993 when, with a pleasing symmetry, Frayling was invited to open the exhibition. Today they are displayed in Hull's Hands on History Museum.[6]

The first wave of Tutat-mania gradually died away so that, by the time of Carter's death, Egyptology was more or less restored to its 'proper' place as the preserve of dry and dusty academics. However, from the 1960s onwards, a series of touring Tutankhamen exhibitions has served to re-ignite public interest on a relatively frequent basis, while raising not inconsiderable amounts of money for Egyptological good causes. The best-known tour, the 1972–9 *Treasures of Tutankhamen* exhibition, visited Britain, the USSR, the USA, Canada and West Germany. The British leg – hosted by the British Museum and sponsored, appropriately enough, by *The Times* – became England's first 'blockbuster' exhibition. I. E. S. Edwards, the Keeper of Egyptology at the British Museum who was instrumental in the planning and implementation of the 1972 exhibition, recognised that the display might signify different things to different people:

> *I used to think at one time that perhaps we had a special claim to have the exhibition, because the tomb had been discovered by a British archaeologist, but Magdi Wahba [Director of Foreign Relations, Ministry of Culture] soon disillusioned me. He said that was not the way the average Egyptian viewed it. The British had been allowed to excavate in what had always promised to be one of the richest sites in Egypt. They had made this marvellous discovery thanks to the generosity of the Egyptians in allowing them to excavate there, a sufficient reward in itself.[7]*

The London exhibition attracted 1,656,151 visitors, happy to pay the adult admission price of 50p. These visitors purchased 458,000 copies of the exhibition *Catalogue* and 306,000 copies of the *Summary Guide,* yielding a net profit from publications alone of £405,000. The British Museum and *The Times* were able to recover their costs and UNESCO received £654,474, which was dedicated to the saving of Egypt's Philae monuments. Meanwhile, indirect profits gave a major boost to the local economy. The current tour, *Tutankhamen and the Golden Age of the Pharaohs* (Britain, USA, Australia), includes fewer Tutankhamen items and lacks the iconic death mask, yet has become the world's most successful touring exhibition, attracting audiences of 1,096,473 at the O2 London venue, 1,270,000 at the Franklin Institute, Philadelphia, and 1,044,743 at Chicago's Field Museum.

Almost ninety years after the discovery of his tomb, exhibitions displaying real and replica Tutankhamen artefacts are as popular as they ever were. Whether this interest extends to Tutankhamen himself, or it is simply a reflection of our modern fascination with consumerism, is very difficult to say. It certainly raises some interesting questions. Do we appreciate Tutankhamen for who he was, or because of the mythology that has transformed him into the consummate ancient world celebrity? Are we, the ultimate consumer generation, simply attracted by his vast array of grave goods and his 'bling', preferring his golden mask to his actual face?

WHO WAS WHO IN ANCIENT EGYPT

Ahmose: acknowledged founder of Egypt's New Kingdom and 18th Dynasty (reigned c.1550–1525 BC).

Akhenaten: late 18th Dynasty king (reigned c.1352–1336 BC); son of Amenhotep III and inspiration behind the 'Amarna Period'; originally known as Amenhotep IV.

Amenherkhepeshef: infant mummy who, in spite of his Ramesside-sounding name, has been identified as the son of the 12th Dynasty king Senwosret III.

Amenhotep I: early 18th Dynasty king (reigned c.1525–1504 BC).

Amenhotep II: 18th Dynasty king (reigned c.1427–1400 BC); his tomb (KV 35) was later used as a mummy cache.

Amenhotep III: Late 18th Dynasty king (reigned c.1390–1352 BC); father of Akhenaten and husband of Tiy.

Amenhotep IV: see Akhenaten.

Anen: son of Yuya and Thuya; brother of Ay.

Ankhesenamen: third surviving daughter of Akhenaten and Nefertiti; consort of Tutankhamen; originally known as Ankhesenpaaten.

Ankhesenpaaten: see Ankhesenamen.

Ankhetkhepherure Neferneferuaten: see Ankhkheperure Neferneferuaten.

Ankhi: owner of a Sakkara tomb.

Ankhkheperure Neferneferuaten (feminine Ankhetkhepherure Neferneferuaten): name discovered in sound archaeological contexts in association with Akhenaten's name; could refer to one individual or two.

Any: 19th Dynasty owner of a magnificent funerary papyrus that is now a part of the British Museum collection.

Ay: penultimate king of the 18th Dynasty (reigned *c.*1327–1323 BC); possible son of Yuya and Thuya and probable father of Nefertiti.

Cheops: Greek version of the Egyptian Khufu; actual builder of the Great Pyramid of Giza, and fictionalised star of Jane Webb's 1827 *The Mummy!*

Cleopatra VII: last queen of Egypt (reigned 51–30 BC).

Diodorus Siculus: Classical historian who wrote about Egypt (*c.* 60–30 BC).

Elder Lady (KV 35EL): later 18th Dynasty female body discovered in the cache tomb of Amenhotep II.

Hatshepsut: 18th Dynasty female pharaoh (reigned *c.*1473–1458 BC).

Hattusaziti: chamberlain to the Hittite king Suppiluliumas.

Henut-Taneb: sister of Akhenaten.

Herihor: general of Libyan extraction who took control of Thebes during the reign of Ramesses XI.

Herodotus: Classical historian who wrote about Egypt (*c.* 484–425 BC).

Horemheb: final king of the 18th Dynasty (reigned *c.*1323–1295 BC).

Ineni, architect to Tuthmosis I.

Isis: sister of Akhenaten.

Kadashman-Enlil I: king of Babylonia (*c.* 1374–1360 BC).

Kiya: secondary queen of Akhenaten; a woman with an important but ill-understood role at the Amarna court.

KV 55 mummy: the male human remains recovered from tomb KV 55; dated to the Amarna period.

Maia (Mayet): wet nurse to Tutankhamen.

Manetho: Egyptian historian and priest; wrote the first official history of Egypt for Ptolemy I and II.

Manhata: one of three foreign wives of Tuthmosis III.

Manuwai: one of three foreign wives of Tuthmosis III.

Maruta: one of three foreign wives of Tuthmosis III.

May: a northern official during the reign of Tutankhamen.

Maya: a courtier who served both Akhenaten and Tutankhamen; his many titles included 'chief of the treasury' and 'overseer of works in the place of eternity'.

Meketaten: second surviving daughter of Akhenaten and Nefertiti; may have died in childbirth.

Merenptah: 19th Dynasty king (reigned *c.* 1213–1203 BC).

Meritaten: the oldest surviving daughter born to Akhenaten and Nefertiti; probably consort of Smenkhkare.

Meryre II: Amarna courtier.

Mutemwia: mother of Amenhotep III and, perhaps, a relative of Yuya of Akhmim.

Mutnodjmet: sister of Nefertiti; may also be the identically named consort of Horemheb.

Nakhtmin: courtier; son or grandson of Ay.

Narmer: first king of the unified Egypt (reigned *c.* 3100 BC).

Nebetah: sister of Akhenaten.

Nebhepetre Montuhotep II: 11th Dynasty king and unifier of Egypt (reigned *c.* 2055–2004 BC).

Neferneferuaten (princess): fourth surviving daughter of Akhenaten and Nefertiti.

Neferneferuaten Nefertiti: see Nefertiti.

Neferneferuaten: an enigmatic Amarna character; see Ankhkheperure Neferneferuaten.

Neferneferure: fifth surviving daughter of Akhenaten and Nefertiti.

Nefertiti: consort of Akhenaten, mother of at least six royal children; probably daughter of Ay; also known as Neferneferuaten Nefertiti.

Pawah: a draughtsman who scribbled a graffito in a Theban tomb (TT 139).

Peteti: owner of a Giza tomb.

Pinodjem II: 21st Dynasty High Priest; owner of a family tomb at Deir el-Bahri (DB 320), which was used as a royal cache.

Pseusennes II: 21st Dynasty king (reigned c. 959–945 BC).

Ramesses I: founder of the 19th Dynasty (reigned *c.* 1295–1294 BC).

Ramesses II 'The Great': 19th Dynasty king (reigned c.1279–1213 BC).

Ramesses III: 20th Dynasty king (reigned *c.* 1184–1153 BC).

Ramesses VI : 20th Dynasty king (reigned *c.*1143–1136 BC).

Ramesses XI: 19th Dynasty king (reigned *c.*1099–1069 BC).

Senwosret III: 12th Dynasty king (reigned c. 1870–1831 BC).

Setepenre: sixth and final surviving daughter born to Akhenaten and Nefertiti.

Seti I: 19th Dynasty king (reigned *c.*1294–1279 BC).

Sitamen: sister of Akhenaten.

Smendes: founder of the 21st Dynasty (reigned *c.* 1069–1043 BC).

Smenkhkare: co-regent of Akhenaten and probable husband of Meritaten (reigned *c.*1338–1336 BC).

Suppiluliumas: king of the Hittites during Tutankhamen's reign.

Tadukhepa: daughter of Tushratta of Mitanni; intended bride of Amenhotep III, actual bride of Akhenaten.

Tera: fictional queen in Bram Stoker's *The Jewel of Seven Stars* (1903).

Teti: 6th Dynasty owner of a Sakkara pyramid.

Thuya: wife of Yuya and mother of Queen Tiy.

Tiy: daughter of Yuya and Thuya; consort of Amenhotep III and mother of Akhenaten.

Tiye: wife and later consort of Ay; nurse to Nefertiti.

Tutankhamen: king of Egypt (reigned *c.*1336–1327 BC); originally known as Tutankhaten.

Tutankhaten: see Tutankhamen.

Tuthmosis (prince): prematurely deceased older brother of Akhenaten.

Tuthmosis I: early 18th Dynasty king (reigned *c.* 1504–1492 BC).

Tuthmosis II: early 18th Dynasty king (reigned *c.*1492–1479 BC).

Tuthmosis III: 18th Dynasty king (reigned *c.*1479–1425 BC).

Tuthmosis IV: 18th Dynasty king (reigned *c.*1400–1390 BC).

'Two Brothers': a pair of Middle Kingdom mummies housed in the Manchester Museum.

Younger Lady (KV 35YL): later 18th Dynasty female body discovered in the cache tomb of Amenhotep II.

Yuya: husband of Thuya and father of Queen Tiy.

Zannanza: Hittite prince, sent to Egypt on an ill-fated mission to marry the queen.

EGYPTOLOGISTS AND 'EXPERTS' AT THE TIME OF THE DISCOVERY

Ayrton, Edward Russell (1882–1914): British Egyptologist; employee of Theodore Davis and excavator of tomb KV 55.

Baikie, Reverend James (1866–1931): widely read Scottish historian of ancient Egypt.

Breastead, James Henry (1865–1935): American Egyptologist, subsequently founded the Oriental Institute at Chicago.

Budge, Sir Ernest Alfred Thompson Wallis (1857–1934): Keeper of Egyptian Antiquities at the British Museum.

Burton, Harry (1879–1940): American archaeologist and photographer employed by the Metropolitan Museum of Art, New York; lent to Howard Carter to record Tutankhamen's tomb.

Callender, Arthur R. (? –1931): retired engineer and architect, friend and colleague of Howard Carter.

Carnarvon, Lady, née Almina Victoria Maria Alexandra Wombwell (1876–1969): held the concession to Tutankhamen's tomb after the death of her husband, Lord Carnarvon.

Carter, Howard (1874–1939): excavator of the tomb of Tutankhamen.

Corelli, Marie (1855–1924): influential novelist with a firm belief in the occult.

Davis, Theodore Monroe (1837–1915): American lawyer, businessman and amateur Egyptologist; held the concession to excavate the Valley of the Kings 1902–14.

Derry, Douglas (1882–1969): Professor of Anatomy in the Medical Faculty of the Egyptian University; the first to examine Tutankhamen's body.

Doyle, Sir Arthur Ignatius Conan (1859–1930): British novelist, and firm believer in 'Tutankhamen's curse'.

Engelbach, Reginald (1888–1946): Chief Inspector of the Antiquities Service and, later, Chief Keeper of the Cairo Museum.

Gardiner, Sir Alan Henderson (1879–1963): British Egyptologist and philologist.

Haggard, Sir Henry Rider (1856–1925): British novelist, and firm unbeliever in 'Tutankhamen's curse'.

Hall, Lindsley Foote (1883–1969): draughtsman loaned to Howard Carter by the Metropolitan Museum of Art, New York.

Hauser, Walter (1893–1960): architect loaned to Howard Carter by the Metropolitan Museum of Art, New York.

Herbert, George Edward Stanhope Molyneux, 5th Earl of Carnarvon (1866–1923): archaeological partner of Howard Carter.

Lacau, Pierre (1873–1963): French Egyptologist and philologist; head of the Egyptian Antiquities Service 1914–36.

Lucas, Alfred (1867–1945): chemist and conservator who worked on the artefacts from Tutankhamen's tomb.

Lythgoe, Albert Morton (1868–1934): American archaeologist; Head of the Department of Egyptian Art at the Metropolitan Museum of Art, New York 1906–29, then Curator Emeritus 1929–33.

Mace, Arthur Cruttenden (1874–1928): English Egyptologist and member of the Metropolitan Museum of Art staff; worked with Howard Carter 1922–4 and co-authored Carter's first (1923) Tutankhamen volume.

Maspero, Sir Gaston Camille Charles (1846–1916): French Egyptologist; head of the Egyptian Antiquities Service 1881–6 and again 1899–1914.

Newberry, Percy Edward (1869–1949): British Egyptologist; mentor to Howard Carter.

Petrie, Sir William Matthew Flinders (1853–1942): British Egyptologist, widely credited with being the first to apply scientific excavation techniques to ancient Egyptian sites.

Quibell, James Edward (1867–1935), British Egyptologist and Inspector of the Egyptian Antiquities Service.

Smith, Sir Grafton Elliot (1871–1937), Australian anatomist and physical anthropologist.

Weigall, Arthur Edward Pearse Broome (1880–1934): British Egyptologist and author, occasional correspondent for the *Daily Mail*.

Winlock, Herbert Eustis (1884–1950): American Egyptologist; director of the Metropolitan Museum of Art 1932–9.

NOTES

Introduction: Tutankhamen's Many Curses

1. Carter describes the almost indescribable moment when he realises that he has discovered a royal tomb. Carter and Mace (1923: 89).
2. Not unnaturally, the Carnarvon family takes a slightly different view. So, for example, Fiona, 8th Countess of Carnarvon, tells 'how an English aristocrat and intellectual and English draughtsman and archaeologist came to meet and pursue their dream of discovering more about the civilization of Ancient Egypt'. Carnarvon (2007: 2).
3. Statistic given by BBC Radio 4 Today programme, 1 February 2011. These figures do not take account of the abrupt drop in visitors following the fall of the Mubarak government, a drop which is bringing extreme hardship to those involved in Egypt's tourism trade. As I write, in July 2011, visitor numbers are slowly increasing.
4. Romer and Romer (1993: 10) identify a second problem which they describe, with perhaps more of an eye for sensation than accuracy, as *The Rape of Tutankhamen*. This is: 'the exploitation of a small valley in a foreign country by a diverse group of specialists who, in return, give precious little to conserve its ancient monuments, and worse, on occasion, even seem to threaten them'.

5. J. H. Breasted writing to Mrs John D. Rockefeller Jr on 23 February 1926, quoted in James (1992: 352); Smith (1923: 11).
6. While the religion of the Amarna Age is often described as 'monotheism' (the worship of a sole god), it is better classed as 'henotheism' (the worship of a sole god while admitting the existence or possible existence of other gods).
7. Both Akhenaten and Nefertiti have developed a similar cultural afterlife. See Montserrat (2000).

1 Loss

1. Carter and Mace (1923: 76).
2. Davis (1912).
3. Johnson (2009).
4. Porter and Moss (1972: 454–9).
5. All measurements are taken from Reeves (1990: 70–71).
6. Carter (1933: 154).
7. James (1992: 202).
8. Statistics given by Romer and Romer (1993: 10).
9. Cross (2008) and personal communication 2011. Cross believes that the flood occurred during the first year of Ay's reign. Bickerstaffe (2009) agrees the importance of the flood, but dates it to 'not long after Horemheb's Year 8'.

2 Discovery

1. The classical historian Diodorus Siculus, writing in the first century BC, tempts historians with a tantalising hint of the Valley's lost past. *Library of History* I: 46.
2. Quoted in Romer (1981: 32).
3. Pococke (1743), quoted in Pinkerton (1814: 246).
4. Newberry (1928: 7). The stela that he describes is in Berlin Museum, inv. 17813.
5. Baikie (1917: 191–3).
6. *The Times,* 1 December 1922.

7. Originally the stela showed Tutankhamen standing with his consort, Ankhesenamen. But during the reign of Horemheb the queen was erased, and Tutankhamen's names were replaced by Horemheb's. For a full translation of the text see Bennet (1939). A small fragment of a duplicate text was discovered in the temple of Montu at Karnak. Both are now housed in Cairo Museum (41504 and 41565).
8. Davis (1907: xxvii–xxviii).
9. Weigall (1912: 175).
10. Borchardt (1905: 254).
11. Davis (1910). Davis's publication should be read in conjunction with Bell (1990) and Reeves (1981). Much of the analysis of the tomb and its contents given here is based on Bell's work.
12. The lost items from KV 55, and their recovery, are discussed in detail on The Theban Royal Mummy Project website presented by W. M. Miller.
13. Weigall (1922: 193).
14. Gardiner (1957: 10).
15. Tyndale (1907: 185–6).
16. Cross (2008: 305) and personal communication 2011.
17. Weigall (1922: 197).
18. Gardiner (1957: 25).
19. Krauss (1986).
20. Martin (1985: 112).
21. Lucas (1931).
22. Engelbach (1931: 98ff.).
23. Davis (1910: 9 and 2).
24. Weigall (1922: 196).
25. Smith (1912: 51).
26. Allen (1988).
27. Gardiner (1957: 19–20).
28. Davis (1910: 2).
29. Tyndale (1907: 193–4).
30. Hankey (2001: 93).
31. Winlock (1941: 21–3).
32. Reeves (1983).
33. Discussed by Arnold, in Winlock (1941: 16–17).
34. Davis (1912: 3).

35. Maspero's contribution, 'Note on the Life and Reign of Touatânkhamanou', to Davis's publication (1912:111–23) tactfully concentrates on Tutankhamen's Theban monuments and more or less ignores the discovery of his 'tomb'.
36. Hankey (2001: 51).
37. Carter and Mace (1923: 76).
38. James (1992: 413–15).
39. Carter (1923: 82).
40. Carnarvon (2007: 14).
41. Frayling (1992: 3).
42. Weigall (1922: 193).
43. Carter and Mace (1923: 86).
44. ibid. (87); Carter diary 1 November 1922; Cross (2008: 308, fig. 4).
45. Carter and Mace (1923: 89).

3 Recovery

1. ibid. (95).
2. The suggestion that a small group of people entered the Burial Chamber before the official unblocking of the inner door is made, among others, by Hoving (1978: 97).
3. Mervyn Herbert Journal, Middle East Centre, St Antony's College Oxford: fol. 369f.
4. Lucas (1942: 136).
5. ibid. (137).
6. The agreement is reproduced in full in James (1992: 418–22). Carnarvon may well have been influenced in his decision by the fact that the Royal Geographical Society had struck a ground-breaking deal for the coverage of the 1921 Everest Expedition, and that had worked out well for all concerned.
7. Both telegrams quoted in Allen (2006: 10).
8. The arguments for and against Adamson's account are summarised in Zwar (2007).
9. Carter and Mace (1923: 134).
10. ibid. (170).

11. Carter gives the date of the opening of the Burial Chamber as 17 February, but independent writings by Mace, Hall and Mrs Burton confirm that it was actually 16 February 1923. (James 1992: 246).
12. Diary of Mervyn Herbert, Cairo Museum. Quoted in Reeves (1992: 82).
13. Carter and Mace (1923: 182).
14. ibid. (143–4).
15. Winstone quoting Breastead (2008: 198).
16. Carter (1927: xiii)
17. ibid. (41).
18. ibid. (45).
19. ibid. (51–2).
20. ibid. (79).
21. ibid. (82–3).
22. ibid. (87–8).
23. Carter and Mace (1923: 184).
24. Carter (1933: 98).
25. Carter believed that he had been born in 1873; his official documents, including his *Who's Who* entries and even his obituaries, carry this date. However, his birth certificate makes it clear that he was born a year later.
26. Bahn (1992).

4 Inventory

1. *The Times*, 30 November 1922.
2. ibid., 4 December 1922.
3. ibid., 14 February 1923.
4. Lucas (1927: 185).
5. Carter (1933: 163–4).
6. Scott (1927: 197–9). There is some confusion between Scott's account and Carter's (1927: 43) as to when the strengthening agent was applied to the cloth.
7. Carter and Mace (1923: 114). The 'shirts' are likely to be tunics.
8. As Vogelsang-Eastwood observes 'there is … a certain prejudice on the side of (the mostly male) Egyptologists as regards the question of whether textiles and costume constitute a serious and "academic" field of study.' (1999: 4).

9. ibid. (1923: 120); *New York Times*, 7 February 1923.

10. Pfister (1937); Crowfoot and Davies (1941).

11. Vogelsang-Eastwood (1999).

12. Measurements calculated by the Tutankhamen Textile Project, Vogelsang-Eastwood (1999: 17–19).

13. Carter (1927: 12–13).

14. Peter Green quoted in Frayling (1992: 265); Reeves (1990: 208).

15. Carter quotes Sir Gardner Wilkinson (1927:139–40). The subheading to this section is taken from Daniel Miller's identically titled publication; an exploration of the importance of personal possessions written from the viewpoint of a social anthropologist. Miller (2008).

16. Carter (1933: 32, 35).

17. He was not the only king confused over this matter; a scene in the mortuary temple of the 19th Dynasty Ramesses III shows the Dead Ramesses performing menial agricultural work before Osiris.

18. Newberry (1927).

19. The ears on Tutankhamen's innermost coffin, and on his gold mask, were also pierced for earrings, but the holes had subsequently been covered with small gold discs.

20. Carter and Mace (1923: 172).

21. Smith (1912: 38–9).

22. Bickerstaffe (2009: 105–112).

23. Hawass *et al.* (2010).

24. Eaton-Krauss (1993); Robins (1984).

25. Carter and Mace (1923: 117).

26. Eaton Krass (2008: 26).

27. Aldred (1978: 57); Arnold (1996: 107).

28. Carter and Mace (1923: 119). Tutankhamen was buried with four thrones, four chairs, eleven stools and twelve footstools: Eaton-Krauss (2008: 21).

29. The scenes on Tutankhamen's shrine are discussed in Troy (1986: 100ff.). See also Bosse-Griffiths (1973).

5 Autopsy

1. Carter prepares for Tutankhamen's autopsy. Carter (1927: 106).

2. Letter from Carter to Derry, 11 July 1926. Quoted in Leek (1972: 1).

3. *The Histories* 2: 86. Translation by A. de Sélincourt (1954:115). It is not actually certain that Herodotus visited Egypt.

4. Experts generally agree that dry natron salt would be used, although some haver argued that natron solution would have been more effective.

5. After discussion with Robert Lonyes and Rosalie David, I have become aware of just how difficult some of the aspects of traditional mummification and bandaging must have been to achieve (pers. comm., July 2011). Loynes is currently addressing some of these difficulties in his ongoing Manchester University PhD thesis.

6. Derry (1927: 145).

7. *The Times*, 3 February 1923.

8. ibid., 13 February 1923.

9. ibid., 20 March 1923.

10. For the fear of being buried alive, and the lengths that some were prepared to adopt to avoid this grisly fate, see Bondeson (2001).

11. For the fear of autopsy and dissection, see MacDonald (2005).

12. See, for example, Dannenfeldt (1985).

13. Brandon (1991: 231).

14. Wolfe (2009: 227). Dr Douglas, at this stage in his life a respected surgeon, had many years earlier been force to flee New York for the crime of body-snatching.

15. Edwards (1888: 450–51).

16. 'Mummies as Bric-a-Brac': the Boston *Congregationalist,*16 August 1882, originally published in *Harper's Magazine*. Quoted in Wolfe (2009: 201).

17. Day (2006: 36); Wolfe (2009: 227–9).

18. David (2007: 99–113) discusses the importance of the original 'Two Brothers' autopsy. Murray had worked as a nurse in Calcutta before realising that she was too short for her chosen profession.

19. Murray (1910: 7).

20. Carter object card/transcription no 256b-05.

21. Carter (1927: 108).

22. ibid. (86).

23. Quoted in Marchant (2011: 45).

24. See, for example, Bucaille (1990).

25. See, for example, Forbes (1992).

26. *Chronicle: Tutankhamen post mortem*, 25 October 1969; Harrison (1971); Harrison and Abdalla (1972). I am very grateful to Robert Connolly of Liverpool University for permission to publish some of these images in this book.
27. Harris and Wente (1980).
28. Hawass *et al.* (2010).
29. Carter diary 11 and 12 November 1925.
30. ibid., 16 November 1925.
31. Derry (1972: 14).
32. ibid. (15).
33. Leek (1972: 17–18).
34. Connolly, Harrison and Ahmed (1976).
35. Quoted in Marchant (2011: 45).
36. *The Times*, 5 May 2006.
37. See, for example, David (2007: 119–20).
38. Mace (1923: 6).
39. Harrison (1971).
40. Boyer, Rodin, Grey and Connolly (2003: 1145–6).
41. Brier (1998: 173).
42. Boyer, Rodin, Grey and Connolly (2003: 1146–7).
43. Harer (2007).

6 Family

1. Maspero (1912: 111).
2. Wente (1995).
3. Bickerstaffe (2009: 97) asks whether this mummy is Nebmaatre Amenhotep III or the similarly named 20th Dynasty Nebmaatre Ramesses VI.
4. The Supreme Council of Antiquities are to be congratulated on their pioneering work in this field.
5. Allen (2009).
6. Ray (1975).
7. See, for example, Van Dijk (2000: 275): 'some scholars have opted for such a period of joint rule lasting for some twelve years, others have at best admitted

the possibility of a short overlap of one or two years, whereas the majority of scholars reject it entirely'.

8. Hawass *et al.* (2010: 639).

9. Reeves (1981: 53) has suggested that 'the possibility of some loss or confusion of the original skeletal material between the time of the discovery in early 1907 and Elliot Smith's examination later that same year cannot be ruled out': it is equally likely that the material may have been misidentified since Elliot Smith's preliminary examination.

10. Smith (1910: xxiv).

11. Smith (1912: 53–4).

12. Derry (1931: 116).

13. Harrison (1966: 111).

14. Quoted in Tyldesley (2000:132).

15. Wente and Harris (1992).

16. 'Dr Selim [radiologist Ashraf Selim] noted that the spine showed, in addition to slight scoliosis, significant degenerative changes associated with age. He said that although it is difficult to determine the age of an individual from bones alone, he might put the mummy's age as high as 60.' Quoted in Mystery of the Mummy from KV 55: Zahi Hawass website www.guardians. net/hawass/articles/Mystery%20of%20the%20Mummy%20from%20KV55. htm.

17. For a consideration of the evidence for Nefertiti's life, including a discussion of the evidence for Nefertiti as king, see Tyldesley (2005).

18. The Lady Tiye has exactly the same name as Queen Tiy; to avoid confusion I have given them different modern spellings.

19. Loeben (1986). The two *shabti* pieces are now in Brooklyn Museum and the Louvre, Paris.

20. Aldred (1988: 229).

21. Alternative theorists have suggested that she may have been reincarnated as, among others, Cleopatra, Marie Antoinette, Isadora Duncan, Marilyn Monroe and Princess Diana.

22. Gabolde (1998: 153–7); Dodson (2009: 36–8).

23. Discussed in Allen (2009).

24. Harris (1973a); (1973b); (1974).

25. Gardiner (1928).

26. Tyldesley (2006: 121–2).

27. The *sistrum* is a sacred rattle shaken by women in praise of Hathor, its slightly metallic sound recalling the rustling of the papyrus thicket from which Hathor the divine cow emerged. An equally pleasing sound could be produced by shaking a beaded *menyt* necklace.

28. Tyldesley (2006: 113–14).

29. ibid. (123–4).

30. ibid. (135–7).

31. A relief recovered from Hermopolis Magna, now housed in the Ny Carlsberg Glyptotek, Copenhagen, appears to show her performing this function.

32. Hanke (1978: 190–91); see also Harris (1974b).

33. *The Times*, 19 December 1922.

34. Martin (1989: 37–41).

35. Gabolde (1998: 107–10).

36. Green (1996: 15 and endnote 56).

37. Pendlebury (1935); Davies (1923: 133). For other references to Nefertiti's 'disgrace', see Seele (1955).

38. For full details of the death of Meketaten, consult Martin (1989: 42–8); El-Khouly and Martin (1984: 8, 16); Arnold (1996: 115).

39. Post (1971).

40. Zivie (2009).

41. Davies (1905: 36–45).

42. Allen (2009: 9).

43. Darnell and Manassa (2007: 44–7).

44. Luban (1999).

45. Fletcher (2004).

46. Hawass *et al.* (2010).

47. Derry, quoted in Leek (1972: 21–3).

48. Reeves (1990: 123).

49. Harrison *et al.* (1979).

50. Chamberlain (2001); Hellier and Connolly (2009).

51. Hawass *et al.* (2010).

52. Phizackerley (2010).

53. Both pieces of circumstantial evidence are suggested by Booth (2007: 80).

54. Darnell and Manassa (2007: 178–84).

55. Güterbock (1959: 94–5).

56. Schulman (1978: 43).

57. Güterbock.
58. Now in the collections of Berlin Museum.

7 Restoration

1. Carter (1927: 20).
2. Some are extremely successful authors in this genre, the best known being, perhaps, Egyptologist Barbara Mertz, who writes the Amelia Peabody series under the pen-name Elizabeth Peters. Amelia, an intrepid late Victorian–Edwardian lady Egyptologist, is present in the Valley of the Kings as many of the events in this book unfold.

Part II: Tutankhamen: Life after Death

1. Goldacre (2008: 243).
2. Aaronovitch (2009: 5).
3. Developed, somewhat tongue in cheek, after consultation with colleagues. Tyldesley's Law can be applied to 'big theories' (aliens, supernatural powers, etc.) and 'small theories' (the use of cosmetics, homeopathy, etc.). Once aware of the law, it is impossible to avoid noticing just how often random inventions and innovations are attributed to the ancient Egyptians.

8 Tutankhamen's Curse

1. Carter and White (1923). The story is retold here in abbreviated form.
2. Letter written by Winlock to Edward Robinson, Director of the Metropolitan Museum, New York, 28 March 1923. Quoted at length in Hoving (1978: 82).
3. James (1992: 94).
4. The development of our fascination with 'the mummy' as a character is discussed in Day (2006).
5. Coates and Bell (1903: 21).
6. Figures taken from UK government statistics.
7. Winifred Burghclere in Carter and Mace (1923: 27).

8. Winifred Burghclere in ibid. (39).

9. Hoving (1978: 229–30).

10. Lord Carnarvon quoted in Vandenberg (1975: 27).

11. Vandenberg (1975: 20).

12. ibid. (20).

13. Carter (1933: 33, 40–41).

14. Hoving (1978: 227).

15. '…the prime function of an ancient Egyptian tomb is to act as a vehicle for salvation in the afterlife, whatever the specific nature(s) of that afterlife': Snape (2011: 212).

16. ibid. (80).

17. Strudwick (2005: 217–18).

18. ibid. (437).

19. Vandenberg (1975: 12).

20. Unpublished article quoted in James (1992: 371).

21. Winlock, *New York Times*, 26 January 1934, 19–20.

22. Nelson (2002).

23. Conan Doyle was firmly convinced by the 'Cottingley Fairies', photographed in 1917 by schoolgirls Elsie Wright and Frances Griffiths. The fairies were exposed as a hoax in the 1980s.

24. *New York Morning Post*, April 1923.

25. Lucas (1927: 165–6).

26. Dean (2002: 95–6).

27. Dean (1975).

28. Comment attributed to Luis Bulgarini (1949): 'the power of radiation' as a tomb defence is discussed in more detail in Vandenberg (1975: 190–94).

29. Weigall's biography, written by his granddaughter Julie Hankey, stresses this link through its title, *A Passion for Egypt: Arthur Weigall, Tutankhamun and the 'Curse of the Pharaohs'* (2001).

30. An often-quoted statement: see, for example, Hoving (1978: 194).

31. Weigall (1923: 136).

32. Smith (1923: 10).

33. Weigall (1923: 316–17).

34. ibid. (138).

35. A mummy board is a decorated mask and open case which formed part of the mummy's funerary provision.

36. Frayling (1992: xiii).

9 Secrets and Lies

1. Howard Carter reflects on the role of the Egyptologist: unpublished account of the robbery of the tomb of Amenhotep II, Archives of the Griffith Institute, Oxford. Quoted in James (1992: 387).
2. Reeves (1985).
3. The *nemes* headcloth, the headcloth seen on Tutankhamen's funerary mask, covers the crown, back of the head and nape of the neck, and has a large flap of cloth descending behind each ear to the shoulder. The *khat* headdress is a simplified version of the *nemes*, and lacks the front flaps.
4. Carter (1927: 41).
5. G. O'Farrell (2001), *The Tutankhamun Deception: The Story of the Mummy's Curse*. Pan Books: 2.
6. Quoted in Hankey (2001: 265).
7. Budge (1920: 143–4).
8. Lilyquist (2003).
9. James (1992: 315).
10. See, for example, Hoving (1978: 323–5).
11. Quoted in James (1992: 353).
12. ibid. (326).
13. Reeves (1988).
14. Winstone (2008: 328).
15. See for example ibid. (330).
16. Foreign Office diary 7 December 1939. Quoted in Winstone (2008: 330).
17. Reeves (1997).
18. Obituary by Randy Kennedy: *New York Times*, 10 December 2009; Hoving (1993: 15).
19. Hoving (1978: 16).
20. New York *Tribune*: quoted in Hoving (1978: 327–8).
21. Quoted in Winstone (2008: 184).
22. Hoving (1978: 350–57: 350): '... despite the nationalists' law, a certain number of treasures from the tomb did leave Egypt – through Carter and Lord

Carnarvon. Their action has been, for more than fifty years, one of the best-kept secrets in the history of Egyptology.'

Epilogue: Tutankhamen Abroad

1. Malek (2007: 3).
2. For post-Tutankhamen Egyptianisation, see Curl (1994: 211–20); for the parallel but more muted Egyptian phenomenon, see Colla (2007: 13).
3. Graves and Hodge (1940: 126).
4. Frayling (1992: 33).
5. ibid. (36).
6. Other permanent British replica Tutankhamen exhibitions are maintained in Dorchester, and at Highclere. It is perhaps not the organiser's fault if some of the visitors to these attractions believe that they have seen the real grave goods. A less faithful reproduction is provided by the 2005–6 installation 'King Tat', by artists Shaun Doyle and Mally Mallison; an artwork inspired by the British Empire Exhibition tomb.
7. Edwards (2000: 271–2). The facts and figures given here are taken from his autobiography (2000: 296).

LIST OF ILLUSTRATIONS

Colour Plate Section

14. The goddesses Isis (left: west) and Serket (south) stand with outstretched arms to protect the gilded canopic chest containing Tutankhamen's preserved internal organs. (Cairo Museum: © Griffith Institute, University of Oxford).
15. Tutankhamen, wearing the White Crown of southern Egypt, and carrying the staff and flail which denote his royal authority, stands on the back of a leopard (Cairo Museum: © Griffith Institute, University of Oxford).
16. The golden face of Tutankhamen (Cairo Museum: © Griffith Institute, University of Oxford).

Black and White Illustrations

While every effort has been made to contact copyright-holders of illustrations, the author and publishers would be grateful for information about any illustrations where they have been unable to trace them, and would be glad to make amendments in further editions.

 Cartouches: The official names of the king known today simply as Tutankhamen: Tutankhamen Nebkheperure.

BIBLIOGRAPHY

Aaronovitch, D. (2009), *Voodoo Histories: The Role of the Conspiracy Theory in Shaping Modern History*. London: Jonathan Cape.

Alcott, L. M. (1869), Lost in a Pyramid, or The Mummy's Curse. *The New World* 1:1.

Aldred, C. (1988), *Akhenaten, King of Egypt*, London: Thames & Hudson.

Aldred, C. (1978), Tradition and Revolution in the Art of the XVIIIth Dynasty, in D. Schmandt-Besserat, ed., *Immortal Egypt: Invited Lectures on the Middle East at the University of Texas at Austin*. Undena: 51–72.

Allen, J. P. (2009), The Amarna Succession, in P. J. Brand and L. Cooper, eds, *Causing His Name to Live: Studies in Egyptian Epigraphy and History in Memory of William J. Murnane*. Leiden: Brill: 9–20.

Allen, J. P. (1988), Two Altered Inscriptions of the Late Amarna Period, *Journal of the American Research Center in Egypt* 25: 117–26.

Allen, S. J. (2006), *Tutankhamun's Tomb: the Thrill of Discovery. Photographs by Harry Burton*. New Haven and London: Yale University Press and the Metropolitan Museum of Art, New York.

Arnold, D. (1996), *The Royal Women of Amarna: Images of Beauty from Ancient Egypt*. New York: Metropolitan Museum of Art.

Baikie, J. (1917), *The Story of the Pharaohs*. London: A. & C. Black, Ltd.

Bahn, P. G. (1992), Honouring Howard Carter, *Archaeology* 45:6: 77.

Bell, M. A. (1990), An Armchair Excavation of KV 55, *Journal of the American Research Center* 27: 97–137.

Bennet, J. (1939), The Restoration Inscription of Tut'ankhamūn, *Journal of Egyptian Archaeology* 25: 8–25.

Bickerstaffe, D. (2009), *Identifying the Royal Mummies: The Royal Mummies of Thebes*. Chippenham: Canopus Press.

Bondeson, J. (2001), *Buried Alive: The Terrifying History of Our Most Primal Fear*. New York: W. W. Norton & Company.

Booth, C. (2007), *The Boy behind the Mask: Meeting the Real Tutankhamen*. Oxford: Oneworld.

Borchardt, L. (1905), D*er Agyptische Titel 'Vater des Gottes' als Bezeichnung für 'Vater oder Schwiegervater des Königs'*, Berichte über die Verhandlungen der Sächsischen Akademie der Wissenschaffen. Leipzig: Teubner.

Bosse-Griffiths, K. (1973), The Little Golden Shrine of Tutankhamen, *Journal of Egyptian Archaeology* 59: 100–108.

Boyer, R. S., Rodin, E. A., Grey, T. C. and Connolly, R.C. (2003), The Skull and Cervical Spine Radiographs of Tutankhamen: A Critical Appraisal, *American Journal of Neuroradiology* 24: 1142–7.

Brandon, P. (1991), *Thomas Cook: 150 Years of Popular Tourism*. London: Martin Secker & Warburg Ltd.

Brier, B. (1998), *The Murder of Tutankhamen: A 3000 Year Old Murder Mystery*. New York: Phoenix.

Bucaille, M. (1990), *Mummies of the Pharaohs: Modern Medical Investigations*. New York: St Martin's Press.

Budge, E. A. W. (1923), *Tutankhamen: Amenism, Atenism and Egyptian Monotheism*. London: Martin Hopkinson & Co. Ltd.

Budge, E. A. W. (1920), *By Nile and Tigris: A Narrative of Journeys in Egypt and Mesopotamia on Behalf of the British Museum Between the Years 1886 and 1913*. London: John Murray.

Carnarvon, F. (2007), *Carnarvon and Carter: The Story of the Two Englishmen who Discovered the Tomb of Tutankhamun*. Berkshire: Highclere Enterprises.

Carter, H. (1933), *The Tomb of Tut.ankh.Amen: The Annex and Treasury*. London: Cassell & Company Limited. Reprinted 2000 with a foreword by Nicholas Reeves, London: Gerald Duckworth & Co. Ltd.

Carter, H. (1927), *The Tomb of Tut.ankh.Amen: The Burial Chamber*. London: Cassell & Company Limited. Reprinted 2001 with a foreword by Nicholas Reeves, London: Gerald Duckworth & Co. Ltd.

Carter, H. and Mace, A. C. (1923), *The Tomb of Tut.ankh.Amen: Search, Discovery and Clearance of the Antechamber*. London: Cassell & Company Limited.

Reprinted 2003 with a foreword by Nicholas Reeves, London: Gerald Duckworth and Co. Ltd.

Carter, H. and White, P. (1923), The Tomb of the Bird, *Pearson's Magazine* 56, November 1923: 433–7.

Chamberlain, G. (2001), Two Babies That Could Have Changed World History, *The Historian* 72: 6–10.

Coates, T. F. G. and Bell, R. S. W. (1903), *Marie Corelli: The Writer and the Woman*. Philadelphia: George W. Jacobs & Co.

Colla, E. (2007), *Conflicted Antiquities: Egyptology, Egyptomania, Egyptian Modernity*. Durham and London: Duke University Press.

Connolly, R. C., Harrison, R. G. and Ahmed, S. (1976), Serological evidence for the parentage of Tutankhamun and Smenkhkare, *Journal of Egyptian Archaeology* 62: 184–6.

Cross, S. W. (2008), The Hydrology of the Valley of the Kings, *Journal of Egyptian Archaeology* 94: 303–10.

Crowfoot, G. M. and Davies, N. de G. (1941), The Tunic of Tut'ankhamūn, *Journal of Egyptian Archaeology* 27: 113–30.

Curl, J. S. (1994), *Egyptomania: the Egyptian revival: a Recurring Theme in the History of Time*. Manchester: Manchester University Press.

Dannenfeldt, K. H. (1985), Egyptian mumia: The Sixteenth Century Experience and Debate, *The Sixteenth Century Journal*: 16:2: 163–80.

Darnell, J. C. and Manassa, C. (2007), *Tutankhamun's Armies: Battle and Conquest During Egypt's Late 18th Dynasty*. Hoboken: John Wiley & Son.

David, R. (2007), *The Two Brothers: Death and the Afterlife in Middle Kingdom Egypt*. Bolton: Rutherford Press Limited.

Davies, N. de G. (1923), Akhenaten at Thebes, *Journal of Egyptian Archaeology* 9: 132–52.

Davies, N. de G. (1905), *The Rock Tombs of el-Amarna* 2, London: Egypt Exploration Society.

Davis, T. M. (1912), *The Tombs of Harmhabi and Touatânkhamanou*. London: Archibald Constable & Co. Ltd. Reprinted 2001 with a foreword by Nicholas Reeves. London: Gerald Duckworth & Co. Ltd.

Davis, T. M. (1910), *The Tomb of Queen Tiyi*. London: Archibald Constable & Co. Ltd. Reprinted 2001 with a foreword by Nicholas Reeves. London: Gerald Duckworth & Co. Ltd.

Davis, T. M. (1907), *The Tomb of Iouiya and Touiyou*. London: Archibald
    Constable & Co. Ltd. Reprinted 2000 with a foreword by Nicholas Reeves.
    London: Gerald Duckworth & Co. Ltd.

Day, J. (2006), *The Mummy's Curse: Mummy Mania in the English-Speaking World*.
    London and New York: Routledge.

Dean, G. (2002), *The Turnstone: A Doctor's Story*. Liverpool: Liverpool University
    Press.

Dean, G. (1975), The Curse of the Pharaohs, *World Medicine*, June 1975: 17–21.

Derry, D. E. (1972), The Anatomical Report on the Royal Mummy. In F. F. Leek,
    The Human Remains from the Tomb of Tut'ankhamūn. Oxford: Griffith
    Institute, 11–20.

Derry, D. E. (1931), in R. Engelbach, The So-called Coffin of Akhenaten, *Annales
    du Service des Antiquités* 31: 98–114.

Derry, D. E. (1927), Appendix I: Report upon the Examination of Tut-Ank-
    Amen's Mummy, in H. Carter, *The Tomb of Tut.ankh.Amen: The Burial
    Chamber*. London: Cassell & Company Limited. Reprinted 2001 with a
    foreword by Nicholas Reeves, London: Gerald Duckworth & Co. Ltd,
    143–61.

Diodorus Siculus, *Library of History* Book I. Translated by C. H. Oldfather (1933),
    Vol. I, Loeb Classical Library, Harvard University Press, Cambridge, Mass.
    and Heinemann, London.

Dodson. A. (2009), *Amarna Sunset: Nefertiti, Tutankhamun, Ay, Horemheb and the
    Egyptian Counter-Reformation*. Cairo: American University in Cairo Press.

Eaton-Krauss, M. (1993), *The Sarcophagus in the Tomb of Tutankhamen*, Oxford:
    Griffith Institute.

Eaton-Krauss, M. (2008) *The Thrones, Chairs, Stools and Footstools from the Tomb
    of Tutankhamun*. Oxford: Griffith Institute.

Edwards, A. B. (1888 revised edition), *A Thousand Miles up the Nile*. London:
    Routledge & Sons Ltd.

Edwards, I. E. S. (2000), *From the Pyramids to Tutankhamen: Memoirs of an
    Egyptologist*. Oxford: Oxbow Books.

El-Khouly, A. and Martin, G. T. (1984), *Excavations in the Royal Necropolis at
    El-Amarna*. Cairo: Supplement aux Annales du Service des Antiquitiés de
    l'Egypte, Cahier 33.

Engelbach, R. (1931), The So-called Coffin of Akhenaten, *Annales du Service des
    Antiquités* 31: 98–114.

Fletcher, J. (2004), *The Search for Nefertiti; The True Story of a Remarkable Discovery,* London: Hodder & Stoughton.

Forbes, D. (1992), Abusing Pharaoh, in C. Frayling, *The Face of Tutankhamen,* London: 285–92. Article originally published in *KMT*.

Frayling, C. (1992), *The Face of Tutankhamen.* London: Faber and Faber.

Gabolde, M. (1998), D'Akhenaton à Toutânkhamon. Lyon: Université Lumière-Lyon 2.

Gardiner, A. H. (1957), The So-called Tomb of Queen Tiye, *Journal of Egyptian Archaeology* 43: 10–25.

Gardiner, A. H. (1928), The Graffito from the Tomb of Pere, *Journal of Egyptian Archaeology* 14: 10–11.

Gautier, T. (1858), *The Romance of a Mummy. The Works of Théophile Gautier Volume 5,* translated and edited by F. C. de Sumichrast (1901). Cambridge USA: University Press.

Goldacre, B. (2008), *Bad Science.* London: Fourth Estate.

Graves, R. and Hodge, A. (1940), *The Long Weekend: A Social History of Great Britain.* London: Cardinal.

Green, L. (1996), The Royal Women of Amarna: Who Was Who, in D. Arnold, *The Royal Women of Amarna: Images of Beauty from Ancient Egypt,* New York: Metropolitan Museum of Art: 7–15.

Güterbock, H. G. (1959), The Deeds of Suppiluliumas as Told by his Son, Mursili II, *Journal of Cuneiform Studies* 10: 41–78, 75–98, 107–30.

Hankey, J. (2001), *A Passion for Egypt: Arthur Weigall, Tutankhamun and the 'Curse of the Pharaohs'.* London and New York: I.B. Tauris.

Harer, W.B. (2007), Chariots, Horses or Hippos: What killed Tutankhamun? *Minerva* 18: 5.

Harris, J. (1974), Nefernefruaten Regnans, *Acta Orientalia* 36: 11–21.

Harris, J. (1973a), Nefertiti Rediviva, *Acta Orientalia* 35: 5–13.

Harris, J. (1973b), Nefernefruaten, *Göttinger Miszellen* 4: 15–17.

Harris, J. E. and Wente, E. F. (1980), *An X-Ray Atlas of the Royal Mummies.* Chicago: University of Chicago Press.

Harrison, R.G. (1971), Post Mortem on Two Pharaohs: Was Tutankhamen's Skull Fractured?, *Buried History* 4: 114–29.

Harrison, R. G. (1966), An Anatomical Examination of the Pharaonic Remains Purported to be Akhenaten, *Journal of Egyptian Archaeology* 52: 95–119.

Harrison, R. G. and Abdalla, A. B. (1972), The Remains of Tutankhamen, *Antiquity* 48: 8–14.

Harrison, R. G., Connolly, R. C., Soheir, A., Abdalla, A.B. and Ghawaby, M. El (1979), A Mummified Foetus from the Tomb of Tutankhamen, *Antiquity* 53: 19–21.

Hawass, Z. *et al.* (2010), Ancestry and Pathology in King Tutankhamun's Family, *Journal of the American Medical Association* 303:7: 638–747.

Hellier, C. A. and Connolly, R. C. (2009), A Re-assessment of the Larger Fetus Found in Tutankhamen's Tomb, *Antiquity* 83: 165–73.

Herodotus, *The Histories*. Translated by A. de Sélincourt (1954), revised with introduction and notes by J. Marincola (1996). London: Penguin Books.

Hoving, T. (1993), *Making the Mummies Dance: Inside the Metropolitan Museum of Art*. New York: Touchstone.

Hoving, T. (1978), *Tutankhamun: The Untold Story*. New York: Simon & Schuster.

James, T. G. H. (1992), *Howard Carter: The Path to Tutankhamen*. London: Kegan Paul International.

Johnson, W. R. (2009), Tutankhamen-Period Battle Narratives at Luxor, *KMT* 20: 4: 20–33.

Krauss, R. (1986), Kija – ursprungliche Besitzerin der Kanopen aus KV 55, *Mitteilungen des Deutschen Archäologischen Instituts Abteilung Kairo* 42: 67–80.

Leek, F. F. (1972), *The Human Remains from the Tomb of Tut'ankhamūn*. Oxford: Griffith Institute.

Lilyquist, C. (2003), *The Tomb of Three Foreign Wives of Tuthmosis III*. New York: Metropolitan Museum of Art.

Loeben, C. E. (1986), Eine Bestrattung der grossen Königlichen Gemahlin Nofretete in Amarna, *Mitteilungen des Deutschen Archäologischen Instituts Abteilung Kairo* 42: 99–107.

Luban, M. (1999), *Do We Have the Mummy of Nefertiti?*, www.geocities.com.

Lucas, A. (1942), Notes on some objects from the tomb of Tut-Ankhamun, *Annales du Service des Antiquités* 41: 135–47.

Lucas, A. (1931), The Canopic Vases from the 'Tomb of Queen Tiyi', *Annales du Service des Antiquités 31*: 120–22.

Lucas, A. (1927), Appendix II: The Chemistry of the Tomb, in H. Carter, *The Tomb of Tut.ankh.Amen: The Burial Chamber*. London: Cassell & Company Limited. Reprinted 2001 with a foreword by Nicholas Reeves, London: Gerald Duckworth and Co. Ltd: 162–88.

MacDonald, H. (2005), *Human Remains: Dissection and its Histories*. Melbourne: Melbourne University Press.

Mace, A. C. (1923), The Egyptian Expedition 1922–23, *Bulletin of the Metropolitan Museum of Art* 18:2:5–11.

Malek, J. (2007), *Tutankhamun: The Secrets of the Tomb and the Life of the Pharaohs*. London: Carlton.

Marchant, J. (2011), Death on the Nile, *New Scientist* 2795: 42–4.

Martin, G. T. (1989), *The Royal Tomb at el-Amarna 2*, London: Egypt Exploration Society.

Martin, G. T. (1985), Notes on a Canopic Jar from Kings' Valley Tomb 22, in P. Posener-Kriéger, ed., *Melanges Gamal-Eddin Mokhtar II*. Cairo: Institut Français d'Archéologie Orientale: 111–24.

Maspero, G. (1912), Note on the Life and Reign of Touatânkhamanou, in T. Davis, *The Tombs of Harmhabi and Touatânkhamanou*. London: Archibald Constable and Co. Ltd. Reprinted 2001 with a foreword by Nicholas Reeves. London: Gerald Duckworth and Co. Ltd: 111–23.

Miller, D. (2008), *The Comfort of Things*. Cambridge: Polity Press.

Montserrat, D. (2000), *Akhenaten: History, Fantasy and Ancient Egypt*. London and New York: Routledge.

Murray, M. A. (1910), *The Tomb of Two Brothers*. Manchester: Sherratt &Hughes.

Nelson, M. R. (2002), The Mummy's Curse: Historical Cohort Study, *British Medical Journal* 325: 1482–4.

Newberry, P. E. (1928), Akhenaten's Eldest Son-in-Law Ankhkheperure, *Journal of Egyptian Archaeology* 14: 3–9.

Newberry, P. E. (1927), Appendix III: Report on the Floral Wreaths Found in the Coffins of Tut-ank-Amen, in H. Carter, *The Tomb of Tut.ankh.Amen: The Burial Chamber*. London: Cassell & Company Limited. Reprinted 2001 with a foreword by Nicholas Reeves. London: Gerald Duckworth and Co. Ltd: 189–96.

Pendlebury, J. (1935), *Tell el-Amarna*. London: Egypt Exploration Society.

Pfister, R. (1937), Les textiles du Tombeau de Toutankhamon, *Revue des Artes Asiatiques* 11: 4: 207–18.

Phizackerley, K. (2010), *DNA Shows the KV55 Mummy Probably Not Akhenaten* http://www.kv64.info/2010/03/dna-shows-that-kv55-mummy-probably-not.html (2 March 2010).

Pococke, R. (1743), *A Description of the East and Some Other Countries* Volume I. London. Full text reproduced in J. Pinkerton, ed. (1814), *A General Collection of the Best and Most Interesting Voyages and Travels in All Parts of the World.* London: Longman, 163–402.

Poe, E. A. (1845), Some Words with a Mummy. *American Review*, April 1845.

Porter, B. and Moss, R. L. B. (1972), *Topographical Bibliography of Ancient Egyptian Hieroglyphic Texts, Reliefs, and Paintings II: Theban Temples, 2nd Edition, revised and Augmented.* Oxford: Clarendon Press.

Post, J. B. (1971), Ages at Menarche and Menopause: Some Mediaeval Authorities, *Population Studies* 25: 1: 83–7.

Ray, J. (1975), The Parentage of Tutankhamun, *Antiquity* 49: 45–7.

Reeves, N. (1997), Howard Carter's Collection of Egyptian and Classical Antiquities, in E. Goring, N. Reeves and J. Ruffle, eds., *Chief of Seers: Egyptian Studies in Memory of Cyril Aldred.* Kegan Paul and National Museums of Scotland, 242–50.

Reeves, N. (1990), *The Complete Tutankhamun: The King, The Tomb, the Royal Treasure.* London: Thames & Hudson.

Reeves, N. (1988), The Search of Tutankhamen: the Final Chapter, *Aramco World* 39: 6: 6–13.

Reeves, N. (1985), Tutankhamen and his Papyri, *Göttinger Miszellen* 88: 39–45.

Reeves, N. (1983), On the Miniature Mask from the Tut'ankhamun Embalming Cache, *Bulletin de la Société d'Égyptologie Genève* 8: 81–3.

Reeves, N. (1981), A Re-Appraisal of Tomb 55 in the Valley of the Kings, *Journal of Egyptian Archaeology* 67: 48–55.

Robins, G. (1984), Isis, Nephthys, Selket and Neith Represented on the Sarcophagus of Tutankhamun and in Four Free-Standing Statues found in KV 62, *Göttinger Miszellen* 72: 21–5.

Romer, J. (1981), *Valley of the Kings*, London: Michael O'Mara Books.

Romer, J. and Romer, E. (1993), *The Rape of Tutankhamun.* London: Michael O'Mara Books.

Scott, A. (1927), Appendix IV: Notes on Objects from the Tomb of Tut-ank-Amen, in H. Carter, *The Tomb of Tut.ankh.Amen: The Burial Chamber.* London: Cassell & Company Limited. Reprinted 2001 with a foreword by Nicholas Reeves, London: Gerald Duckworth and Co. Ltd, 197–213.

Schulman, A.R. (1978), Ankhesenamen, Nofretity and the Amka Affair, *Journal of the American Research Center in Egypt* 15: 43–8.

Seele, K.C. (1955), King Ay and the close of the Amarna Age, *Journal of Near Eastern Studies* 14: 168–80.

Shaw, I. (2000), *The Oxford History of Ancient Egypt*. Oxford: Oxford University Press.

Smith, G. E. (1923), *Tutankhamen and the Discovery of His Tomb by the Late Earl of Carnarvon and Mr Howard Carter*. London: Routledge & Sons Ltd.

Smith, G. E. (1912), *The Royal Mummies*. Cairo: Service des Antiquitiés de L'Égypte.

Smith, G. E. (1910), A Note on the Estimate of the Age Attained by the Person whose Skeleton was Found in the Tomb, in T. M. Davis, *The Tomb of Queen Tiyi*. London: Archibald Constable & Co. Ltd. Reprinted 2001 with a foreword by Nicholas Reeves. London: Gerald Duckworth & Co. Ltd, XXIII–XXIV.

Snape, S. (2011), *Ancient Egyptian Tombs: the Culture of Life and Death*. Oxford: Wiley-Blackwell.

Stoker, B. (1903), *The Jewel of Seven Stars*. London: Heinemann.

Strudwick, N. (2005), *Texts from the Pyramid Age*. Atlanta: Society of Biblical Literature.

Troy, L. (1986), *Patterns of Queenship in Ancient Egyptian Myth and History*. Uppsala: Acta Universitatis Upsaliensis.

Tyldesley, J. A. (2006), *Chronicle of the Queens of Egypt*. London: Thames & Hudson.

Tyldesley, J. A. (2005 revised edition), *Nefertiti*. London: Penguin.

Tyldesley, J. A. (2000), *Private Lives of the Pharaohs*. London: Channel 4 Books.

Tyndale, W. (1907), *Below the Cataracts*. London: Heinemann.

Vandenberg, P. (1975), *The Curse of the Pharaohs*, trans. T. Weyr. London: Book Club Associates.

Van Dijk, J. (2000), The Amarna Period and the Later New Kingdom, in I. Shaw, ed., *The Oxford History of Ancient Egypt*. Oxford: Oxford University Press, 272–313.

Vogelsang-Eastwood, G. M. (1999), *Tutankhamun's Wardrobe: Garments from the Tomb of Tutankhamun*. Leiden: Van Doorn & Co.

Webb, J. (1827) *The Mummy! Or a Tale of the Twenty-Second Century*. London: Henry Colburn.

Weigall, A. E. P. B. (1923), *Tutankhamen and Other Essays*. London: Thornton Butterworth Ltd.

Weigall, A. E. P. B. (1922), The Mummy of Akhenaten, *Journal of Egyptian Archaeology* 8: 193–200.

Weigall, A. E. P. B. (1912), *The Treasury of Ancient Egypt: Miscellaneous Chapters on Ancient Egyptian History and Archaeology*. Chicago and New York: Rand McNally & Co.

Weigall, A.E.P.B (1910), *The Life and Times of Akhenaten, Pharaoh of Egypt*. London: Thornton Butterworth Ltd.

Wente, E. F. (1995), Who Was Who Among the Royal Mummies?, *Oriental Institute News and Notes* 144.

Wente, E. F. and Harris, J. E. (1992), Royal Mummies of the Eighteenth Dynasty, in N. Reeves, ed., *After Tutankhamun: Research and Excavation in the Royal Necropolis at Thebes*, London and New York: Routledge.

Winlock, H. E. (1941), *Materials Used at the Embalming of King Tutankhamun*, New York: The Metropolitan Museum of Art Papers 10. Reprinted 2010 with a foreword by D. Arnold, as *Tutankhamen's Funeral*. New York: Metropolitan Museum of Art.

Winstone, H. V. F. (2008, revised and updated), *Howard Carter and the Discovery of Tutankhamen*. Manchester and Beirut: Barzan.

Wolfe, S. J. with R. Singerman (2009), *Mummies in Nineteenth Century America: Ancient Egyptians as Artefacts*. Jefferson, North Carolina and London: McFarland & Company.

Wynne, B. (1972), *Behind the Mask of Tutankhamen*. London: Souvenir Press.

Zivie, A. (2009), *La Tombe de Maïa, mère nourricière du roi Toutânkhamon et grande du harem*. Toulouse: Caracara Edition.

Zwar, D. (2007), Tutankhamun's Last Guardian, *History Today* 57:11.

Internet Resources

Theban Mapping Project: http://www.thebanmappingproject.com/

Theban Royal Mummy Project: http://anubis4_2000.tripod.com/mummypages1/introduction.htm

Tutankahmun: Anatomy of an Excavation: www.griffith.ox.ac.uk/gri/4tut.html

INDEX